THE DEVELOPMENT
OF VISUAL
PERCEPTION

GOODYEAR DEVELOPMENTAL PSYCHOLOGY SERIES
Alexander W. Siegel, Series Editor

Evolution, Development, and Children's Learning
Harold D. Fishbein

The Development of Visual Perception
Richard R. Rosinski

THE DEVELOPMENT OF VISUAL PERCEPTION

Richard R. Rosinski
University of Pittsburgh

Goodyear Publishing Company, Inc.
Santa Monica, California

Library of Congress Cataloging in Publication Data
Rosinski, Richard R.
    The development of visual perception.
    (Goodyear developmental psychology series)
    Bibliography: p. 206
    Includes indexes.
    1. Visual perception.   2. Child psychology.   I. Title.
BF723.V5R6   152.1′4   76-21558
ISBN 0-87620-221-0

Y-2210-6

Current printing (last digit):
10 9 8 7 6 5 4 3 2

Printed in the United States of America

Cover and interior design: Jacqueline Thibodeau

CONTENTS

Preface   ix

Chapter 1   DEVELOPMENT AND THE STUDY OF
                       PERCEPTION   1
Defining Perception   2
An approach to Perception   2
    Potential and Effective Information   4
The Concept of Stimulus Information   5
Components of the Study of Perception and
         Development   7
    The Perceptual Component   7
    The Developmental Component   8
Methods of Studying Perceptual Development   9
    Judgmental Methods   10
    Discrimination Learning   12
    Preference Methods   13
    Habituation and Dishabituation Techniques   16
The Principle of Converging Operations   19
Basic Concepts in the Study of Perception   20
Summary   22

Chapter 2   SPATIAL LAYOUT: PERCEPTION OF DEPTH
              AND DISTANCE   24

              Childrens' Perception of Depth and Distance   25
              Binocular Vision   30
                 Convergence   30
                 Binocular Disparity   32
              Motion Parallax   37
              Motion Perspective   39
                 Looming   41
              Redundancy in Perceptual Systems: Texture
                 Gradients   46
                 Texture Gradients and Development   49
              Summary   54

Chapter 3   OTHER ASPECTS OF SPATIAL LAYOUT
              PERCEPTION   57

              The Perception of Slant   57
              The Perception of Size   62
              The Perception of Motion   68
                 Velocity   69
              The Perception of Kinetic Depth   70
              Summary   74

Chapter 4   THE DEVELOPMENT OF VISUALLY GUIDED
              BEHAVIOR   75

              The Effects of Light Deprivation on Perceptual
                 Development   77
              The Effects of Partial Light Deprivation   80
              The Role of Self-Produced Movement   83
                 Self-Produced Movement and Visual Information   85
              The Role of Other Forms of Stimulation   89
                 Eye-Limb Coordination   90
              Research with Infants   93
              Summary   97

Chapter 5   CONTROL OF VISUALLY GUIDED BEHAVIOR   99

              Visual Control and Control Systems Theory   101
                 Reversing the Sign of Feedback   105
                 Disturbing the Input to the System   105
                 Examining Reaction Times   105
                 Opening the Feedback Loop   106
                 A Simple Demonstration of Control Principles   106
              Control Systems in Adaptation and Development   107

Organization and Reorganization of Visual-Motor
    Coordination   109
    Array Motion and Self-Produced Movement   109
    Other Forms of Feedback   112
Changes in Control Systems   115
Summary   120

Chapter 6   PATTERN PERCEPTION: PROCESSES AND
    EARLY DEVELOPMENT   122

Differences between Spatial and Pattern Perception   122
Types of Pattern Perception   125
    Discrimination   125
    Recognition   125
    Identification   126
Models of Pattern Perception   127
    Template Matching   127
    Feature Testing   128
Information for Pattern Perception   130
Pattern Perception in Infants   134
    Discrimination   134
    Recognition   140
    Identification   143
Summary   144

Chapter 7   PATTERN PERCEPTION: FURTHER
    DEVELOPMENT   146

The Nature of Early Development   147
    Perception of Form   147
    Effects of Maturation and Experience   151
Pattern Perception in Older Children and Adults   154
    Discrimination   154
    Recognition   163
Summary   168

Chapter 8   REPRESENTATIONS AND SYMBOLS   169

Pictorial Perception   170
    Perception of Objects in Pictures   172
    Perception of Spatial Layout in Pictures   175
    Perception of Actions and Events in Pictures   178
Pattern Perception and Reading   181
    Perception of Letters   182
    Higher-Order Units—Bigrams and Trigrams   184
    Higher-Order Units—Words   187
Summary   190

Chapter 9   GENERAL PRINCIPLES OF PERCEPTUAL
                 DEVELOPMENT   192
                 Changes in Information Pickup   193
                   Eye Movements   193
                   Selective Attention   195
                   Differentiation   199
                 Changes in Informational Specificity   201
                 Summary   204

References   206

Author Index   220

Subject Index   223

PREFACE

My purpose in writing this book is to introduce the undergraduate or beginning graduate student in psychology to important phenomena of visual perception from a developmental perspective. In many courses, students are exposed to the classic experiments in perceptual development. Often, these experiments present isolated facts without supplying a framework to organize these facts and convey their significance. Students learn that children will not crawl off cliffs, that they will look at certain patterns, and that their perceptual abilities improve with age, but they do not learn how to integrate these facts into a conceptual framework.

This framework became clear to me from examining two questions that may tie together many aspects of psychology and development. The first is a conceptual-theoretical question: What is a particular phenomenon or process like; how does it operate? Related to this is a developmental question: How did that phenomenon or process get to be that way; how does it develop to a particular level? The theoretical question is often approached independently of the second. Many psychologists are concerned with theoretical explanations that may ignore development.

It seems to me, however, that developmental questions cannot be dealt with in isolation. Development is not a phenomenon that can be studied out of context. To be meaningful, research in development must be closely related to a conceptual framework that encompasses the processes being studied.

This book has been organized around a conceptual account of perceptual processes and an interrelated description of the developmental changes that occur in perception. In each of the chapters dealing with spatial perception, visually guided behavior, and pattern perception, I have attempted to present the problems that have stimulated interest in the area, summarize the explanations of perceptual processes that have proved fruitful, and review the developmental research within this context. The goal of this organization is to integrate perceptual processes and developmental changes.

As is apparent from the research cited in the text, I owe a substantial intellectual debt to Eleanor J. Gibson and James J. Gibson. I have benefited enormously from discussions with them, and their theories have played a large role in my thinking. I am indebted also to many people who read parts of the manuscript and commented on it: Alexander Siegel, David Warren, Hubert Dolezal, Thomas Toleno, James Farber, Kirk Wheeler, Roberta Golinkoff, Joseph Fagan, and Robert Fantz. Their advice and encouragement are greatly appreciated.

I am especially grateful to my wife, Frances, who has acted as assistant, typist, editor, proofreader, and reviewer throughout. She has encouraged my writing and tolerated my preoccupation. She makes it all worthwhile.

Richard R. Rosinski

THE DEVELOPMENT
OF VISUAL
PERCEPTION

Chapter 1

DEVELOPMENT AND
THE STUDY OF PERCEPTION

How does a child come to know about the sizes, shapes, orientations, distances, and identities of the objects that fill his or her environment? One of the earliest answers to this question was that knowledge about the world must come through the senses. If we wish to determine how knowledge is gained about the environment, we must first determine how our senses provide us with this knowledge. For this reason, the study of perceptual processes—that is, how organisms register and react to stimulation from the environment—is one of the oldest aspects of the field of psychology, dating perhaps from 1879, when Wilhelm Wundt, a German psychologist, established the first psychological research laboratory in Leipzig. To gain an understanding of the psychological processes that underlie an individual's knowledge of his or her environment, then, the study of perception is the best place to begin.

Many fields of psychology were initially part of the general study of perception. For example, the Rorschach Psychodiagnostic Test and the techniques of discrimination learning were originally devised to study perception in the clinic and the animal laboratory. In recent years, however, psychology has been compartmentalized into many different areas, and perception is no longer an all-encompassing discipline; but the relationships and interactions between perception and other areas of psychology are still recognized. These interactions form the bases for many different approaches to psychology. The relations between perception and memory, perception and learning, perception and motivation, and perception and social influences are all established fields of psychological study.

DEFINING PERCEPTION

Given such a large domain in which the study of perception is some-how concerned, what exactly is *perception*? Defining an area adequately is often difficult. In a broad sense, the entire history of a subject, because it outlines the important problems and the approaches taken in studying them, forms the definition. For our purposes, this method of definition is clearly the long way around. Instead, since an approach or a set of questions has implicit in it a definition, let us define *perception* by the specific approach taken and the way in which questions are framed.

In this sense, much of this book defines perception: it outlines a certain approach, poses certain questions, and provides some answers. Summarizing this approach, then, would reveal a summary definition of perception. Our primary concern is to determine how an individual uses stimulation to guide his normal activities in the world. Our interest will be centered on such problems as: How is an object located? How is locomotion guided? How are dangerous events avoided? How are patterns perceived? All these questions relate to an individual's ability to perceive the world and guide his behavior appropriately. These questions imply a particular view of perception as an internal process of the organism. Perception is not simply what an individual sees or how an individual responds; it is one mechanism that provides the individual with knowledge about the world. Since perception is the acquisition and utilization of knowledge about the world, it involves an active interaction with the environment.

Let us restrict this definition of perception still further. Since this book is also about development, perception within the context of human development will be emphasized, although it will sometimes be useful to look at perception in other organisms as well. Moreover, perceptual processes will be narrowed to visual perception. Because vision is one of the most important perceptual systems in the development and acquisition of knowledge, and because most of what is known about perceptual development involves vision, limiting our study to visual processes seems justified.

For a close look at how perception works, let us start by determining how children acquire knowledge about the world. Clearly, the study of development is intertwined with an understanding of perception.

AN APPROACH TO PERCEPTUAL DEVELOPMENT

Kurt Koffka (1935) formulated the most succinct question underlying the study of perception: "Why does the world look as it does?" In one form or another, this question has been the focus of most theoretical and experimental work in perception. Two general answers might be offered. The first asserts that things look as they do because specific information exists in the light that enters an eye. This aspect of perception has been most fully developed by J. J. Gibson (1966), E. J. Gibson (1969), and their colleagues. Formulated slightly differently, the question becomes: Why does the world look as it is? In other words, why are our perceptions accurate and in correspondence with the world?

Although this reformulation of Koffka's question may, at first glance, seem relatively minor, it has a number of far-reaching implications for the study of perception, for it directs our attention to the basic causes of *veridical perception*, that is, the accurate correspondence between perception and the structure of the world. The Gibsons hypothesize that the physical energy from an environment potentially provides an organism with information about that environment; that is, there is some correspondence between the structure of the environment and the structure of the light that is available to our eyes. The physical features of objects in the world determine the nature of information which, in turn, affects perception. An example will show the relationship that can exist between the structure of the environment and information.

Consider a textured, slanted surface such as the one depicted in Figure 1–1. Each of the elements of texture has a particular size. As you look from the bottom edge of the surface to the top, you notice that the size of those elements changes and becomes smaller as you near the top. The rate at which this size change takes place is exactly related to the amount that the surface is slanted. For each different slant of the surface there is a different rate at which the element size changes. This rate of change,

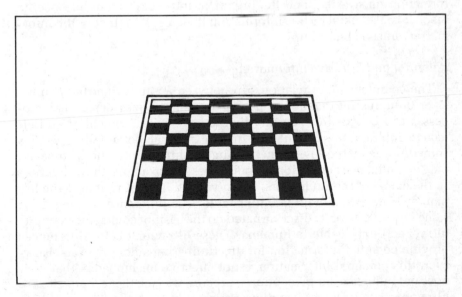

Figure 1–1
The change in size and density of texture elements specifies a slanted surface. For a regularly textured surface, each rate of change in size and density is uniquely related to a particular surface slant.

then, could be information for perceiving slant. If we were able to discern the rate at which the elements change size, we could know what the slant of the surface was. Since this information can tell us something about the arrangement of the environment (in this case, the slant of a surface), using this information could provide a basis for perception.

A second response to Koffka's question, "Why does the world look as it does?" stresses another aspect of perception. Things look the way they do because of specific mechanisms and processes in the perceiver (Neisser 1967). A perceiving organism is not simply a passive receiver of information. Perception is an active process in which the organism searches for, selects, computes, compares, and stores the information that specifies an object or event. As we have said, to be able to understand perception, we must understand the way information is picked up and used by an organism. To use the example of slant again, the rate at which texture elements change potentially specifies slant. To perceive slant, the organism must learn the set of invariants that relate optical texture to physical slant. There must be some stimulus-specific correlation the organism uses to tell that a certain rate of size change *means* a certain slant.

These two answers to Koffka's question are complementary; neither in isolation adequately explains the nature of perception. For visual perception to occur, there must be a correspondence between the structure of the environment and the structure of visual stimulation (that is, information must exist), and the organism must have stimulus-specific mechanisms that relate this information to perception (that is, the information must be picked up).

Potential and Effective Information

The complementary relationship between an approach that emphasizes stimulus information and one that emphasizes perceptual processes can be examined in the distinction between *potential* and *effective information*. Stimulation may exist that potentially specifies something about the environment. This potential information, however, may not influence perception in some cases. For example, the differences in the colors of certain flowers, when viewed in light visible to the human eye, are virtually indistinguishable. The differences among these same flowers are easily discriminated on the basis of colors (for example, ultraviolet) not visible to humans. These ultraviolet color differences provide potential information for discriminating among flowers. However, this potential information is not effective for humans—that is, it does not influence our perception—because we lack the receptors to see ultraviolet colors. For other animals such as bees, these colors are effective since the bee has the receptors necessary to pick up this potential information. In this example, potential information is not effective for humans because of the lack of an appropriate receptor mechanism.

There are other circumstances in which potential information and a receptor system for this information both exist, but no stimulus-specific correlation relating this information to the environment is present. Under these conditions, information is not effective. For example, the plane of polarization of light potentially specifies the location of the sun, even on overcast days. This information could be potentially important in navigation, since once the direction of the sun is known, compass direction can be calculated. You can demonstrate to yourself that you possess the sensory ability to perceive the plane of polarization of light by looking at a brightly illuminated white surface through one lens of a pair of Polaroid sunglasses. Slowly rotate the lens while you look at the surface. You will observe a faint yellow "hourglass" shape on a faint blue background. The appearance of this hourglass is due to the structure of the retina. The long axis of the hourglass is always oriented perpendicularly to the plane of polarization. Despite the fact that this information exists and that you have a receptor apparatus in the eye for polarization, it is useless in perception because there is no mechanism in the brain to relate this information to any aspect of the environment.

The distinction between potential and effective stimulation is important even when both sensory mechanisms and perceptual abilities exist. Although a sensory and perceptual capacity may exist, a person may fail to notice or pay attention to the information that is available. In this case, the information is not effective.

Thus, the two answers to Koffka's question, "Why does the world look as it does?" (because of the information available and the processes that register it) and the distinction between potential and effective stimulation point out that the study of perception must be based on two congruent approaches. First, such study must analyze the information that is available to a perceiving organism; second, it must determine the way this information is picked up and used by the organism. When we know what the potential information for perception is, in addition to knowing how this information is made effective, a complete understanding of perception will emerge.

THE CONCEPT OF STIMULUS INFORMATION

In the preceding section, the notion that stimulation contains information about the world is interwoven with the discussion of approaches to the study of perception. Clearly, *stimulus information* is a crucial concept for much of perception. Any theory of perception must concern itself with the sources of perceptual knowledge. In this section, we will examine the concept of stimulus information and its relationship to perceptual processes.

The use of the term *information* in psychology derives from work in communications engineering. To analyze the characteristics of a communications system, a quantitative measure of information—called a *bit*—was defined as the amount of information needed to distinguish between two equally likely alternatives. Specifying this unit of information allowed computer engineers to characterize the limitations of their machines. For example, one can specify the limitations of a computer memory bank as "so many thousand bits of information," or the limits of a pattern recognition device as "bits per second."

For many psychologists, the similarities between the capacities of a computer and human limitations were striking. As a result, psychologists attempted to apply the concept of bits of information to human perception and thought. Research attempted to fix the limits of human ability in terms of a certain amount of information. Despite a great deal of work on the measurement of information, the notion of a quantitative unit of information for human processing has not been very successful, and adequate measures of information that are meaningful in relation to human perception have not yet been devised.

Even though the amount of information available to an organism cannot be easily specified, we can describe both quantitatively and qualitatively what perceptual information is. The description that we will use here was provided by Gibson (1966). He pointed out that *information about* something means only *specificity to* something. Thus, when we say that stimulation provides information about a certain condition in the environment, we mean that there is some specific relationship between that environmental condition and some characteristic of stimulation. This concept of *information about* something can be demonstrated using the example of surface slant illustrated in Figure 1–1. The rate at which the angular size of texture elements changes is related to the slant of the surface. Each possible slant has a unique rate of change associated with it. That is, the rate of change is specific to a particular slant. Because of this specificity, we can say that the rate of change of angular size provides potential information about the slant of the surface.

Viewed in this way, the concept of stimulus information has several aspects. First, information arises from an abstract characterization of the physical world. In the example of slant, the information does not arise from the specific texture that might be on a surface, the actual size of the elements, their color or brightness, or any particular feature of the surface itself. The information is provided by the rate at which the element size changes. Second, information must be invariant over a number of changes, since information about something exists because of the specific relationship between a property of stimulation and a property of the world. Again using the example of slant, the specific relationship between rate of change of element size and slant is unaffected by (is "invariant over") any particular characteristic of the surface. As long as a regular texture exists on the surface, the information is present. Changing the makeup of the surface, the size of the elements, and so forth, does not affect the information. Third, any particular kind of information can be mathematically characterized. That is, since information is specific to a situation, this specificity can be exactly described.

This discussion concentrates on what might be called a strong, ideal concept of information. On a theoretical level, several instances have been found in which an exact specificity exists between a property of stimulation and a property of the environment. In other cases, such exact specificity seems to be lacking, and information must be considered more broadly. In either case, the concept of stimulus information is useful, for it draws our attention to those characteristics of the world that form the basis of our perceptual knowledge.

COMPONENTS OF THE STUDY OF PERCEPTION AND DEVELOPMENT

Outlining a definition and an approach to the study of perception directly suggests a number of areas that are important in studying perceptual development. These theoretical areas form the basis for much of the discussion in the following sections of this book. In addition, they organize and relate the areas of perception and development.

The Perceptual Component

Several perceptual questions have already been discussed in the context of perception and perceptual analysis. Clearly, one of the most important questions that we must deal with relates to the information available for perception. Examining the potential sources of information available to an observer tells us what possible bases perception might have. Then we may determine whether this information is actually used by an observer, that is, whether the description of available information is a description of the information that is actually effective in perception.

Once an adequate characterization of the stimulus information is available, we can then ask how the perceiving organism uses this information, or what kinds of selection and analysis are performed by the perceiver. As pointed out in the description of information, an exact relationship between the environment and a property of stimulation may exist. With texture information for slant, for example, the specificity between rate of change of texture and physical slant is so great that a perceiver could, theoretically, determine the angle at which a surface is slanted with extreme precision. If the information could be picked up, slant could be known to within a fraction of a degree. Yet, we know that humans are not perfect perceptual computers. One facet of perceptual study, then, is to determine how well stimulation can be analyzed, and how exact the correspondence is between stimulus information and perception.

The Developmental Component

In examining perceptual development, we will be concerned with the problems of stimulus information and information pickup. One way to approach these problems is to look at how perception develops. There is a great deal of redundant information available to an observer. It is known that these different kinds of information interact. However, little is known about the nature of this interaction. Whether an individual selects one type of information and excludes others, or whether different types of information are combined in some way to result in a final *percept* is, in many cases, unknown. The means by which the perceptual system utilizes independent sources of information for veridical perception cannot yet be specified.

Developmental psychology is particularly suited to examining these questions, since young children are in the process of developing the perceptual abilities that adults possess. Therefore, studying the course of this development should reveal how perceptual information is picked up and used. By determining how a perceptual ability develops, how it changes with experience, and how it reaches adult levels, we gain insight into the basic nature of perceptual development. Understanding the basic course of perceptual development may, in turn, prove useful in examining some of the practical problems of developmental psychology. If, for instance, we understand the developmental basis of space perception and visual-motor coordination, we might be able to correct impairments in these abilities or structure experience to assure optimal development. Similarly, understanding pattern perception may ultimately contribute to solving educational problems involving reading. Before an attempt can be made to solve either the basic or applied problems of perceptual development, though, we must know how perceptual processes change over the course of development.

One of the first developmental concerns is when certain abilities first appear. Is the ability to perceive space, to know about the spatial arrangement of the environment, present in infants? Are certain kinds of perceptual knowledge available to very young children and other kinds not available? At any point in perceptual development, what limitations are present?

It is well known that the perceptual abilities of infants differ from those of adults. A second consideration, then, is in what ways these perceptual abilities change, or what the differences are between what a child can perceive at one point in development and what he or she can perceive at a different point.

Since developmental changes in perception do occur in childhood, a third concern is why these changes occur. Are differences in the ways children pick up and use information related to changes in ability? Does the ability to pick up information change? Does the effectiveness of certain kinds of information change? Does the relationship between information and perception become more precise—that is, does stimulus information become more precisely related to perception over the course of development? For an adequate description of perceptual development, all of these questions must be approached.

A final developmental problem is related to the generality of the perceptual changes that occur. Do the developmental changes found in perception obey some set of general principles, or do totally different rules govern the development of different abilities? In other words, we must ask whether the process of perceptual change in development can be described within a simple theoretical framework—that is, can we formulate a theory of perceptual development and perceptual learning?

This enumeration of problems in perception and perceptual development forms the organization for this book. For each aspect of perception discussed, these considerations will provide the basis of our examination. In many instances, we will not be able to answer all of the questions posed, since the study of perceptual development is a relatively new discipline in psychology. Although psychologists have been concerned for many decades about the changes that occur in development, an intensive study of perceptual development has occurred in only the last few years. Because of the newness of this field, research data that provide definitive answers to many of the questions about perceptual development are not available. Although a complete description of perception in development is still many years off, organizing our study around questions in perceptual development points out some of the holes that need filling in our knowledge of development and generates a number of interesting speculations about the course of development.

METHODS OF STUDYING PERCEPTUAL DEVELOPMENT

If perception is indeed an internal process that is involved in the organism's gaining knowledge about the world, how can this process be studied? The methodological problems encountered in studying perceptual development are by no means unique to developmental psychology. Rather they seem to be an amalgam of the problems encountered in a number of different areas. Many of the experimental problems involved in studying children's perception are parallel to those involved in studying other psychological processes and other organisms.

As in the study of other internal cognitive processes, one basic problem in perceptual research is to determine the meaning of a particular response made by an organism. An experiment gives us only a sample of our subjects' behavior under certain conditions. Yet perception is not simply the study of behavior. We are uninterested in the particular responses that a subject makes. These behaviors are of interest only to the extent that they provide us with some means of determining the nature

of the organism's internal processes. In other words, experimental behaviors are important because they allow us to infer something about the
nature of the perceptual system.

Developmental psychology also shares a methodological problem
with comparative psychology. Especially in the study of infants and
young children, there is no direct way to "question" a child about what
he can see. To meet this problem, both comparative and developmental
psychology have developed methods to assess the capabilities of nonverbal organisms. These indirect means of study form one set of procedures used in perceptual experimentation. A number of procedures have
been applied to the study of perceptual development. In the section that
follows, these methods are discussed and evaluated as means of gather-
ing data on perceptual capacity.

Judgmental Methods

Probably the most direct method of determining what a verbal child is
able to perceive is simply to ask him or her. If a child is able to make a
judgment about a particular aspect of the world, this judgment may
provide the researcher with some knowledge about the child's perceptual abilities. There is a vast number of different *judgmental methods*
used to determine the perceptual capacities of a subject. These
psychophysical methods involve different kinds of judgments, different
ways of presenting stimuli, and different ways of statistically analyzing
the judgments made. Many of these techniques are described in a text by
Guilford (1954). Although there is a variety of judgmental techniques
used to explore perceptual development, the experiment described
below illustrates the nature of one approach and shows how judgmental
techniques can reveal perceptual abilities.

Wohlwill (1965) showed elementary school children and college-aged
adults pictures depicting toys arranged on the ground as in Figure 1–2. A
very simple judgment was required of the subjects. They were asked to
imagine they were in the field in which the picture was taken and to say
whether the cow or the horse was closer to the fence. The position of the
fence varied in different photographs, sometimes being closer to the
cow, sometimes to the horse, and sometimes exactly in the middle between them. This task asks the subject to bisect the interval between the
two animals. He must be able to compare the space between the cow and
the fence with the space between the horse and the fence and to determine which is greater. From a large number of such judgments,
Wohlwill calculated at which point these two spaces seemed equivalent
to a child. By comparing this estimate of a child's judgment of equivalence to the actual (physical) point at which the two spaces were equivalent, Wohlwill determined how accurate children's judgments were and
compared them to adult judgments. Using such a technique, Wohlwill

Figure 1–2

Sample stimuli used in Wohlwill's study. Children were asked to judge whether the cow or horse was closer to the fence. (From Wohlwill, 1965.)

determined the effect of a number of different variables on the accuracy of judgment in both children and adults.

In principle, similar data could be generated by a number of other judgmental experiments, such as asking the subjects to match the distance to the fence depicted in one photo with the distance shown in a second photo, to ask the same type of experimental question: How accurately can distances be judged?

Although using judgmental methods for studying perceptual development may seem straightforward, there are a few drawbacks. For example, the number of separate judgments required to determine accuracy is fairly large. Depending on specific procedures, more judgments than a child can make in a reasonable amount of time may be necessary. Thus, in a long experiment the effects of fatigue and boredom may influence the results. Since fatigue may be related to the age of the child, age differences in judgment may appear that are unrelated to perceptual processes but are the result of the long session. Consequently, in some situations judgmental techniques are not appropriate with children.

A second caution related to using judgmental methods is that developmental changes in judgmental data may be difficult to interpret.

Consider a result that indicated young children were much poorer at a judgmental task than were older children. How should this be interpreted? Do children's perceptual abilities become better with increasing age, or are older children simply better at understanding the instructions and performing the task? In fact, both of these effects could be operating at once, and some studies have found differing results based on the specific judgment required of the child.

A third difficulty in using judgmental procedures involves the ages with which they can be used. Clearly, there is a lower age limit at which children could be expected to perform such a task. In Wohlwill's experiment, it was appropriate to ask elementary school children to make distance judgments; they could be expected to understand the task and to respond verbally to the experimenter's questions. But if one wished to investigate children's perceptual abilities at an earlier point in development, these techniques could not be used. Preverbal children certainly could not be tested using these procedures. Other methods have been developed, however, that enable nonverbal subjects to indicate their judgments.

Discrimination Learning

One set of methods devised to study the perceptual ability of nonverbal subjects is *discrimination learning*. The logical connection between perceptual ability and discrimination learning is very simple. If a subject can learn to respond differentially to different stimuli (for example, objects or patterns), he must possess the perceptual ability to discriminate between those stimuli. The essential aspect of discrimination learning techniques involves the training procedure used to determine whether learning can occur. For example, to determine whether a child could discriminate between two patterns, the child would be rewarded for responding to one of the patterns but not rewarded for responding to the other. In one situation, a child may have to push aside the pattern to receive candy as a reward. The experimenter changes the position of the patterns between trials so that simply responding to one position is not an adequate basis for consistently receiving a reward. If the child can learn to respond in such a way as to gain the reward whenever the patterns are presented, he has learned the problem and therefore must be able to distinguish between them. If the patterns were not distinguishable to the child, there would be no way he could learn to receive the reward consistently.

The advantages of discrimination learning procedures lie in their extreme flexibility. Since no verbal instructions are given to a child and no verbal response required, these methods are not dependent on a child's ability to use or understand language. Furthermore, in discrimination learning studies of perception, the important data involve whether a problem can be learned. The response that indicates learning is irrelevant. Any response the child can make can be used as a measure of learning. In testing young infants, for example, one might train a child to turn his head in one direction when one pattern is presented, but to turn his head in another direction to a different pattern. If the right responses are made, the child is rewarded. Since any response can be used in these techniques, the only limitation lies in the experimenter's ingenuity in finding a response that a young child can make.

A problem that arises in using discrimination learning procedures is similar to one involved in using the judgmental techniques. How do we interpret results that indicate the child cannot solve the learning problem? For example, an experiment by House (1964) assessed size discrimination by using discrimination learning procedures. Three objects were presented to the subjects, two of the same size and one of a different size. The children were to learn to respond to the different-sized object. Retarded children were given thirty-three training trials per day for twenty days. Performance levels of six children in the experiment were only about 80 percent correct at the end of training. Clearly, these children experienced some difficulty in solving the size problem. After 660 training trials, they still made substantial errors in size judgment.

Can we conclude from these results that the children's difficulty with the problem lies in the fact that they could not perceive the size differences between the objects, or could they perceive the size differences but not learn to respond consistently to them? Do the results indicate the lack of a perceptual ability or of a learning ability? The inability to learn a discrimination problem is often taken to be the same thing as an inability to perceive differences in the patterns.

Equating discrimination learning performance with perceptual discrimination ability is erroneous, however. This can be seen in a second part of House's experiment. After the children completed the discrimination learning phase of the experiment, they were questioned verbally. Two different-sized objects were presented and the child was asked, "Which is bigger?" The differences between the learning and verbal test procedures were striking. Some of the children who had difficulty with the original discrimination problem performed almost perfectly during the verbal testing.

The implication of this experiment is clear. Discrimination learning measures require both a perceptual and a learning ability. Some of the children in House's experiment were able to discriminate size differences correctly but could not learn the oddity problem. There are other means of assessing perception based on differences in responding that do not require training or learning a problem.

Preference Methods

Preference methods are similar to discrimination learning procedures in that they both take as their basic data the child's ability to respond differently to stimuli as an indication of perceptual ability. As the name implies, preference methods are based on the child's tendency to prefer to respond to certain patterns more than to others. These methods were developed and refined by Robert Fantz (1967) in his work on infant perception. Since control of eye movements is one of the few response systems well developed in infancy, Fantz chose to measure the amount of time that infants spent looking at different patterns. The rationale behind this choice was simple. A child is presented with a pair of patterns whose right-left position is changed from trial to trial. If the child looks at one stimulus reliably more than another, he must be able to see differences between the two. The only way that a consistent preference for one stimulus could be shown is if differences were perceived. If the

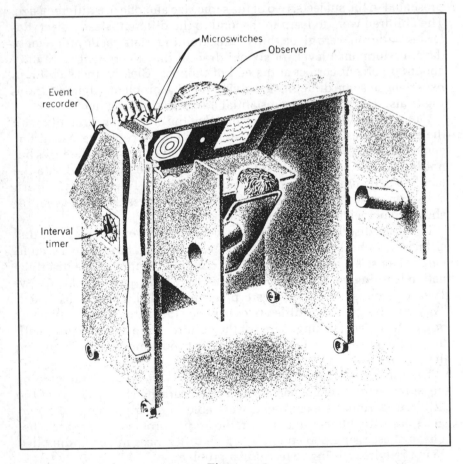

Figure 1–3

An experimental apparatus used to determine the visual preferences of infants. From R. L. Fantz, "Visual perception and experience in early infancy: a look at the hidden side of behavioral development." In *Early behavior: comparative and developmental approaches,* edited by H. W. Stevenson, E. H. Hess, and H. L. Rheingold. Copyright © 1967 John Wiley & Sons, Inc. Reprinted by permission of John Wiley & Sons, Inc.

two stimuli were perceived as identical, there could be no basis for differential looking.

In one experiment (Fantz 1967), an infant was placed in an inclined restraining seat and surrounded by a boxlike apparatus that entirely filled his visual field. A pair of patterns were placed slightly above and on each side of the infant. A peephole located between the two patterns enabled the experimenter to observe the infant's eyes. Because of the construction of the apparatus, the experimenter could see a reflection of the pattern being looked at on the infant's cornea. Timers were used to record the amount of time spent looking at each of the patterns, and a comparison of these times indicated whether there was a preference for one pattern. Figure 1–4 presents some data drawn from an experiment by Fantz and Nevis (1967), which show infant preference and, consequently, their discrimination ability for a set of patterns.

The preference method can be used with infants immediately after birth and requires no training of the subjects, but there is an important limitation on the interpretation of preference results. If a child shows no preference for a pattern, this fact does not necessarily imply that the child cannot discriminate between the two patterns. He may see them as different but find both equally attractive, or he may be bored or sleepy

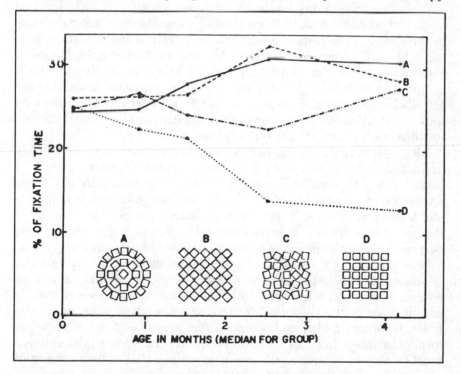

Figure 1–4

Infants' relative visual preferences for four arrangements of squares. (From Fantz and Nevis, 1967. Reprinted by permission of the author and the *Merrill-Palmer Quarterly of Behavior and Development*.

and not care to look at any pattern. Consequently, preference data can indicate only what abilities a child possesses. They cannot give an indication of what abilities are lacking.

A study by McGurk (1970) has demonstrated the limitations of the preference procedure. This experiment studied whether infants have the capacity to discriminate between two patterns that differ in orientation. To study this question, McGurk first used a standard preference technique. Lifelike models of a human face were constructed, and a pair of these models was presented in a preference apparatus. The faces were identical except in their orientation. One was presented normally (right side up) and the other one presented upside down. When the amount of time spent looking at each of the two stimuli was compared, no significant preference was found. Infants spent about the same amount of time looking at the upright face as they spent looking at the upside-down face. One might be tempted to conclude from these results that infants are unable to discriminate faces on the basis of orientation. McGurk also used a second technique, however, in which discrimination of orientation was assessed by means of a habituation procedure.

Habituation and Dishabituation Techniques

When an unchanging stimulus is presented repetitively, an individual may react briskly at first. With succeeding presentations, the magnitude or the speed of the response may decrease until it reaches some low, stable level. This decrement in responsiveness is known as *habituation*. Habituation is one of the most ubiquitous of all behavioral phenomena. It occurs in animals having no nervous system as well as in animals having a well-developed brain; amoeba habituate to repetitive stimuli as do humans. Habituation will occur in any organism that has certain characteristics, such as several behavioral states.

Although the underlying mechanisms for habituation must differ in various kinds of organisms, we can identify general characteristics of the phenomenon. Habituation is a relatively enduring decrement in responsiveness that is stimulus specific and is distinct from response fatigue and sensory adaptation. These characteristics are especially relevant to the use of habituation in developmental research. Since the response decrement is stimulus specific, the occurrence of habituation can provide an indication of an organism's perceptual ability. If a single pattern is presented repeatedly, and the subjects' response to this pattern decreases over trials, some aspect of that pattern must be perceived. In addition, since the response decrement takes place over successive trials, habituation also demonstrates the presence of some primitive form of memory. In order for habituation to occur over trials, a subject must be able to categorize the stimulus on one trial as being the same one perceived on the previous trials.

The fact that habituation is stimulus specific and not due to the fatigue of the response mechanism provides another important way in which habituation techniques can be applied to perceptual development research. This technique involves *dishabituation,* or a recovery of the habituated response. Assume that a stimulus has been repeatedly presented to a subject and habituation has occurred. What would happen if a new stimulus were substituted for the old one? Since habituation is stimulus specific and not due to sensory adaptation, we should expect that the original response would recover. This phenomenon of dishabituation also provides a means for assessing an organism's perceptual capacities. If dishabituation occurs to a change in stimulation, then that change must have been perceived by the organism; the two stimuli must be discriminable.

An example of how habituation and dishabituation can be used to assess a child's perceptual ability is provided by McGurk's study (1970). In using the preference method, he found no evidence that infants were able to discriminate between upright and inverted faces. In a second study, McGurk showed infants a face in one orientation for six successive trials of twenty seconds each. In each trial, the amount of time the infant spent looking at the face was recorded. Habituation was found; looking time decreased over the six trials. This result suggests that the infants were able to perceive the face and could "remember" it from trial to trial.

In a third experiment, McGurk used a dishabituation technique to verify the results obtained with habituation measures. A face in one orientation was presented for eighty seconds. Fixation of the face habituated over this time period, as might be expected from the results of the previous study. After this habituation period of eighty seconds, however, the face was exposed in a new orientation for twenty seconds. Dishabituation occurred in this twenty second period: the infants spent more time looking at the face in a new orientation. This dishabituation resulting from a change in orientation demonstrates that the infants could distinguish a difference between the patterns.

McGurk's studies illustrate how the habituation paradigm can be used with young infants. The change in the children's looking behavior over habituation and dishabituation clearly demonstrates that discrimination capacity is present in infancy. Of course, fixation is not the only response that can be investigated with a habituation procedure. Any response measure is potentially useful.

One measure of discrimination capacity that has been used even with very young infants is the heart rate. The general techniques used in heart rate habituation studies are the same as those used in fixation habituation. In both cases, the relevant question concerns whether the child's responsiveness (heart rate) will change as a result of his experience with particular stimuli. On the first presentation of a stimulus, heart rate may accelerate greatly (for example, if the infant is startled), but with succeeding presentations the change in rate may decrease as habituation takes place. Also, as in the preference studies, a perceptible change in the stimulus may then result in a recovery of response rate. Such results indicate that the child was able to perceive the pattern, remember it over the intertrial interval, and notice a difference between the original pattern and the changed one. An acceleration in heart rate is not necessary for use of the habituation measure. Under some conditions, heart rate may decrease when a stimulus is presented. A change in this deceleration with successive stimulus presentations would then indicate habituation, and a recovery of response with a novel stimulus would indicate dishabituation and thus discrimination.

Some psychologists (for example, Lacey, Kagan, Lacey, and Moss 1963) suggest that the direction of change in heart rate is itself an important indicator of perceptual and cognitive ability: an acceleration is correlated with a startle response, whereas a deceleration is correlated with curiosity or interest. Thus, heart rate habituation measures potentially reveal not only the ability to discriminate but also the specific way in which a child interacts with a stimulus.

Using habituation techniques provides several advantages in assessing perceptual capacity. The procedures themselves are not limited in their usefulness to any particular stimulus or response. Therefore, a wide range of abilities may be investigated. Since any responses (including involuntary ones) the child can consistently make are appropriate for use in habituation, children at all ages can be tested with these procedures. Habituation techniques are as applicable to neonates as to adolescents and adults.

One difficulty in using habituation and dishabituation procedures, especially with infants, lies in the interaction between measures of habituation and the child's behavioral state at the time of testing. Habituation and dishabituation are processes that involve a change in the organism's state during testing. For example, in the preference studies, during habituation an infant goes from a state of high responsiveness or attentiveness to one of low responsiveness. In dishabituation, there is recovery of a state of high responsiveness. Clearly, the state of the infant at the beginning of the test period influences results. If the infant is initially very unresponsive (is sleepy or bored, for example), no further decrement may occur. The absence of habituation and dishabituation may be the result of either a lack of perceptual ability or of an initially unresponsive state of the child.

An interaction is also present between the kinds of stimuli used and a change in state. Certain stimuli may be perceived, but they may be so attractive or so attention grabbing that habituation does not occur over a short period. For example, a pattern made of fluorescent colors may be so attractive to an infant that he gazes intently at this pattern over a number of trials and habituates only after an extremely long exposure period. As a result, the absence of habituation over the short run of an experiment may not indicate the lack of a perceptual ability. Similarly, when a stimulus is changed, the change may be noticed but not result in a change in state. The difference between the original and the changed stimulus may be perceptible but not large enough to result in significant response recovery.

THE PRINCIPLE OF CONVERGING OPERATIONS

All of the methods discussed above share a common limitation: none can prove that a perceptual ability is lacking. Experimentation cannot prove that an infant of a certain age does not possess a particular ability. As many of the examples in the preceding section show, the failure of a child to perform successfully in a task may indicate either the lack of a perceptual ability or a performance difficulty specific to the task. We are unable to decide between these alternatives on the basis of a single experiment. This fact has one important implication for the study of development—one experiment can never tell us when a certain ability first appears in development. Any result indicating that a certain ability (such as pattern discrimination) appears at x months should always be qualified in its interpretation to read that the ability is present "*at least by x months.*" The perceptual ability might have been found earlier if different methods and techniques had been used.

The use of *converging operations* provides a partial solution to this difficulty. Converging operations use a set of different experiments designed to rule out alternative explanations of a study. The experiments of McGurk (1970) and of House (1964) cited earlier demonstrate the use of converging operations in developmental research. McGurk's first preference study did not determine whether the infants' difficulty in discriminating orientation was due to a perceptual deficit or to a problem related to the use of preference techniques; both of the facial orientations may have been equally attractive to the children. McGurk's habituation and dishabituation experiments, however, permit us to eliminate one of these hypotheses. If the preference results were due to methodological problems, habituation measures would provide different results. Since the habituation results showed that pattern differences associated with orientation could be perceived by infants, the preference results were affected by methodology. The dishabituation procedure McGurk used substantiates this conclusion and shows further that infants are capable of noticing a difference between faces at different orientations.

Similar reasoning underlies the analysis of House's data. The children she tested could not use oddity to learn the solution to a size discrimination problem. Taken by itself, this result has several interpretations. The children might not be able to discriminate among sizes; they might not be capable of understanding the abstract concept "odd"; or they might not be able to learn discrimination problems. By verbally questioning the children later in the experiment, the first two of these alternate hypotheses were ruled out. The children could discriminate among patterns based on oddity, but they had difficulty with the specific learning task.

Sets of converging experiments could be used in many cases to determine whether the lack of a perceptual ability was real or the result of the particular method used. By enabling us to rule out alternative methodological hypotheses, converging operations allow firmer conclusions to be drawn concerning the appearance of a perceptual ability in development. Strictly speaking, converging operations do not provide a total answer to the problem of determining when an ability first appears. It is at least possible that a series of converging operations involving all techniques would yield negative results even though the child did possess a certain ability. An experimental series, however, decreases the chances that a particular result is due to methodological idiosyncracies.

The use of a set of converging operations also allows a psychologist to assess interactions of perceptual ability with specific tasks. Using one method (such as a preference task), an ability may be found present. With another procedure (such as discrimination learning), the ability may not be found. Comparing these results and examining the parameters of discrimination learning that influence performance could give some insight into the relationship between perception and learning in children and thus permit the connection between these two processes in development to be studied.

BASIC CONCEPTS IN THE STUDY OF PERCEPTION

Most of the concepts necessary for a discussion of perceptual development are introduced in relation to specific topics. Several general concepts (based on Gibson's theoretical framework) are used throughout this book, however, and are closely related to the specific approach to perception taken here.

The Optic Array. In any illuminated space, environmental surfaces reflect light in many directions. These light rays converge on an infinite number of points in space and form the basis of vision. When a set of light rays from an object is available to the eye, perception can occur. An eye positioned in this space receives a bundle of light rays projected to it from surfaces in the world. This set of light rays is a sample of the array of light that is projected to any point in space. Information for perception is contained in this array of light. The concept of the *optic array* refers to this projection of light to a point.

The Station Point, or Viewing Point. The sample of an array of light that the eye can receive is partially determined by the position of the eye in space. Each different location of the eye results in a different sample of the array. Figure 1–5 shows how the sample array changes with changes in eye position. The particular point occupied by an eye sampling the

Figure 1–5

Different viewing points provide an observer with different optic arrays.

array is called the *station point*, or *viewing point*. To specify the light available to the eye, the station point must be known.

Display. An array of light projected to an eye need not come from objects and surfaces in space. An artifact may be constructed that also projects an array of light to an eye. A picture or a photograph is an example of such an artifact. Since the array that reaches the eye from a photo depends on the viewing conditions, specification of the point of observation is especially important in picture perception.

Visual Angle, or Angular Size. There are two ways to describe the physical size of an object in the world. The first is the normal way, in standard units of length such as feet and inches. Such a description is often of little use in perception. Since the array of light projected to the eye is the basis for visual perception, a description of size in terms of the geometry of the array, or the *visual angle*, is more useful. As shown in Figure 1–6, because the array is a solid angle of light rays that are available to the eye,

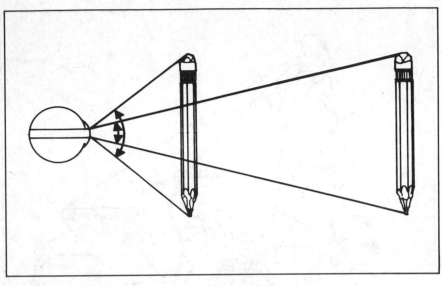

Figure 1–6

The angular size of an object is related to both its physical size and its distance.

specifying size in terms of angle relates object size to the array. Since an object of a certain physical size occupies a different amount of the array depending on its distance, angular units, not metric units, relate size to the array. Specifying the angular size of an object (for example, we could say that an object is 15 degrees high) tells how much of the array the object fills and how large the projected size of the object is.

Gradient of Size. As objects of equal physical size recede into the distance, their angular size changes (it gets smaller). If these objects are evenly distributed over a surface, this change in angular size is very regular. The rate at which these changes occur is called the *gradient of size*. This gradient provides important information for two aspects of space perception—distance and slant.

Visual Acuity. There are several operational definitions of *visual acuity*. In general, the term applies to the ability of the eye to resolve fine detail. The importance of visual acuity for perceptual development is that it places a limit on the information that can be used by an individual. An object or detail that is smaller than the limit of visual acuity cannot be perceived, since its size is less than the eye's capacity to see detail. The implication for developmental perception is that variables of stimulation that are potentially informative may not influence perception since they cannot be distinguished by the eye.

SUMMARY

The basic question regarding perception was asked by Koffka: Why does the world look as it does? Contemporary psychology offers two complimentary answers. First, the world looks as it does because of the specific relationship between the structure of the world and the information available to an observer. Second, the world looks as it does because there exist, in the observer, processes which select, compare and store information. The available information and the processes that register it conjointly determine our perceptions.

Within this approach, the concept of stimulus information is crucial. The most fruitful use of the information concept is in the work of J. J. Gibson, who pointed out that *information about* something means only *specificity to* something. When there is a specific relationship between some environmental condition and some characteristic of stimulation, we say that that stimulation can provide information about that environmental condition.

In studying perceptual development, we are interested in what information is available to an observer, whether this information is effective, and what kind of selection and analysis is performed by the perceiver, as well as when in development perceptual abilities first appear, how they change over age, and whether general principles could describe developmental changes.

Several methods have been developed to address these questions: judgmental methods, discrimination learning methods, preference methods, and habituation techniques. All these procedures have a common weakness. They cannot prove that a child lacks a particular perceptual ability; inability to perform in a task may indicate either a perceptual deficit, or a difficulty specific to the task. A partial solution to this problem in inference is provided by the principle of converging operations. Several studies using different methods allow us to rule out certain conclusions and thus converge on the nature of perceptual processes.

Chapter 2

SPATIAL LAYOUT: PERCEPTION OF DEPTH AND DISTANCE

A visual organism must possess the ability to determine the arrangement of objects and surfaces in the world to function in its environment. The size of objects, their distance away, their orientation, and whether they are moving or stationary are all important perceptual facts. The significant developmental consideration involves the nature of early perceptual abilities and the way these abilities change with growth and experience. That is, what information do young children use, and how does the use of this information change during development?

The logic underlying the notion of converging operations, discussed in Chapter One, implies that there may be a large set of different behaviors closely related to one another simply because they all rely on a common core of perceptual knowledge. If the perception of distance develops in a particular way, for example, we might expect that a number of different behaviors that depend on distance perception would follow a similar developmental course. From this standpoint, we might assume a high degree of congruence among different behavioral indexes of distance perception. This expected convergence, however, has not always been found. Part of the reason for this lack of convergence is simply that the different kinds of information available to a child have not always been clearly defined. As we will see, there are a number of different bases for the perception of distance. Consequently, to speak of distance perception as a single phenomenon without considering the different kinds of information and the different perceptual activities involved does not increase our understanding of the means by which development affects the use of information. Since different kinds of information may be effective at different points in development, each source of information should be considered separately.

CHILDREN'S PERCEPTION OF DEPTH AND DISTANCE

In this chapter and the next, we will consider the various types of information that potentially specify spatial layout and how that information is used over the course of development. Since the topic of spatial layout perception is broad, let us begin with a particular facet of layout perception—the ability to perceive depth and distance.

Early studies investigating children's depth perception used an apparatus called the *visual cliff*. The visual cliff consists of a glass-topped table bisected by a center board on which a subject can crawl. A surface may be placed beneath the glass at varying distances from the table top, on either side of the center board. For example, a textured surface is placed directly beneath the glass on one side of the center board, and a second surface is placed on the other side of the center board forty inches below the glass. The experiment is calculated to discover whether subjects are able to distinguish between the shallow and the deep sides of the "cliff." Determining an answer to this question is fairly simple. A subject is placed on the center board and the experimenter records

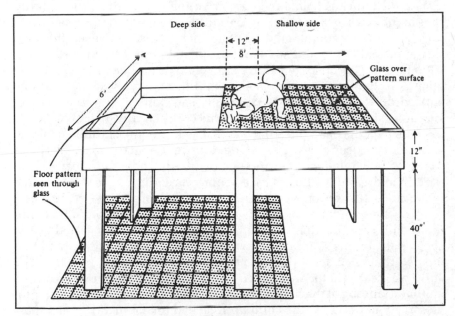

Figure 2–1

By showing a preference for the shallow side of the visual cliff, an infant demonstrates that he can perceive the difference between the two sides. (From Gibson, 1963. Copyright © 1963 by The Society for Research in Child Development, Inc. Reprinted by permission.)

whether the subject descends to the shallow side or the deep side. The major assumption is that if a consistent choice of one side is made, the subject can distinguish between the two depths. If no consistent preference is observed (that is, if the subject goes off the deep side as often as off the shallow side), the experimenter infers that the two sides are indiscriminable to the subject. A wide variety of animals have been tested on the visual cliff, and with few exceptions (notably, aquatic animals) a preference for the shallow side, implying discrimination of depth, has been demonstrated in all species. For a review of the animal literature see Walk (1965).

When children are tested on the cliff, the procedures take the general form described above. A child is placed on the center board and his mother attempts to entice him on to either the shallow side or the deep side by calling to him and presenting a toy. If the child is able to discriminate between the two sides of the cliff, he should crawl to his mother more frequently when she calls from the safer shallow side.

Using this technique, Walk and Gibson (1961) have demonstrated that infants are able to perceive the difference between the two sides. In this experiment, the shallow side of the cliff was positioned directly below the surface of the glass and was covered with green, patterned linoleum. The deep side was covered with the same linoleum pattern but was placed forty inches below the surface of the glass. Since the lighting caused the glass to be invisible to the child, the shallow side appeared to present a small stepping-off drop of an inch or two. However, the deep side appeared to drop off suddenly to a distance of forty inches.

Walk and Gibson tested thirty-six infants ranging in age from six months to fourteen months. Of these children, twenty-seven could be enticed off the center board. All twenty-seven crawled to the shallow side at least once, while only three of the children tried to crawl to their mothers over the deep side. The fact that so few of the children could be enticed to the deep side of the cliff demonstrates that the vast majority of the children could discriminate the potentially dangerous deep side of the cliff and avoid it. Thus, at least by the time children are able to crawl, they are able to discriminate differences in depth of at least forty inches.

Using a modification of the visual cliff, Walk (1969) found that children's ability to discriminate depth is even finer than suggested by the above data. In this series of experiments, Walk used a center board that tapered from 35.3 cm at the wide end to 7.6 cm at the narrow end. The child was placed at the wide end of the board and enticed to crawl to his mother, standing at the narrow end. Since the center board became progressively narrower as the child approached his mother, it was impossible for him to remain on it throughout the trial. In order to reach his mother, the child had to leave the center board and descend to the glass. This necessitated a choice, and the interesting findings are whether the child chose to descend to the shallow or the deep side.

Walk tested children from 6½ months to 15 months old in this situation. The deep side of the cliff was either five, ten, twenty, or forty inches under the glass; the shallow side was directly beneath the glass. Regardless of the distance of the deep side, children showed a significant preference for the shallow side. However, there were differences in the proportion choosing the shallow side, depending on the depth of the deep side. When the deep side of the cliff was five inches under the glass, children chose the shallow side on 73 percent of the trials. When the deep side was ten or more inches below, a preference for the shallow side was demonstrated on 93 percent of the trials. These results indicate that infants are able to discriminate between one depth zero to five inches away and a second depth ten or more inches away.

In other studies done by Walk (1966), texture of the surfaces beneath the glass was found to be an important variable affecting cliff performance. One side of the cliff stayed at zero depth (surface directly beneath the glass), but the other was varied from zero to forty inches. When a textured surface was used, the proportion of children crossing over to the deep side decreased as the distance was made greater. When an untextured, gray surface was used under the glass, however, the actual depth of the surface did not influence the children's responses. For example, when the gray surface was directly beneath the glass, 50 percent of the children crossed over to the deep side. When the surface was fifty inches below, 41 percent would cross to the deep side. Thus, a nontextured surface under the glass does not provide the child with sufficient information for depth discrimination.

Taken together, the studies of Walk and Gibson (1961) and of Walk (1966, 1969) demonstrate that children are able to differentiate between surfaces at different depths as soon as they are able to crawl. Can children make such a discrimination before they can locomote? Using the cliff studies would be inappropriate because they require a gross locomotor response (crawling) as an indication of differential perception. A locomotor response is not mandatory, however, since any differential response to the shallow and deep sides will indicate that depth is differentially perceived.

Campos, Langer, and Krowitz (1970) developed a method for assessing depth perception in prelocomotor infants by recording their heart rates when placed directly on the glass over either the shallow or the deep side of a visual cliff. Both sides of the cliff were patterned with red and white checks, and the deep side was forty inches below the glass. Children too young to crawl (median age of fifty-five days) responded differently on the two sides of the cliff. When these children were placed on the shallow side, Campos et al. found a small, generally nonsignificant change in heart rate. However, when the children were placed on the deep side, a large deceleration in heart rate was observed.

It is clear from these results that even young infants can discriminate between two depths on the visual cliff. A second interesting aspect of the Campos data concerns the heart rate deceleration observed when the children were on the deep side of the cliff. Since the deep side elicited a deceleration rather than an acceleration of heart rate, Campos et al.

suggest that the perception of depth results in an orienting response, or an attention to depth, rather than fear. Corroborating evidence also indicates the children were not afraid when placed on the deep side. There was significantly less crying and fussing when on the deep side than when on the shallow side. This also suggests that depth elicited orientation, or curiosity, rather than fear.

This finding was later replicated by Campos and Langer (1971), who again found highly reliable heart rate deceleration on the deep side of the cliff, but no change in heart rate on the shallow side. This pattern of behavioral and heart rate responses suggests that human infants react quite differently from the young of other species. Research conducted by Gibson and Walk (1960) and by Rosenblum and Cross (1963) on young kittens, goats, and neonatal monkeys found that being placed on the deep side of the cliff was very stressful; the animals showed very stereotyped fear and distress. Such distress and fear were clearly absent in the human infants tested.

Schwartz, Campos, and Baisel (1973) studied the development of fearfulness in the visual cliff experiment and found the direction of heart rate change of the infants placed on the deep side of the cliff different at different ages. By the time the infants were nine months old, they showed a pronounced acceleration of heart rate when placed on the deep side of the cliff. Schwartz et al. interpret these results as indicating that fearful or emotional responses to the depth of the cliff do not appear until later in infancy.

This later development of the fear of depth raises an additional complexity in the perceptual interpretation of the results of Campos et al. Previous studies using the visual cliff with human infants capable of crawling and neonates of other species conclusively demonstrated the existence of depth perception, because they found both a consistent preference for one side of the cliff as well as a fear of the potentially dangerous deep side. How should we interpret the ability to discriminate the two sides without an attendant fear of the deep side? One possibility is that the infants could perceive depth but simply had not yet come to fear depth. Equally plausible would be the argument that infants could discriminate some difference between the two sides of the cliff, but that this difference was not necessarily related to the perception of depth. In other words, a discriminable difference in stimulation might exist but not be an effective determiner of depth perception in early infancy. In sum, these studies may indicate either that young infants can discriminate depth but do not fear it, or that they can discriminate some difference in stimulation but cannot perceive depth.

Fortunately, we can turn to other research that uses a totally different method of examination, which converges on the question of depth perception in early infancy. Bower (1964, 1965) has provided evidence that children are able to perceive differences in depth before they can locomote. Bower used a discrimination learning paradigm to determine whether infants could discriminate differences in distance. Infants between seventy days and eighty-five days old were conditioned to turn their heads in the presence of a twelve-inch cube located three feet away. As a reinforcement during training, an experimenter popped up and said "peekaboo" whenever the infant responded appropriately. After training, the infants were tested using four different stimulus situations (see Figure 2–2): (1) the original training stimulus at three feet; (2) the original cube at nine feet; (3) a thirty-six-inch cube at three feet; and (4) a thirty-six-inch cube at nine feet. Notice that with this set of test conditions, both the size and the distance of the stimulus are the same as the training stimulus in test condition 1. The size of the stimulus is the same in condition 2, but the distance is changed. The distance is the same in condition 3, but the size is changed. In condition 4, both the actual size and the distance of the stimulus are changed; however, the retinal size (projection of the stimulus on the retina) is the same as in the training situation.

Using these four tests, Bower could determine which aspects of the situation the infants could perceive—size, distance, or retinal projection. Bower's results are presented in Table 2–1. As one might expect, the original training stimulus resulted in the greatest number of responses during testing. An important aspect of these data is that the actual size and actual distance of the cube were detected by the infants. Changing either distance or size (conditions 2 and 3) affects performance. In condition 4 (changed size and distance), infants responded the fewest number of times. Although the stimulus in this condition had the same projected size as the training stimulus, it was not responded to in the same way. Since there were clear differences in the number of responses in conditions 1 and 4, actual size and distance must control responding rather than retinal size. These results provide an unambiguous interpretation of the visual cliff studies: infants are able to perceive distance to a surface or object before they are afraid of falling.

These few studies present adequate evidence that infants are able to perceive at least one aspect of spatial layout, the distance or depth of

Table 2–1

The Number of Responses Made in the Various Test Conditions of the Bower Study (1965)

Test Stimulus	Stimulus Size	Stimulus Distance	Number of Test Responses
1	Same as in training	Same as in training	102.70
2	Same as in training	Different than in training	66.03
3	Different than in training	Same as in training	54.10
4	Different than in training	Different than in training	22.92

Source: Adapted from T. G. R. Bower, "Stimulus Variables Determining Space Perception in Infants," Science 149, (1965): 88–89.

surfaces and objects. Although it is clear that this perceptual ability exists even in two- and three-month-olds, the basis of this ability is not specified by these studies. Next we will consider what information can be used to determine the distance of an object.

BINOCULAR VISION

Convergence

Binocular vision provides an important source of information about spatial layout. The fact that our eyes are slightly separated (about 6.5 cm in adults) has a number of implications for depth perception. One potential source of information about distance comes from the fact that the lines of sight of the two eyes must converge on a particular object in fixation. When an object is far away, the angle formed between the two lines of sight is small. When an object is close, the angle between the lines of sight is large. This fact is illustrated in Figure 2–2. If the points represent a row of objects extending away from the observer, the eyes must converge much more to fixate a point nearby than to fixate one far away from the subject. Once an object is fixated, convergence may supply information for the perception of distance. In converging the eyes, receptors in

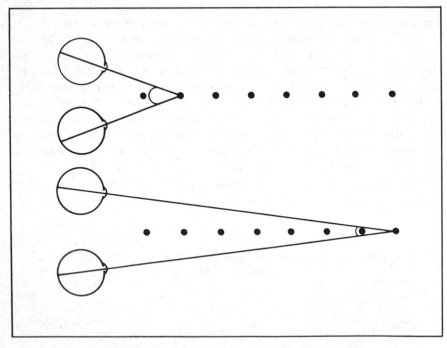

Figure 2–2

The eyes must converge more to fixate a near object than to fixate a far one. The amount the eyes have to converge could provide a cue for depth.

the eye muscles could indicate the amount of rotation undergone by the eyes and, consequently, the angle of the line of sight of each eye. Distance could then be determined on the basis of these two angles. For example, each pair of angles of convergence could specify a particular distance.

Although these simple geometrical relationships between the lines of sight of the two eyes could be used to specify distance, there is little agreement about whether convergence can actually be used in perception. Grant (1942), using adult subjects, found convergence of the eyes did influence judgments of distance. Others, however, have concluded that distance perception based on convergence is impossible or unreliable (Ogle and Reiher 1962) or is at best a minor aspect of perception (Graham 1965).

Recent research with adults has suggested that the ability to use convergence in distance perception exists in some subjects, at least. Gogel and Sturm (1972) found a relationship between convergence and perceived distance for most subjects; perception was influenced by the degree of convergence of the eyes. Similar results are reported by Richards and Miller (1969). The latter found that 60 percent of their subjects used convergence in estimates of distance, but 40 percent did not. Richards and Miller suggest the use of convergence in distance perception is an aptitude that represents a particular property of the perceptual system, and the presence of this aptitude differs among individual subjects. On the basis of other data, they also suggest this aptitude may be an innate property of an individual's mechanisms for distance perception.

There are, however, no developmental data that bear on the use of convergence as a cue for distance. We do not know if certain children are able to use convergence whereas others are not, or whether this ability occurs very early in development. In addition, there is some question of whether infants possess the requisite ocular-motor abilities necessary to use convergence in distance perception. Before being able to use the information provided by ocular-motor adjustments for perception, it is first necessary to be able to converge the eyes on a point being fixated— and psychologists disagree about whether infants can appropriately converge the eyes in fixation. For example, Hershenson (1964) reported that convergence and conjugate eye movements were observed in two- to four-day-old infants. Wickelgren (1967), however, found convergence was absent during a large proportion of the time spent looking at a target. She photographed infants' (two to five days old) eyes while they were looking at two, six-inch-square panels positioned five inches apart. In one of the experiments, she found that 22 percent of the time one eye was oriented toward one of the panels while the other eye was oriented toward the other panel. In a second experiment, the eyes fixated different panels 50 percent of the time, and the eyes were converged only 9 percent of the time. These results suggest that neonates cannot use con-

vergence information for perception simply because they cannot converge the eyes on a single point while fixating.

More recent research indicates that the extent to which infants can
perform convergent eye movements lies somewhere between the extremes suggested by the research of Hershenson and of Wickelgren.
Slater and Findlay (1975) found that newborn infants reliably converged
their eyes sufficiently to maintain binocular fixation when they viewed
arrays of lights ten and twenty inches away, but could not do so with targets five inches away. In a further experiment, Slater and Findlay used
different stimuli: a strip of lights, a triangle and square, and an array of
squares. With these patterns, nine out of fifteen newborns demonstrated
convergence sufficient for binocular fixation, but six did not.

Aslin (1976) tested convergence abilities of one-, two-, and three-
month-olds. He found that although even the youngest children showed
convergent eye movements to a moving target, these eye movements
were not sufficient to maintain binocular fixation. The convergence
movements of three-month-olds were sufficient to maintain binocular
fixation of the moving target, however. Thus it appears that newborn
infants do have some ability to converge the eyes. In early life, performance is rather inaccurate and inconsistent and improves in accuracy,
at least up until three months of age (Aslin 1976).

Binocular Disparity

In addition to convergence, binocular vision provides another potential source of information about depth and distance. Since our eyes are
slightly separated, each eye sees a slightly different view of the world;
that is, each eye picks up a different array. You can observe these differences by alternately closing one eye and then the other, noting the
changes that occur. They are very small but can be detected. Depending
on which eye is open, different portions of objects are covered over or
hidden by other objects, and the position of objects seems to shift a little
as you switch to the other eye. These subtle differences between the two
arrays are an important condition of binocular vision. Figure 2–3 illustrates how different views of an object result in binocular depth perception. Following the instructions in the figure caption will provide the
experience of binocular depth for about 98 percent of the population. (If
you do not have binocular depth perception, you will have to accept on
faith that it exists.)

The disparate arrays projected to the eyes do not normally result in
double vision. Instead, they result in a unitary perception of objects in
depth. In some way, the two arrays are combined and the disparity
between the two arrays is used by the nervous system to compute depth
relations. A great deal of psychophysical work has been done relating
disparity and depth (Ogle 1950) and determining a metric for binocular
stimulation (Luneberg 1947). Although research on binocular vision has

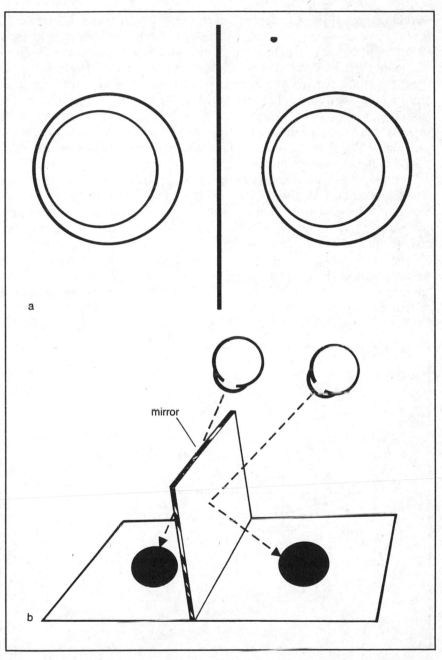

Figure 2-3

To see depth binocularly in the figure, place a mirror on the center line in (a) as shown in (b). Move the mirror slightly until the reflection of the drawing on the right merges with the drawing on the left. The small and large circle should appear at different levels.

a long history, little is known about the process by which the disparate arrays to the eyes are converted into a perception of depth. Hochberg (1971) outlined the major theoretical alternatives involved in explaining binocular vision. Each alternative has some difficulty explaining the existing data, however, and none seems to provide a sufficient explanation of binocular vision. Part of the difficulty is that the mechanism for binocular vision is very complex. Binocular depth perception can occur even when the two arrays are intricate and appear virtually indistinguishable. The slight differences between two arrays that seem identical result in depth perception.

Young children are also able to use disparity information for binocular depth perception. A simple way of demonstrating this ability is provided by a stereoscopic projector, which works in the same way as projectors for three-dimensional movies. In this apparatus (see Figure 2–4), two slightly disparate images are projected on a screen in front of a subject. Cross-polarized filters are placed in front of the projection lamps and in front of the subject's eyes so that the right eye sees one of the images and the left eye, the other. Under these circumstances, a person with binocular vision sees a single object located in space part of the way between himself and the screen. If a subject localizes the image in space,

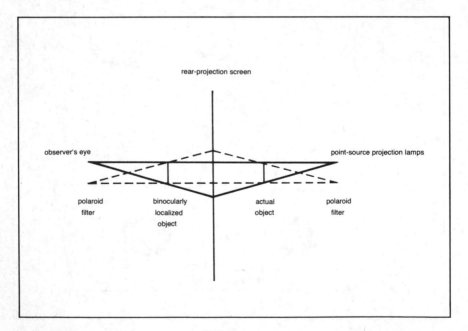

Figure 2–4

In one form of binocular projection, lamps project two images of an object onto a screen. Polarized filters aligned and placed in front of the lamps and the subject's eyes, allow one eye to view one image and the other eye to view the other image. Consequently, as in Figure 2–3, each eye receives a different array and the object appears in front of the screen.

he must have binocular vision. Johnson and Beck (1941) used such an apparatus to test children ranging in age from two to six years. Each child was seated twenty inches away from a screen on which a photograph of a doll was stereoscopically projected. To an adult observer, the doll was seen ten inches in front of the screen. After some preliminary questioning, each child was asked, "Would you like to touch the dolly?" As the child reached out, Johnson and Beck noted the point the subject reached toward and recorded any spontaneous comments.

The results indicated that all children had stereoscopic vision. All of them reached out about ten inches when trying to touch the doll. Furthermore, many of the comments showed that the children were surprised when they could not touch the doll: "I'm touching her nose but I can't feel her." When one of the projectors was blocked off so only a single image was projected, children localized the doll on the screen. When asked to touch the doll, they touched the screen.

These data demonstrate that the ability to use disparity information for depth perception is present by the time a child is two years old. There is also some indication that this ability may be present even earlier. Appel (1971) tested eight-week-old children on the ability to discriminate between projected stereograms with and without binocular disparity. When the stimulus that a subject was matching was changed from a stereogram without disparity to one with disparity, heart rate deceleration and sucking suppression were observed, indicating that the difference between the two conditions could be discriminated by eight week olds. From this study, it is not clear whether depth was perceived or whether the stereograms were discriminated on some other basis such as double versus single images.

However, a further study suggests that the use of disparity information for binocular depth perception may occur in very young infants. Bower, Broughton, and Moore (1970) studied children from six days to six months old. A cube was stereoscopically projected in front of the children, and the experimenters noted the infants' behavior. Bower et al. report that "anticipatory hand shaping [partial grasping] . . .occurred at all ages. . . . Seventy-two instances of anticipatory hand shaping were discernible in the seven-day-old group" (Bower, Broughton, and Moore 1970, p. 52). Although this study was not directed at assessing binocular abilities, the results directly imply that binocular vision is present even in neonates.

Since there were several reasons for assuming that neonates could not possess binocular abilities, these results are surprising and raise several important questions for the study of perceptual development in infants. First, it is apparent that the ability to use binocular disparity information is a highly cortical process. Julesz (1971), for example, has argued that neural processing of binocular disparity must take place in the cortex, at least seven synapses away from the retina. Neonatal behavior has been thought to be primarily under the control of subcortical mechanisms, and the cortex has been believed to be little developed at birth (Peiper 1963). Although newborns do have some cortical function, as can be seen in a rudimentary ability to perceive patterns, the presence of binocular stereopsis would suggest a more highly developed nervous system than was previously believed.

Second, as we pointed out earlier, there is some question whether neonates have the ability to converge the eyes in conjugate fixation. Julesz has found that even adults cannot maintain binocular vision over the divergence found (Wickelgren 1967) in neonates. In adults, such divergence would lead to double vision rather than stereoscopic perception. The presence of stereopsis in infants would imply a high degree of ocular motor control.

Third, Bower et al. report that all of their neonates showed anticipatory hand shaping to the binocular image. Such fine motor coordination had not previously been found. White (1971), for example, found that infants begin to swing at an object with a closed fist sometime during the second month of life; and both Piaget (1952) and White had not found hand shaping or attempts at grasping until several weeks after birth. Thus, finding binocular perception in newborns raises a number of important questions about the neural and visual motor abilities of young infants, suggesting strongly that the phenomenon be explored in greater detail. (Further investigation is especially important since some of the results of the Bower et al. study have been difficult to duplicate.)

To avoid the problems of fine muscle control discussed above, Gordon and Yonas (1976) assessed infants' stereoscopic ability without relying on accurate grasping. To do this, they determined whether infants' movements were directed to the depth of a binocular visual object or were simply random activity. Although reaching toward an object was very inaccurate, infants' body and hand movements indicated that five-month-olds are sensitive to binocular information for depth. Yonas (in a personal communication) has been unable to verify binocular depth perception in younger infants.

Regardless of the state of infants' binocular abilities, we do know that binocular vision is not necessary for the perception of distance and depth. You can demonstrate this easily for yourself. If you close one eye, binocular vision is no longer possible. Yet you can still perceive depth and distance and perform complex visual tasks, such as walking, driving an automobile, or even flying an airplane. Several studies indicate that children can also perceive depth and distance without binocular vision. Obviously, some other source of information must be sufficient for accurate perception.

Walk and Dodge (1962) tested a ten-month-old child who had vision in only one eye. Performance on the visual cliff was not found to be different from that of normally sighted children. Similarly, Walk (1968) tested normally sighted children either with both eyes open or with one eye occluded. When the deep side of the cliff was 25 cm or more away, 93 percent of the monocular infants chose the shallow side; 94 percent of the binocular infants also chose the shallow side. In a follow-up to the discrimination learning study, Bower (1965) found that monocular and binocular vision produced almost identical results. Smith and Smith (1966), using older children as subjects, also found no consistent differences between binocular and monocular performance. All of these studies indicate that monocular vision is sufficient for perception of depth and distance. Although binocular disparity may be an important source of depth information for children, other kinds of information must be picked up as well.

MOTION PARALLAX

The studies discussed above imply that some source of monocular information must be a sufficient basis for the perception of surface layout. Walk and Gibson (1961) have suggested that sufficient effective information for appropriate cliff performance is provided by motion parallax. Subjects on the cliff do not merely remain passive and motionless while looking over the edge. Instead, they normally walk or crawl up and down the center board or move their heads from side to side while looking at the textured surface under the glass. As such movements are made, regular changes occur from moment to moment in the array of light projected to the eye. With each change in the position of the eye, a slightly different view of the world is obtained. During this movement, a person can observe an apparent relative movement of objects in the field. Although such movement occurs every time the position of the eye is shifted, it usually goes unnoticed; objects in the world normally retain a constant position regardless of our movements. It is only when we are moving fairly rapidly that we notice objects streaming past our eyes.

Such movement occurs with any displacement of the head, however, and can easily be observed. With one hand, hold a pencil in front of you at arm's length; with your other hand, hold a second pencil about a foot from your eyes. With one eye closed, move your head about six inches from side to side. As you move, you will notice that the pencils change their relative position. If you fixate the farther pencil while moving to the right, the nearer pencil will be displaced to the left. If the nearer pencil is fixated, the farther one will move off to the right. If you fixate on the far wall as you move to the right, both pencils will move to the left. This apparent movement of the objects is related to the distance of the objects from the eye. As you move your head you should notice that the nearer pencil is displaced more, and its array velocity is greater than the farther pencil. There is a close relationship between the array motion and distance.

It has long been known that such motion of objects in the array provides information for distance. Helmholtz (1910) described the changes that occur in the array with motion and pointed out the exact relationship between array motion and distance. Under normal conditions of side-to-side head motion (that is, when the head moves with a constant velocity, when the eyes are a constant distance above the ground, and the line of sight is perpendicular to the direction of the head motion), the distance to an object is inversely proportional to the velocity of its array motion. The more accurately head motion velocity and angular displacement can be determined, the more accurately distance can be judged.

This relationship between array motion and distance provides sufficient information for the perception of depth on the visual cliff. As a subject moves his head, the array displacement of texture elements on the near and far sides of the cliff specifies their distance. Clear, unblurred vision of the texture may not be necessary, since the movement of the blurred texture elements would still specify depth in the same way. Even accurate estimation of the array motion may not be necessary. If a subject can only distinguish between two relative velocities—one specifying a safe stepping-off depth and the other specifying an unsafe falling-off depth—successful avoidance of the deep side would result.

Several experiments have demonstrated that children are able to use motion parallax information for the perception of depth. One of the most convincing of these experiments was performed by Bower (1965). The first portion of the study consisted essentially of a replication of the Bower experiment described earlier in this chapter. Fifty- to sixty-day-old infants were conditioned to turn their heads to one side when a twelve-inch cube three feet away was presented. After training was complete, three different test stimuli were used to isolate the effective information used by the children in their perception of depth. In one condition, children were tested binocularly; in a second, they were tested monocularly; and in the third, they were tested while viewing a photograph of the stimulus situation. The choice of these three test conditions allowed Bower to determine what information the children were using. As Table 2–2 shows, children in the binocular test situation could have used binocular disparity information, monocular motion parallax information, or pictorial cues such as retinal image size for judgments of size and distance. In the monocular condition (since binocular vision was eliminated), only motion parallax and the pictorial cues could have

Table 2–2
Information Available in Each Condition of the Bower Study (1965)

Test Condition	Binocular Disparity	Motion Parallax	Static Pictorial
Binocular viewing	Yes	Yes	Yes
Monocular viewing	No	Yes	Yes
Pictorial stimulus	No	No	Yes

Source: Adapted from T. G. R. Bower, "Stimulus Variables Determining Space Perception in Infants," *Science* 149, (1965):88–89.

been effective. In the third situation, a static photograph was presented, thus eliminating both binocular and motion parallax information.

Bower found the responses in the binocular and monocular test conditions did not differ, whereas relatively few responses were made in the photo condition. From these data, we can conclude that pictorial cues were minimally effective, at most, since few responses were made in this condition. We can also see that these children could not have been relying solely on binocular vision. In the monocular condition and perhaps in the binocular condition as well, these children must have been relying on motion parallax information to discriminate the size and distance of the cube. These results suggest that children are able to use motion parallax, at least to some extent, in perceiving spatial layout before they are two months old.

MOTION PERSPECTIVE

The relationship between distance and parallactic motion is not restricted to the conditions of normal head movement cited above. As one moves about, the array motion is not limited to objects near a perpendicular line of sight or to conditions of constant velocity or constant eye height. The stimulus situation in motion parallax is, in fact, a special case of motion perspective described by Gibson, Olum, and Rosenblatt (1955). As one moves over a textured surface such as the ground, virtually all objects undergo regular array motion. The ground ahead seems to expand from a point on the horizon, flow past the observer, and contract to another point on the horizon behind. The apparent velocity of all points in this flow is completely regular, as shown in Figure 2–5. In this more general case, the velocity of these points does not specify their distance in a simple inverse relationship.

Without the constraints that we placed on head motion in the prior description of motion parallax, velocity of a point in the field is a joint function of the velocity of the observer, height of the observer's eye, and the angle between that point and the path of locomotion. The effect of observer's velocity operates in a simple way. The greater the velocity (V) of the observer, the faster the points in the flow field will move. As one is traveling in a car, an increase in the speed of the car increases the rate at which objects stream past. As the height of the observer's eye is increased, the apparent velocity of points decreases. This effect is easy to observe. Traveling at a certain speed (say, 30 mph), one sees objects flow past at a faster rate when one is in a low sports car than when in a truck or bus. Since the velocity of points in the flow field affects the impression of speed, one seems to be traveling slower in a truck or bus than when traveling at the same velocity in a car. The same effect can also be observed in an airplane. Pilots report that flight speed appears greater as they near the ground.

These two factors work in a complementary way. Any combination of

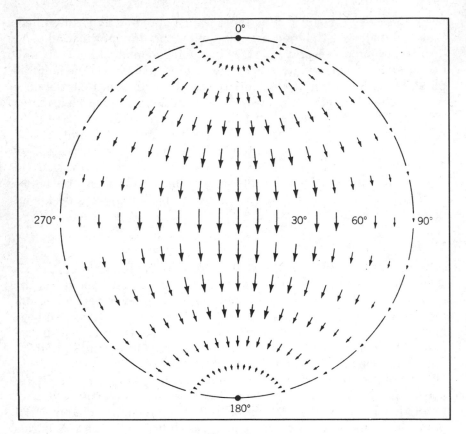

Figure 2–5

An idealized representation of the flow pattern experienced by an observer at the center moving along a straight line. The arrows represent relative velocities and directions of points in the array at different distances and positions. Notice that array motions are least at the greatest distances. (From Gibson, Olum, and Rosenblatt, 1955. Reprinted by permission.)

velocity (V) and height (h) that results in a constant fraction V/h produces the same flow field. For example, a velocity of 10 mph at a height of 10 feet gives the same flow field as a velocity of 5 mph at 5 feet. Consequently, unless changes in height can be compensated for, alteration in height should affect velocity estimates based on the flow field. This is what happens in the truck versus sports car anecdote, which suggests at least on an intuitive level that motion perspective information does influence our perception.

Other aspects of motion perspective play an important role in perception. If you drive rapidly down a long straight road, you can notice the motion of points, as shown in Figure 2–5. Objects farthest away seem to move the least. In addition, you will notice a point on the horizon that does not appear to move at all. In fact, it seems that the motion originates here and flows around you. This point is called the *focus of expansion*, and on a straight road it always lies directly in front of your car. Since the line of locomotion intersects the focus of expansion, the flow field specifies the future path of the observer. If the focus of expansion is within the contours of an obstacle, there will be a collision with that obstacle. To avoid a collision, therefore, the observer need only keep the focus of expansion outside the contours of objects along the path. To collide purposely with an object (for example, in attacking a prey animal), it is necessary to keep the focus of expansion on the object.

Looming

Although there have been no investigations directly concerned with perceptual development and motion perspective, there is evidence that a specific aspect of motion-carried information is used by a number of animals very early in life. Consider for a moment the changes that occur in the optic array as an observer moves directly toward an object. As pointed out earlier, there is a flow field with its focus of expansion at the point where the eye will hit the object. In addition, as the distance between the observer and the object decreases, the angular size of the object gets larger. This is shown in Figure 2–6. Schiff (1965) has shown that the flow field and the change in size of the object provide information about motion and the point of collision. An optically similar situation arises when an object moves or is thrown at a stationary observer. There is a flow field within the contours of the object, and the projected size of the object increases. If the object will hit the eye, the focus of expansion is within the contours of the object.

The rate at which changes occur in the flow field and in the projected size indicates the time to collision with an object. These changes occur

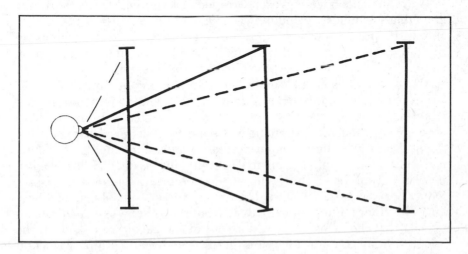

Figure 2–6

The increase in angular size of an object as it looms toward the eye specifies whether collision will occur.

rather slowly when the object is far away and increase in rate as the object approaches. The projected size increases geometrically with approach, filling the entire visual field at collision. This rapid expansion can be said to indicate that collision is imminent. Furthermore, the rate of expansion specifies the time remaining to collision. For example, if the angular size of the object doubles in one second, there remains one second to collision. The rapidly increasing change in the optical size of an object that occurs before collision is called *looming* by Schiff. The motion perspective information involved in looming potentially specifies the approach of an object, whether it will hit the observer, and how much time will elapse before collision will occur.

The ability to use this potential information is important for many organisms. Instances of looming in an organism's natural environment may occur under potentially dangerous circumstances. For example, the collision may be with a predatory animal hunting the observer or with a falling or thrown missile such as a rock. In either case, the ability to use looming information and thus detect imminent collision has great survival value. Organisms that could not avoid impending collision would be in constant danger. It seems reasonable to expect, then, that looming information is used by many (if not all) animals. Because of its importance for survival, little direct learning may be involved. There would seem to be few opportunities for an animal to "learn" looming information and use it to guide his avoidance behavior, since an animal might not survive the first time he fails to avoid a looming predator. If the failure to respond appropriately on the first trial could be lethal, no avoidance learning mechanism could protect the animal. Learning in one trial would be learning too late.

The argument above suggests two specific hypotheses. First, virtually all animals should show looming avoidance ability. Second, this ability should be present even in very young animals, since it provides an important means of avoiding danger. Several experiments have been conducted to test these suppositions. One such experiment by Schiff, Caviness, and Gibson (1962) was performed on infant monkeys. To assure that only the optical expansion pattern of looming was the effective stimulus for avoidance, the experimenters projected a silhouette of an object on a screen. The silhouette was made to undergo rapid expansion (magnification) while the experimenters watched the monkeys' behavior. Eight infant monkeys from five to eight months old and fifteen adult monkeys were tested individually. Pronounced avoidance responses were observed in nineteen of the twenty-three animals tested. These animals either rapidly jumped away from the silhouette (sometimes so rapidly that they crashed into the wall of the cage) or ducked. In the younger animals, alarm cries were often uttered. Schiff et al. suggest that the failures to avoid were probably the result of the monkeys' looking away from the screen when looming occurred. No differences were observed between the infants' responses and those of the older subjects.

A second important finding of this study lies in the responses of the subjects to repeated looming. In most perceptual situations, frequent repetition of the stimulus results in habituation, or a reduction in the magnitude and number of responses given to the stimulus. Although habituation occurs in all perceptual systems, we can see that rapid habituation of the response to looming would not be adaptive for any animal. Avoiding only the first few of a series of impending collisions would certainly not result in the animal's avoiding danger. Schiff et al. presented a succession of fifteen loomings spaced ten seconds apart. On all trials, the animals avoided the apparent collision. No evidence of habituation was found over this stimulus series.

Schiff (1965) continued the investigation of looming avoidance with a number of different species. Using the optical expansion of a silhouette, Schiff found that four species representing four different taxonomic classes (crabs, frogs, chicks, and human adults) responded appropriately to a looming stimulus. The nonhuman species actively avoided by jumping or ducking from the expanding shadow. Human subjects reported the apparent approach of an object but did not actively avoid.

These two studies demonstrate that many animals can use the optical information that specifies impending collision and can respond appropriately to avoid the looming object. For many animals, the pattern of optical expansion provides effective information for the perception of an approaching object. As noted above, the rate of change of the flow gradient also potentially specifies the time to collision with the looming object. To determine whether subjects can pick up the information for time to collision, using crabs and chicks as subjects Schiff manipulated the rate of expansion of the shadow so that it corresponded to four different rates of approach of the object (and consequently to four different times to collision). The author found the response times for avoidance were influenced by the rate of approach. There was a close correspondence between the response times and the theoretically predicted time to collision. Subjects avoided much more rapidly as the time to collision was decreased. For example, an expansion pattern that specified a collision in 4.0 seconds elicited avoidance in 3.0 to 3.5 seconds, and a collision time of 1.75 seconds elicited a response in 1.4 to 1.6 seconds.

Human infants have also been tested in the looming avoidance situation and have been found to register looming. Ball and Tronick (1971) exposed infants between two and eleven weeks old to two different kinds of looming stimulus displays. In this experiment, infants were seated upright in an infant chair with an adult's support, and either an optical loom (an expanding shadow on a screen) or a real loom (an actual object moving toward the child) was produced. These children gave very pronounced avoidance responses to both of the displays. When looming occurred, the infant's eyes opened wide, his head pulled back, and his arms were brought up to cover his face. The adult holding the infant often reported that the child also stiffened his body during the looming. These responses were observed only when the looming object was apparently headed directly at the infant.

When the stimulus situation was altered to indicate the approach of an object that would not hit the child but pass beside him, a totally different response was observed. Stiffening did not occur, and the infant commonly turned his head and eyes along the path of the shadow or object. These responses were apparently quite distinct. Ball and Tronick noted that visitors who were unaware of the stimulus situation watched videotapes of the infants' responses and commented that the children seemed to be avoiding something or watching something in the two conditions. Even very young infants respond with reflexlike withdrawal to a looming object, and they can easily distinguish between an expansion pattern that specifies a hit and one that specifies a near miss.

This latter result is particularly important. Since the children could distinguish between impending collision and a near miss, they must be able to differentiate between two aspects of looming information. When the optical expansion of an object is symmetrical, collision is specified. When the pattern is asymmetrical (beyond certain limits), the object will miss. Ball and Tronick's results indicate that the form of the expansion pattern is the important factor for infants' responses, not simply gross changes in size.

A similar experiment was performed by Bower, Broughton, and Moore (1971). They used infants as young as six days old, and reported results similar to those reported by Ball and Tronick. Even neonates showed the stereotyped avoidance response described above. The Bower et al. findings also show that looming resulted in a considerable degree of emotional upset. In one study of the effect of nearness of approach, the infants were so violently upset that the experiment was discontinued.

The studies of Ball et al. and Bower et al. have an interesting implication. Research has shown that an infant under one month old has virtually no ability to focus its eyes (White 1971). The eyes appear to be fixed at one focal distance of about 19 cm. If objects are presented farther away than 19 cm, their contours appear increasingly blurred. Information for collision, however, is not dependent on sharpness of vision. Rather, information is carried by the rate of change of an object's projected size, regardless of whether the object's contours are sharp or blurred. Theoretically, then, the ability to perceive looming should not be greatly affected by visual acuity. The findings of Ball et al. and of Bower et al. seem to verify this hypothesis.

Young infants including neonates show a response to the optical stimulation that specifies looming. This should not be interpreted as indicating that they possess well-developed looming avoidance abilities or that the response is a defensive one. Bower et al. report that the response of neonates is, in some way, dependent on the posture and orientation of the infant. (Yonas, in a personal communication has reported some difficulty replicating the study, perhaps because of these postural effects.) If the infant's ability to respond to the looming object is dependent on his posture, the behavioral pattern cannot be taken as an indicator of adaptive avoidance but rather merely as an indicator that looming information can be registered. Other research makes it clear that the integration of other responses with the ability to register looming information takes several months to develop.

White (1971), for example, measured the eye blink response to imminent collision. White's subjects were tested while lying on their backs. To minimize air currents, a sheet of plexiglass was placed a few inches above each infant tested. In such a position, the subjects could not make the kinds of responses that were reported by Bower et al. and by Ball and Tronick. Under these specific conditions, White found that infants did not respond consistently to looming until after three months of age. It seems to take several weeks for the optical stimulus of looming to control a simple eye blink response.

Integrating more complex behavioral patterns into the response to looming seems to take even longer. One such pattern is the visual placing response. As pointed out earlier, the optical expansion pattern in looming is the same regardless of whether the object moves toward an observer or the observer moves toward the object. Consequently, either movement should result in an avoidance response. When an animal or human infant is brought rapidly toward a surface, he will extend his forelegs or arms before collision. With human infants, this visual placing response takes from several weeks to several months to develop. Walk reported (in an unpublished paper) testing 3½-month-old infants and found that none demonstrated the visual response to impending collision; however, 7-month-olds did. It appears that the placing response does not develop and come under the control of optical expansion until some time between the third and seventh month of life.

The research conducted thus far on looming avoidance in children indicates that the ability to register the optical expansion pattern is present shortly after birth, but maturational and experiential factors are necessary for this information to control behavior effectively. This is suggested also by Hein, Gower, and Diamond (1970), who reared kittens in a diffuse light environment for four weeks. At the end of this period, the kittens were tested by being brought rapidly toward a solid surface. All the animals exhibited reflexive paw placing to the approaching surface. In the absence of any visual experience, they were able to detect looming. However, experience was necessary for this reflexive response to be adaptively guided. Thus, in kittens and perhaps in humans as well, the ability to detect looming information requires no visual experience, but the ability to use this information in avoidance does.

The study of looming avoidance in children is in its very early stages; further research to determine how this ability develops is needed. Bower, Broughton, and Moore (1971) found that infants' responsiveness to looming decreased if the rate of approach increased. There may be stimulus-specific limits to infants' abilities to pick up looming information, though these abilities improve with age. Increasing accuracy in differentiating the parameters of motion perspective should be closely related to the accuracy of looming avoidance. In addition, research may determine the accuracy possessed by both children and adults in the looming situation. Although we know that even infants can distinguish between collision and a near miss, we do not know how accurately this distinction can be made. How large are the errors that people make in determining collision, and how are these errors related to the actual avoidance behavior that subjects demonstrate? Is avoidance behavior controlled in such a way that errors are compensated for?

Although there is a great deal to be learned about the nature of looming avoidance in children, the few data we now have are very informative. It is clear that motion-carried information is used to direct behavior even by neonates. Since looming results in a stereotyped, almost reflexive, response, detection of looming may be prewired into the nervous system of infants at birth. Later experience may refine this ability and allow its generalization. After some perceptual learning, the information contained in motion perspective and motion parallax may be used in other perceptual activities. The nature of this experience will be considered in later chapters.

REDUNDANCY IN PERCEPTUAL SYSTEMS: TEXTURE GRADIENTS

Until now, we have limited the consideration of depth and distance perception to conditions in which an organism can look at the world with two eyes or with one eye and with movement of his head or body. Although binocular vision and motion parallax provide accurate information for the perception of distance and depth, they do not provide the only available information. Other kinds of information also contribute to the perception of spatial layout. This can easily be verified. If you close one eye and keep your head motionless while looking across a room, the impression of depth and distance is not lost. Even though in this case there is no binocular or motion-carried information available, you can still perceive the distance and arrangement of objects in the room. This simple fact demonstrates that there must be some form of static, monocular information that specifies distance.

You might think it strange that there are so many different ways to perceive distance. In our experience, the perception of distance seems to be a very simple ability, yet it involves many different and complex mechanisms. Another unusual aspect of distance perception is that all of the different kinds of abilities that provide information about distance are redundant. Binocular and motion-carried information specify exactly the same distance as monocular information. On the face of it, it seems inefficient to have three separate means of determining the same distance, so we might ask why such redundancy exists.

An absolute reason for this redundancy or an explanation for why evolution has taken a particular course can never be precisely known, but we can speculate about the benefits of redundancy. A key lies in the fact that distance perception is a crucial ability. A visual animal without it could scarcely survive in its normal environment. An animal must be able to perceive distance under a variety of circumstances. Binocular vision would certainly provide a basis for distance perception. But relying on binocular vision alone would make an animal quite vulnerable. Impairment or loss of one eye would mean the loss of distance perception. The presence of a second distance system would offset this loss. In addition, some animals appear to have no binocular vision, and even those that do, do not have complete overlap of the area seen by the two eyes. There is always some portion of the periphery that does not have binocular distance perception. This partial or total lack of binocular distance perception is unimportant if motion-carried information can be used. An added advantage is that motion perspective enables distance to be perceived accurately when the animal is moving.

But there are other conditions in which distance must be perceived. When avoiding a predator, for example, many animals remain motionless in an attempt to escape being noticed. Binocular vision and motion parallax enable the predator to find the prey. Both kinds of information indicate the distance between the prey and the background and thus make the prey animal stand out in relief against the background. While remaining motionless, however, the prey must be able to tell how far away the predator is. The ability to use static, monocular information enables the animal to do this even if it has limited binocular vision. We cannot be sure that this speculation describes the evolutionary pressures leading to multiple systems of distance perception, but there are clearly some advantages to being able to determine distance in a variety of ways. In this section, we will consider a source of monocular information and how its use develops in children.

One source of static, monocular information for spatial layout depends on a particular characteristic of surfaces in the world. They are textured—that is, they are made up of elements that are slightly different from each other in color or brightness. The changes that occur in these texture elements as we look over a surface can indicate distance. Figure 2–7 shows how this effect can occur. You can easily see that the surface recedes into the distance. Any one of the texture elements can be judged to be nearer than, farther than, or the same distance as, any other element.

The information that allows you to make this judgment lies in the way texture changes with distance. The angular size of the texture elements closer to you is larger than the angular size of the elements farther away. If you run your eye from the bottom of the figure to the top, you can see

Figure 2–7

A texture gradient made up of equal size elements extending to the horizon.

how the size changes in a regular way. The rate at which these changes occur is called a *gradient*. For any textured surface there are a number of gradients. In Figure 2–7, you can see that the angular size (area) changes as your eye sweeps upward. This is a *size gradient*. The height of each element gets more compressed as you look nearer the top of the picture. This is a *compression gradient*. The width of each element also changes, and the rate of this change is called a *perspective gradient*. In addition, the density of the elements change. You can see in Figure 2–7 that there are many more elements in the area at the top of the picture than at the bottom. The rate of this change is the *density gradient*. These four gradients are closely interrelated in that if the angular height and width of the texture elements change, their areas (size) must change also; and if the angular size changes, so must the density.

These gradients directly indicate distance. If one element is smaller in angular size than another, it must be farther away. If two elements have the same angular size, they must be the same distance away. In this manner, relative distance can easily be determined. The absolute distance (the actual distance in feet or in some other unit) can also be determined from the texture. If one can perceive the gradient (the actual rate at which the elements change) and the height of the eye, then the actual distance of an object is exactly specified. Thus, the gradient of texture provides a basis for the perception of distance.

Texture Gradients and Development

Two questions about texture gradient information are worth investigating. First, are children able to use texture gradient information in distance perception? Second, what features influence the ability to use texture in perception? Wohlwill (1963a) asked college-aged subjects to make judgments of distance while viewing a stimulus display through a single eyepiece. (Such monocular viewing eliminates binocular and motion-carried information.) While looking into the apparatus, they saw a textured surface over which were suspended two conical markers. The subjects indicated where to position a third marker (an arrow) so that it bisected the distance between the two cones (see Figure 2–8 for an illustration of this apparatus). To assess the effect of texture on the judgment that each subject made, six differently textured surfaces were used. Both

Figure 2–8

Viewing condition in Wohlwill's bisection study. (Reprinted with permission of author and publisher: Wohlwill, J. F. Overconstancy in distance perception as a function of the texture of the stimulus field and other variables. *Perceptual and Motor Skills*, 1963, 17, 831–846.)

the regularity of the texture (from totally random spacing to regular rows and columns) and the number of texture elements (from no texture to one-fourth of the surface area covered with texture elements) were varied. Wohlwill found some effect of texture on distance bisection. When a regularly textured surface with a large number of texture elements was used, judgments were significantly more accurate than when any of the other textures were used. A replication of this study using six- to sixteen-year-old subjects provided similar results (Wohlwill 1963b). When texture was varied, Wohlwill found that only the highly regular, heavily textured surface resulted in accurate bisections of the surface.

These results suggest that texture information was used to arrive at judgments of distance. However, some aspects of Wohlwill's data indicate that other kinds of information may have affected the results of this experiment. For example, subjects were also able to make bisections when an untextured surface was used. Since in this case no texture information was available, judgments must have been based on some other kind of information.

To remove any extraneous depth information, Wohlwill (1965) performed a third experiment on the influence of texture on bisection judgments. In this experiment, subjects from first, fourth, eighth, and eleventh grades made bisection judgments of distances represented in photographs. The use of photographs in this situation provides an easy means of assessing the effect of texture in the absence of other spatial information. Since the array projected to the eye from a photograph is static, moving the head provides no parallectic information. Additionally, binocular information cannot indicate distance.

Subjects viewed a photograph of three wooden toys (horse, fence, and cow) standing on a textured surface (see Figure 2–9). They were asked to imagine they were standing in a field and to judge whether the horse or the cow was closer to the fence. In each photograph, the position of the fence was varied, and subjects made judgments on several series of photographs. As in the previous studies, the regularity and number of texture elements were also varied. In this experiment, the effect of texture on judgment was highly significant. First, the highly regular, heavily textured surface resulted in considerable accuracy (as in the other studies). In addition, Wohlwill found accuracy increased as the number of texture elements on the surface increased. A slight age effect was also found. Although even the younger children were able to make consistent judgments, accuracy was greater for older children and adults.

These results indicate that textural information is picked up by children, and the nature of the texture influences bisection judgments. Increasing the number of texture elements in the display improves accuracy. Perceptually, however, a gradient can be extracted more easily when many texture elements are present.

These results suggest another fact about the use of texture information. Theoretically, the arrangement of the texture elements on a surface does

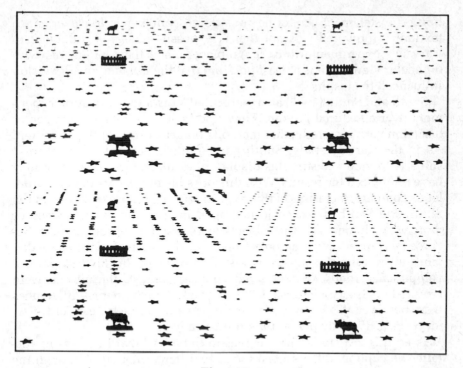

Figure 2–9

Textured surfaces varying in the number and spacing of texture elements.
(From Wohlwill, 1965.)

not affect the available information carried by the gradient. For example, regardless of the arrangement of the elements, the changes in width and height that occur with distance precisely define the gradients of linear perspective and compression. However, although the arrangement does not affect the availability of potential information, it does affect subjects' ability to use that information. When texture elements were regularly arranged in rows and columns, accuracy was substantially increased. It seems that the size changes that define the gradient are more striking and easier to pick up when a regular arrangement of elements is used.

Harway (1963) had subjects from five to twenty-three years old make judgments of successive one-foot distances over a grassy field. The subjects stood at one end of the field and directed the experimenter to mark off successive intervals of one foot. Harway found a significant age effect on the accuracy of judgment. Five-, seven-, and ten-year-olds made substantial errors, and performances did not differ within this age range. Twelve-year-olds and adults were significantly more accurate than were the younger children. These results suggest the same sort of developmental trends in distance perception as were found by Wohlwill. It would appear that in this second test situation, the ability to use texture information improves with age in the same way as in the bisection situation. The statement cannot be considered conclusive, however, since textural information was not the only possible basis of judgment in Harway's experiment. Since his subjects made their judgments with binocular viewing, it is at least possible that the use of binocular vision influenced the results.

Smith and Smith (1966) also performed a distance estimation experiment over a textured ground. They, too, made a direct comparison of bisection versus reproduction methods of measuring depth perception. As in the Harway study, Smith and Smith apparently allowed their subjects to view the stimulus display binocularly, and this again may have influenced the results. With this possible binocular effect in mind, let us compare the results of this experiment with those of others. In the Smith and Smith study, subjects ranged in age from five to sixteen or more years. In one task, the subjects were asked to reproduce a set distance by indicating which object of a row of objects was the same distance away from the subject as a standard target. In this task, no developmental trends were observed. In a second task, the subjects were required to bisect an interval. With this task, developmental differences were observed. The younger children (five to thirteen years old) performed significantly poorer than did the adults.

From this last study, there is reason to believe that in assessing distance perception, different tasks lead to different results. Although the presence of texture gradient provides sufficient information for the perception of distance, the ability to use this information may be affected by the experimental task. Extremely accurate, precise judgments of distance based on texture gradient information have been reported by Levine and Rosinski (1976). Observers ranging from first-graders through college-aged students were asked to make judgments of the distance of a target lying on a textured surface. To assure that only monocular information for distance was available, subjects viewed photographs of the stimulus display; and to eliminate response problems, the subjects made judgments by adjusting the distance of a second object to match the distance of the target. In this situation, no developmental differences were found; judgments at all grade levels were very accurate and very precise. Judgments based on texture gradient information were virtually perfect, with an average error of less than 1 percent.

These studies indicate that texture gradient information is used by children in perceiving distance. Furthermore, this ability is influenced by a number of factors, such as the number of texture elements that are visible, the regularity of their spacing, the age of the subjects, and the type of judgment being made. One other factor that may influence judgments based on texture information is the height of the viewing point. Given a particular height of the viewing point, the value of the texture gradient will exactly specify distance. This specific relationship between texture gradient value and distance holds only for that one particular height. Using a viewing point at a different height, there is a different relationship between the gradient and distance. This suggests that certain errors should result if the height of the viewing point is changed. For example, if a subject bases his judgments of distance on one height of the viewing point, when, in fact, he is viewing the surface from half that height, judged distance should be twice the actual distance. Texture gradient theory is explicit on this point.

Such an effect, however, leads to a paradox. Our perceptions of distance are based on gradients that change their relationship to distance depending on viewing height. Yet our perceptions should not change in this way. People must judge distance from a variety of heights. We need to be accurate regardless of whether we are sitting, kneeling, standing on the floor, or standing on a platform. The perceptual system must reconcile this contradiction in some way. The reconciliation takes place simply. The relationship between the gradient and distance is influenced by height, but people can compensate for changes in height and remain accurate over a variety of different viewing heights.

The experimental data related to this point suggest that such a compensation occurs both with children and adults. Harway's (1963) study of distance perception in children and adults was also concerned with the effect of the height of the viewing point on distance perception. For adults, height was varied by having the subjects make their judgments from either a standing or a kneeling position. Children's height was varied by having them judge distance while standing on the ground or while standing on a platform that raised them to a height of 5 feet 6 ½ inches. Harway found that changing the height of the viewing point in this way did not affect the accuracy of judgment at any of the age levels tested.

Height of the viewing point was also manipulated in the Wohlwill (1963) studies. Subjects made judgments of distance while looking through an aperture that was either 12 cm or 36 cm above the floor. In this study, changing the viewing point did not increase errors; in fact, errors decreased considerably.

Both of these studies show that changing height does not affect distance judgments as predicted by gradient theory. In both cases, the subjects were able to compensate for the changes in height. The subjects' knowledge that different viewing heights were being used may have influenced the way in which distance was perceived.

If such compensation occurs, the only way the effect of height on distance judgment can be evaluated is to manipulate height without providing the subject with information for the correct height. One way to do this is to use photographs taken from different viewing points. Rosinski has performed such an experiment (unpublished), and the preliminary results suggest that errors of the type predicted do occur. In this experiment, adult subjects were shown two photographs of objects on a textured surface. When both photographs were taken from the same viewing point, subjects had little difficulty matching the distances. When one photo was taken from twice the height of the other, errors resulted that were in accordance with those predicted. In this case, a distance of twenty feet in one photo might be matched with a distance of forty feet in the second photo. All errors did not exactly match those predicted theoretically, but all errors were in the predicted direction. The experimental situation is depicted in Figure 2–10. This preliminary result provides some indication that height of the station point does affect judgments as predicted by gradient theory. Further research is being conducted to explore this effect and to determine any developmental differences in the ability to judge distance accurately when height is varied.

SUMMARY

An examination of depth and distance perception reveals that this ability is an extremely complex one. Distance is specified by a wide variety of perceptual information that is used in different ways. Because of this multiplicity, it is inaccurate to speak of distance perception as a single ability that has a single developmental course. In fact, there are several abilities that underlie distance perception, and each may develop in unique ways. These different abilities involve the use of at least four different kinds of information: binocular disparity, motion parallax, motion perspective, and texture gradients.

Binocular Disparity. Since each eye receives a slightly different view of the environment, distance information is provided. The two different views available are related in precise ways that allow the visual system to "calculate" distance. The relative position of an object as seen by the eyes is directly related to the distance of that object from the observer.

In adults, this ability is highly developed and forms one of our most accurate means of perceiving distance. Little is known about the developmental course of binocular disparity information. It appears that the ability to perceive depth is present at least to some degree in newborns. Five-month-old infants can use binocular vision to locate an object projected in front of them. Accuracy at this age is unknown, and the developmental course of binocular distance perception from infancy to adulthood has not yet been determined.

Motion Parallax. As an observer moves his head, the objects in the array projected to the eye change their positions and appear to move. The amount of this movement is inversely proportional to the distance between an observer and an object. The ability to use this information is present at fifty-five to sixty days of age, and at this age it is accurate enough to allow the infant to distinguish between large differences in depth and distance. Depth differences of at least forty inches and distance differences of at least six feet can be discriminated before the third month of life. Within the first year, some children are able to discrimi-

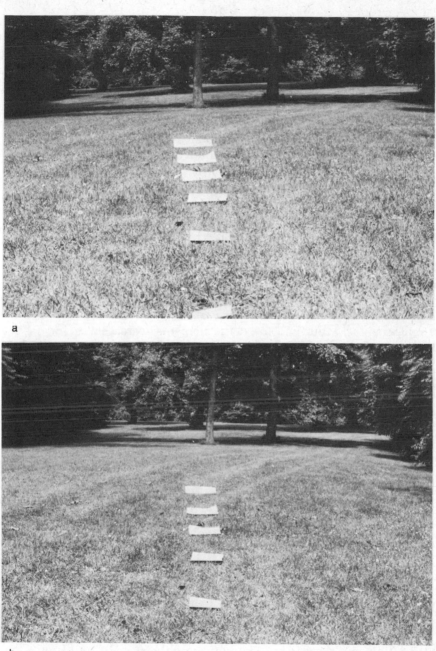

a

b

Figure 2–10

The height of the station point influences perceived distance. Which squares in
(a) are the same distances away as the squares in (b)? The two farthest squares,
the two next farthest, and so on, in each photo are equidistant.

nate between depths on the visual cliff that differ by five inches. Whether this degree of accuracy is present initially or develops over time is not known. The developmental course of the ability to use motion parallax information has not been studied.

Motion Perspective. In addition to the motion changes that occur in motion parallax, other objects in the world appear to move as the observer moves about. The general changes that occur are referred to as motion perspective. Motion perspective provides potential information for a variety of perceptual tasks. Distance, path of movement, impending collision, rate of motion, and time to collision are all specified by motion perspective. Only one aspect of motion perspective has been studied in children, the ability to avoid a looming object. This ability is present in newborns; a symmetrical expansion of an object's contours results in a stereotyped response. Infants are able to use motion perspective information that specifies looming to determine whether an approaching object will hit them, and they respond to it. No satisfactory studies of looming avoidance ability have been done with adults or with older children, so it is not known whether this ability changes with age.

Texture Gradients. As an observer looks at a textured, flat surface, the angular height, width, and size of the elements decrease with increasing distance. The rate at which these changes occur defines the gradients of size, compression, perspective, and density. These gradients can be directly related to distance. Several factors have been shown to influence accuracy of distance judgments based on texture. Among them are the number of elements present, the regularity of spacing of elements, the type of task employed, and the age of the subject. It is not known how early this ability appears in the course of development, but is already present in first-grade children. The ability to use gradient information in perceiving distance may improve with age, but the exact course of this development is not clear. Some experiments suggest that there is little improvement in early childhood but marked changes in later childhood or adulthood. Others suggest a more gradual course of development. Still others have found no developmental trends.

This chapter has concentrated on the four aspects of distance perception summarized above. Several other sources of information for distance have been suggested by perceptual psychologists; for example, the muscle tension required for the eyes to focus on an object and the calculation of distance from the angular size of a familiar object. These other sources of information appear to play a relatively minor role in adult perception, and there is little known about their use by children.

Chapter 3

OTHER ASPECTS OF SPATIAL LAYOUT PERCEPTION

The ability to perceive depth and distance is not the only ability we possess related to spatial layout. Simply being able to perceive the location of an object (its depth or distance from an observer) provides merely a partial description of our perceptual abilities. If we conceive of spatial layout in the total context of how an organism is able to get around adequately in the world, we can see that many other important perceptual abilities must be involved. For example, the size of objects, the slant of their surfaces, and their movement all play a role in our perception of the world. Consequently, an approach to the study of perception must be able to account for more than the perception of flat surfaces. In this section, we will consider other aspects of spatial layout perception and what is known about their development.

THE PERCEPTION OF SLANT

One obvious characteristic of objects and surfaces in the world is their slant—that is, their orientation relative to some horizontal or vertical reference axis. If we are to explain fully how the visual system is able to interpret the information available to it, the phenomenon of slant perception must be considered. In addition, the study of slant perception is interesting because the kinds of information that specify the slant of a surface area are also crucial in the perception of distance; that is, an explanation of how slant is perceived cannot be formulated in isolation. In fact, many of the problems implicit in explaining the perception of distance are also present in explaining the perception of slant. Since there seem to be many similarities between slant and other aspects of spatial layout perception, we might expect a number of similar experimental phenomena involving the two. Thus, if the perceptual mechanisms underlying the perception of slant are the same as those underlying some other aspect of spatial layout perception, then an investigation of slant perception provides a ready-made procedure that we can use to converge on these basic mechanisms. Further, as more developmental data are available, we should expect that certain aspects of the developmental trends in the use of information for perceiving slant and distance will be similar.

How is the slant of a surface perceived? What kinds of information are available to an organism to specify slant? To begin with, monocular slant information is provided by the texture gradients that were discussed in Chapter Two. Over a flat horizontal surface, the angular size of texture elements decreases as distance increases. The rate of this decrease defines a gradient of texture. For the perception of distance, the important fact is that over such a surface a texture gradient is present, and any value along this gradient is directly related to distance. A crucial fact for the perception of slant is that the gradient (the rate of change of texture elements) also depends on the slant of the surface. For each unique surface slant, there is a correspondingly unique gradient of texture. Consequently, if gradient information can be extracted, slant is specified.

An example will help clarify this relationship. We pointed out in the section on texture gradients (in Chapter Two) that a flat surface—one having a slant of 90 degrees relative to the vertical—projects a particular gradient. If the same surface were vertical (at zero slant), the texture elements would change only negligibly, and there would be essentially no gradient. As the slant of the surface varies from 0 to 90 degrees, the gradient varies, as depicted in Figure 3–1. As the slant of the surface increases, the rate of change of texture elements (the gradient) increases. A mathematical description of this effect shows that gradients and slant are precisely related. This analysis demonstrates that each slant angle

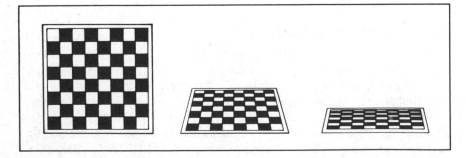

Figure 3–1

The gradients of texture specify three different slants for the three surfaces.

has associated with it a unique gradient. Again, if the gradient can be picked up, the slant of the surface is specified (Flock 1964).

Psychologists have known for many years that texture gradients specify the slant of a surface (Gibson 1950). However, the effectiveness of gradient information has been analyzed only within the last few years. In fact, because of a number of methodological errors, early studies failed to find any effect of texture gradients on slant perception. Much of this early literature is summarized by Flock (1965), who points out the problems experienced in this early work. Later research, however, has shown that texture gradients directly affect the perception of slant, and that each slant is specified by a gradient.

Perhaps the most ingenious and convincing demonstration that texture gradient information is used in the perception of surface slant was provided by Purdy (1960). He showed not only that judgments of slant were in correspondence with texture information but also that an optical change in the gradient influenced judgments, just as predicted by gradient theory. Purdy used magnification to determine the effect of texture information on judgments. In general, magnification alters stimulus information in such a way that the gradient projected to a station point specifies a steeper (more nearly vertical) physical slant than actually exists. For example, a texture gradient projected from a surface inclined at 45 degrees from the horizontal will, when magnified 1.5x, specify a slant of approximately 56 degrees. For this reason, a slanted surface seems to look steeper when it is seen through binoculars or a telescope, the telescope changes the gradient to appear more vertical.

Consequently, if subjects rely on texture gradient information for the perception of slant, readily predictable errors should occur under magnification. The purpose of Purdy's experiment was to determine whether such errors did occur. Subjects judged the slant of a regular grid either with or without magnification. When constant error was statistically controlled, subjects' judgments almost exactly matched the predictions. These results indicate that adult subjects used gradient information in the perception of slant, and that the relationship between judged slant and texture gradient closely follows the prediction of gradient theory. Purdy's experiment demonstrates two things about the character of slant perception in adults. First, adults have the ability to pick up the gradient information that specifies slant; second, specific invariant relationships have been formed that connect gradient information with perceived slant.

Until now the discussion of slant perception has centered on the effectiveness of texture gradient information. Textures do not provide the only source of slant information, however. Since a slanted surface recedes in distance, any information for distance could potentially specify slant. For example, since motion parallax information specifies distance, it should also be an effective basis for slant perception. Similarly, binocular depth perception should also play a role in slant perception. Recent research investigating these hypotheses has supported these ideas. Braunstein (1968) tested adult subjects and found very high levels of accuracy when slant was specified by motion parallax information.

Although adults' perception of slant is quite accurate, there is little experimental evidence about its development. Two studies that have attempted to assess the abilities of children suggest that infants are able to perceive slant, but that this ability may be relatively ineffective in controlling some behaviors. Bower (1966) studied fifty- to sixty-day-old infants by operantly conditioning a head turning response to a rectangle slanted at 45 degrees. Transfer testing was used to determine which aspect of the experimental situation controlled the infants' responses. Bower found that the rectangle at a different slant angle resulted in a large number of responses being made in testing. When a different shape (a trapezoid) was presented at 45 degrees, infants responded the least. These results indicate that the slant of the object relative to the shape of the object had little control over the infants' responses. There are two possible interpretations of these results. First, it is possible that infants at this age have little or no ability to use visual information for the perception of slant. Second, it could be argued that the infants have the ability to perceive both the slant and the shape of the objects but that in this learning situation, shape is the more salient property of the object.

An experiment by Fantz and Nevis (1967) using the visual preference technique suggests that the ability to perceive slant is present in infancy, and that consequently, the latter interpretation of Bower's results may be appropriate. Fantz and Nevis measured visual fixation behavior of two-week-old infants when shown an unslanted surface and one slanted at 45 degrees. The children showed a reliable preference for one of the targets in testing, thus demonstrating that they were able to perceive differences between the two surfaces.

In both the Bower and the Fantz experiments, the infants could have been using binocular, motion-carried, or textural information, so it is not possible to determine the effective stimulation for infants' perception of slant. A study of the development of slant perception in older children has been performed which isolates effective information. Rosinski and Levine (1976) measured elementary school children's ability to perceive slant solely on the basis of texture gradient information. A special rear projection technique was used to present texture gradients that specified slants of 30, 40, 50, 60, and 70 degrees. In each trial, the child set the inclination of a surface with his hand to match the slant as seen on the screen. It was found that even first-grade children were able to perform this task, although accuracy of judgment improved with age. Fifth-graders were considerably more accurate than were first-graders.

Of particular interest in this experiment is the effect of different kinds of gradient information on children's judgments. Different groups of children made their judgments on the basis of compression gradient information, perspective gradient information, or all four gradients combined. Results are presented in Figure 3–2. Compression gradient information, however, had very little effect on slant judgments. At all grade levels, children's judgments were most inaccurate when only compression information was available. The information provided by linear perspective was considerably more useful; children using this information were significantly more accurate than those using compression information. When the slant of the surface was specified by all four gradients (compression, perspective, size, and density), judgments were most accurate. It is clear that the availability of other forms of gradient information substantially affects perceptual accuracy.

Although all four of the texture gradients provide the same information (they all specify the same slant), some forms of the gradients are more effective in influencing perception than are others. Rosinski and Levine found that compression had little effect on slant perception in children. Braunstein (1968) found that information provided by a density gradient had little influence on slant perception in adults. From these two studies, it appears that the gradients of size and perspective are most influential in slant judgments. It is known also that the relative effectiveness of the four gradients changes with age, and that such

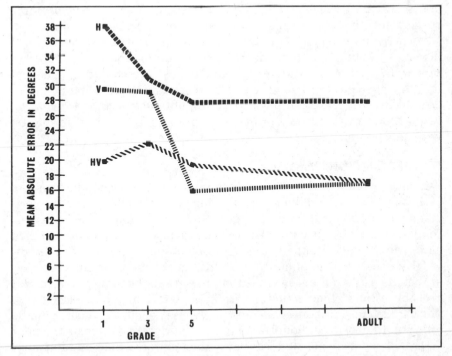

Figure 3–2

Absolute error in children's judgments of slant based on compression (H), perspective (V), or all gradients (HV). (From Rosinski and Levine, 1976.)

changes extend over several years of development (Rosinski and Levine 1976).

The age changes that occur in slant perception are similar to those observed in children's distance perception based on texture. This suggests that the ability to extract gradient information may be a general factor that influences both perceptual tasks. Other evidence supports this implication. For example, the number of texture elements that can be seen on a surface influences both the judgment of distance (Wohlwill 1965) and the judgment of slant (Flock, Tenney, and Graves 1966). A regular arrangement of elements that accentuates linear perspective improves both distance judgments (Wohlwill 1965) and slant judgments (Flock and Moscatelli 1964). Flock and Moscatelli have found that the variability of texture element size influenced slant judgments, and an identical effect was predicted for distance by Purdy (1960).

Furthermore, the gradient of textural compression is relatively ineffective in the perception of slant (Rosinski and Levine 1976) for children as well as adults; very similar results have been reported for judgments of distance (Levine and Rosinski 1976).

There are no developmental data on the use of binocular disparity or motion parallax in the perception of slant. However, assuming that similar mechanisms underlie the perception of both slant and distance, several predictions can be made. Most important, there should be some correspondence between the development of distance perception and slant perception when a single source of information is available. If neonates are able to use binocular disparity information, as the results of Bower, Broughton, and Moore (1970) suggest, we should expect that binocular perception of slant would also appear in early infancy. Similarly, if the use of motion parallax information takes some time to develop, then both slant and distance perception based on this information will appear later.

THE PERCEPTION OF SIZE

Explaining how children are able to perceive the size of objects is one of the most difficult problems in studying perception. Dozens of experimental studies have been done, yet little is understood about size perception. Let us begin with an initial description of a paradox in size perception. Take a group of objects (perhaps some pencils) and distribute them across the floor at different distances from your chair. As you look at them, it is quite easy to see that they are all the same size. You can probably estimate their actual size in inches with considerable accuracy. The paradox results if one considers how these pencils are imaged on the retina of the eye. Even though a pencil on your desk and one on the floor across the room are perceived as being the same size, their angular sizes (and consequently, the size on the retina) differ greatly. The nearer pencil may be ten or more times as large as the farther one. The paradox is this: How can we see these pencils as equal in size when the retinal images are vastly different? Why is perceived size virtually constant when retinal size is not?

One possible answer is that this variation of retinal size can be taken into account if one knows the distance to an object. For example, if an object has an angular size of 1 degree, and we know that it is three feet away, then we can calculate that the real size of the object is about one-half inch. If the angular size is 1 degree and the distance is six feet, then the object size must be larger. Since the relationship between real size and retinal size is affected by distance, knowing the distance would enable a perceiver to calculate size. This notion is appealing for its simplicity and also because it involves an ability that we know even young children possess—the ability to perceive distance.

Figure 3–3 demonstrates this effect. Although the cylinders in the drawing all have the same visual angular size, the one that appears farthest away is perceived as being largest. Although the size-distance hypothesis may be attractive in many ways, there has been considerable difficulty in demonstrating that size is in fact computed from retinal size and known distance. (See Hochberg 1971 for a review of these issues.) One alternative to the theory that size is computed from distance relationships is simply that some sort of information for size is available to a subject, and thus he need not compute size but merely pick up this size information. At least three sources of invariant information for size have been defined that involve the relationship between an object and the background.

Consider a set of equal-sized objects lying flat on a textured surface, such as books on a tiled floor. The nearest book might cover over one-and-a-half floor tiles. A book twice as far away would also cover one-and-a-half floor tiles. A book at ten times that distance would still cover one-and-a-half floor tiles. Regardless of distance, the same number of tiles would be covered. In this example, all the books would have to be the same size. If one of the books (at any distance) covered more of the tiles, it would have to be bigger than the others. In other words, although the retinal size of an object changes with distance, the relationship between the object and the texture that it covers is invariant over distance. This relationship between the size of an object and the amount of texture it occludes provides one explanation for the problem illustrated in Figure 3–3. Since the cylinders cover different amounts of the wall and floor texture, they are seen as different in size.

A second kind of invariant information for perception of size is similar to the first. Imagine an object with a textured surface. Assume that along its length it has five textural elements. That object would have five textural elements along that side regardless of its distance. Similarly, objects having the same texture would have the same number of elements along that side only if they were all the same size. In other words, for any size object, the number of inherent textural elements is invariant over distance.

Figure 3–3

Although the two children have the same retinal size, they are perceived to be very different in size because one appears further away and covers more of the wall and floor than does the other.

A third source of invariant information can be described for object size. When seen from a particular viewing point, some objects (for example, the stakes represented in Figure 3–4) seem to protrude over the horizon. It happens that the relationship between an object and the horizon could specify size. For example, if one-third of an object protrudes over the horizon, and two-thirds lie below the horizon, this ratio is unaffected by distance. Regardless of how far away that object is, it will have one-third of its length above the horizon and two-thirds below. Comparing this ratio for different objects could reveal whether they are the same size or different sizes.

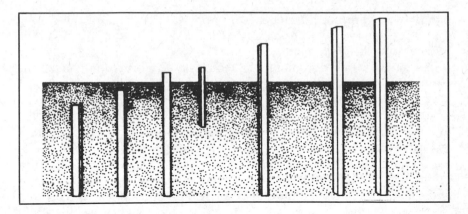

Figure 3–4

Size information is provided by the invariant relationship between object size and the horizon. Match the size of the center object with the size of one of the others. (After Gibson J. J., 1950.)

In addition to this relationship between the relative size of an object and the horizon, potential information can also specify the actual size of an object. Sedgwick (1973) has shown that a simple ratio exists between an object's position relative to the horizon and its actual height. If an object (such as one of the stakes in Figure 3–4) extends two-thirds of its height over the horizon and one-third under the horizon, it can be shown that the object's height must be three times the height of the observer's eye above the ground (assuming the object is on the ground and not floating in the air). Consequently, potential information for the actual size of an object relative to one's own height is provided by horizon information.

It must be stressed that these invariant relationships are potential sources of information and may not be used by all individuals or under all conditions. Research does indicate, however, that these invariants are effective determiners of size in some situations. Sedgwick (1973) found that adults used information provided by the relationship between an object and the horizon. His subjects were able to make accurate size judgments based on horizon information, and they made predictable errors when the position of the horizon in a display was artificially manipulated.

Further evidence comes from the work of Smith (1958). He asked adult subjects to match sizes of the stakes depicted in Figure 3–4. Subjects were to indicate which of the stakes in the foreground was the same size as the more distant one. In addition, the photos were presented so that the apparent distance of the stakes was 75, 100, or 250 percent of the real distance. Size matches were extremely accurate. For example, the average height of the stakes to be judged was 69 inches. The average judgment was 68.4 inches. More striking than this level of accuracy was that judgments were not affected by the apparent distance of the stakes. Clearly, some form of information invariant over distance provided the basis for the size judgments.

Although we do not know what sources of information control the perception of size, many experiments have been conducted to determine children's ability to judge size, and several clear generalizations can be made. The Bower (1965) experiment referred to previously shows that infants have some ability to perceive distance and to perceive constant size over different distances. Seventy to eighty, fifty-five-day-old infants were conditioned to respond to an object of a particular size at a distance of three feet. When the size of the object was changed, fewer responses were made. As Bower points out, these results indicate that the children were capable of determining the size of the object. However, this study gives us little idea of infants' accuracy. Extremely crude estimates of size could have been made. The minimum ability that Bower's subjects demonstrate involves discriminating between a one-foot cube and a three-foot cube. Although infants may have the rudiments of size perception, it may exist at a very undeveloped level.

The suggestion that size perception is poorly developed in young children is supported by a series of experiments that found developmental improvements of size perception. Wilcox and Teghtsoonian (1971) conditioned three- and seven-year-old children and college-aged students to respond to the larger of two geometric figures presented in an otherwise black display. In testing, the geometric forms were superimposed on backgrounds (perspective drawings, photographs, and texture gradients) that provided distance and relative size information. If distance or relative size information or both were not effective determiners of perceived size, the subjects' judgments should not have been influenced by the test backgrounds. In fact, Wilcox and Teghtsoonian found that the performance of the three-year-olds was not affected by the size information in the backgrounds; rather, their judgments were apparently based on visual angle. The performance of nine-year-olds was partially affected by the background information; and adults' judgments were substantially affected by the backgrounds. These results indicate that the effectiveness of static monocular information for size changes over the course of development.

In an extension of this study, Yonas and Hagen (1973) found that three-year-olds did show some sensitivity to textural information but often tended to judge on the basis of retinal rather than actual size. When verdical motion parallax information for distance was present, the children's accuracy improved. Moreover, developmental improvements in accuracy were found.

Other studies show that accuracy in perceiving the actual size of objects improves over childhood. Zeigler and Leibowitz (1957) showed that substantial improvements occurred with age when seven- to nine-year-olds were compared to adults. Subjects saw a stick at one of several distances (10, 30, 60, 80, 100 feet) and were asked to adjust the height of a comparison stick so that it matched the height of the one in the distance. Adults were highly accurate in this task. Their estimates closely approximated perfect size judgments. The children, on the other hand, were much less accurate. Although there was a correspondence between the actual height of the sticks and their judged height, errors were substantial. Zeigler and Leibowitz conclude that these results support the view that size constancy increases with age.

There have been a great number of studies of size perception in children (see Wohlwill 1960, for a review of the literature). Although these studies generally agree that children's ability to perceive the size of an object changes with age, there is little agreement on the exact developmental course of this change. The reason for this lack of agreement lies in the number of methodological problems encountered in studying size perception. One source of these problems is the task the subject thinks he is to perform. Depending on how he interprets the experimental instructions, different attitudes can be adopted which influence results. For example, assume you are asked to judge the sizes of two objects, one near and one far away. You could approach this task either in a naive way or in an analytical way. Naively, you could look at the two objects, see their real sizes are equal (for example, both are six inches long), and judge that both are the same size. Or, you could adopt an analytic framework and make rough estimates of angular size. In some sense, an object does look smaller when it is farther away. We can tell that equal-sized objects seem to get smaller as they recede into the distance.

Depending on which of these two strategies was adopted, judgments would or would not show size constancy. With a naive framework, a high degree of size constancy would be evident in the judgments. With the analytic framework, however, it would appear that judgments were based totally on retinal or angular size; that is, size constancy was not present. Since these two attitudes can clearly influence results, the attitude that a subject had would play a large role in how he perceived size. This point has been demonstrated by Smith and Smith (1966), who asked children to make size judgments of a baseball. When the size judgments were analyzed, the results fell into two distinct clusters. Some of the judgments were based on a naive attitude and indicated size constancy; other judgments were based on the angular size of the baseball. Adults, however, interpreted the instructions in terms of actual size matches; none of them used angular size as a basis of judgment.

In addition to the effect of attitude on size judgments, there is also a large number of other methodological considerations affecting developmental data. In 1946, Lambercier (cited in Gibson 1969) found that many seemingly trivial experimental variables influenced children's performance. Judgments were found to be affected by the test methods used, practice, instructions, subjects' height, lateral position of the objects, background, arrangement of a series of objects to be judged, type of comparison required, type of object, as well as attitude toward the task.

In view of all these variables influencing a child's performance in a size judgment task, it is not surprising that different experiments do not agree on the developmental course of size perception. Perhaps a more productive course for future work on size perception would be to identify the variables of stimulation (the invariant information) that specify size and then to determine whether children are able to use this information. Such an approach would indicate not only the abilities children have at different ages but would also indicate what the perceptual basis of these abilities was. Until we know more about size information, size perception will not be completely understood.

THE PERCEPTION OF MOTION

In the layout of the world, objects have particular locations, orientations, slants, and sizes. They also move or remain stationary. For some reason lost in evolution, these last characteristics seem very important. Humans are unusually attuned to the presence of motion. One of the most attention-grabbing stimuli that exists for us is a sudden motion in the periphery of our visual field. Regardless of what activity we are engaged in, a sudden movement usually distracts us. To demonstrate this with a concentrated task such as reading, arrange a pendulum to swing in such a way as to just be seen out of the corner of your eye. You will find it very difficult, even uncomfortable, to read. Even though your attention is focused on a small area of a page, you still see the pendulum peripherally and your attention is drawn to it. It is as if there were a special mechanism in the visual system that detects motion and forces us to pay attention to it.

Movement is very important, yet we know little about how it is perceived. There may be stimulus information for movement (Gibson 1968), but movement may also be seen when no movement exists. If a small light is positioned in a totally dark room, that light appears to move even though it is completely stable. Similarly, if a set of lights is flashed on and off in the right way, movement is seen where none exists.

Evidence indicates that infants are able to distinguish motion from stability with both real and apparent motion. An early test of newborns' responsiveness to visual stimuli involves the ability to follow a moving spot of light with the eyes. Although it is well known that infants immediately after birth are able to follow moving light and thus can perceive motion, there is little known of infants' ability to perceive real movement or of the conditions under which infants can detect real movement.

Primarily for experimental convenience, most studies of motion perception in children have used apparent motion. One type of apparent motion, called the "phi phenomenon," has been used extensively in development. In this experiment, two lights are positioned a short distance apart. First one is lit and then extinguished, and after a brief interval the second one is lit. If the time interval between the two lights is appropriate, one sees a single light that changes its position. If the time interval is too short, two lights are seen simultaneously; and if the time interval is too long, the two lights seem to flash successively.

Tauber and Koffler (1966) presented neonates with a pattern of stripes that were illuminated to give the appearance of a stripe that moved across the field of view. The majority of the infants responded by following the moving stripe with their eyes. Haith (1966) also found that neonates responded to a moving pattern of lights. When a sequence of lights was presented under conditions in which adults saw movement, the infants stopped sucking. Reduction of sucking did not occur when only a stationary light was presented. Both of these sets of results suggest that children are able to perceive apparent movement virtually from birth.

Within the context of real movement, the experiments on looming are again relevant. Since neonates are able to pick up information for impending collision and react to it, they must be able to discriminate simple motion. Additionally, because the infants were capable of discriminating between a condition that specified a direct hit versus one that specified a near miss, subtle differences in direction of movement must also be accurately perceived. From these studies, we can conclude that children are able to perceive both real and apparent motion and can discriminate the direction of motion within the first few days of life.

Velocity

Children's perception of velocity has been studied extensively by Piaget, Feller, and McNear (1958). They suggest that children's perception of speed is based on simple comparisons of one speed relative to another. Since perception of speed depends on the relationship between two objects (according to Piaget), physical events such as one object's passing another affect children's judgments. Piaget (1946) suggested that the ability to judge velocity might pass through three stages. In the first, the ordinal stage, actual passing of one object by another is crucial. If two mobiles are moving and one passes the other, it is seen as traveling faster. In the second stage, the hyperordinal, actual passing is unnecessary for the perception of differential velocity. As long as the space between two moving objects shortens (implying passing at a later point), differential velocity is perceived. Fraisse and Vautrey (cited in Gibson 1969) performed a series of experiments in which various factors, such as amount of distance covered, time, overtaking of one object by another, and passing were manipulated. They found that children between the ages of four and one-half and five and one-half were able to judge relative velocity correctly even if the greater speed did not correspond with passing. These results suggest that Piaget's hyperordinal stage may be useful in categorizing young children's abilities.

Beyond this level, Piaget suggested a higher level of functioning characteristic of older children. When direct passing or overtaking did not occur, children could judge differences in velocity by operating within a metric stage. Without actual passing or overtaking (for example, with successive presentation of two moving objects or with motion along a circular track), Piaget suggests that velocity (V) is determined by means of the equation $V = d/t$. The subject estimates the distance (d) traveled and the time (t) taken and uses these estimates to compute velocity. The evidence presented for this third stage is very preliminary and deserves replication. It would be worthwhile to determine whether children do become conscious calculators of velocity at some point in development. Regardless of the actual existence of this third stage, however, it is clear from other evidence that children are able to perceive differences in velocity as early as four years old.

Piaget and his colleagues have contributed many other studies of motion perception in children, which concern the relationship of rather esoteric laboratory phenomena (for example, a square seems to change its shape when traveling very rapidly) to Piaget's general theory of cognitive development. These theoretical notions are well developed in three monographs (Piaget 1946, 1969; Piaget, Feller, and McNear 1958).

THE PERCEPTION OF KINETIC DEPTH

An individual's ability to perceive orientation, relative depth, and direction of motion are interrelated in a particular way. A certain kind of motion-carried information potentially specifies each of these aspects of spatial layout. A phenomenon that demonstrates the interrelationship between these aspects of layout and the effectiveness of motion-carried information is the Kinetic Depth Effect (KDE).

To experience the KDE, take a three-dimensional wire model of an object, such as the skeleton cube depicted in Figure 3–5, and place it in front of a light bulb so it casts a shadow on a wall. This shadow will clearly be two-dimensional and might look something like the cube in Figure 3–5. By itself, this two-dimensional projection tells you little about the actual object casting the shadow. That *particular* shadow pattern could arise from any one of a large number of different objects. For example, a cube at one orientation could cast that shadow, as could a rhomboid at a different orientation, as could a pattern of lines drawn on a flat sheet of glass. The two-dimensional projection itself provides no information for the actual object.

If you slightly rotate the wire figure, you will notice that its shadow changes. We can say that the shadow has undergone a transformation as a result of this slight rotation. If you slowly and continuously rotate the

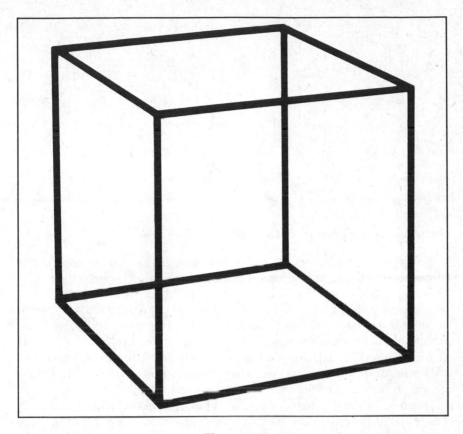

Figure 3–5

Reversible skeleton cube.

object, the shadow pattern continuously changes. A transformation of the pattern occurs from instant to instant, and as the object rotates, the shadow pattern undergoes a particular sequence of transformation, as shown in Figure 3–6. If you perform this experiment, you will notice the motion of the object allows you to determine its actual shape, its thickness compared to its height, and the orientation or slant of its surfaces. In fact, you would be able to perceive the shape, thickness, and orientation of an unfamiliar figure given the sequence of transformations of its shadow.

This esoteric laboratory phenomenon is relevant to everyday perception. As the wire figure is rotated, it undergoes a sequence of transformations. In a similar way, the shape of an object undergoes a sequence of transformations as you walk around it or walk past it. Consequently, the transformation sequence that provides information in the Kinetic Depth Effect is the same kind as the transformation sequences that occur when we normally move about. In both cases, these sequences provide potential information for spatial layout.

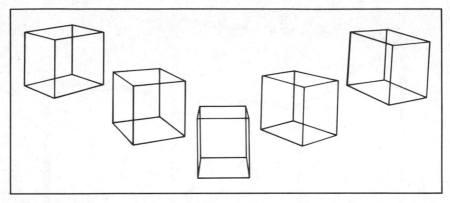

Figure 3–6

Sequence of transformations of a rotating skeleton cube.

Hay (1966) and Farber (1972) demonstrated that under certain cir-cumstances, these transformation sequences affect perception. Al-though an analysis of the information given by any arbitrary motion of any arbitrary object is not available, Farber has shown that in two special cases, the transformations produced by motion of a rigid object are uniquely related to its shape and internal depth. The first of these cases is the movement (translation) of the point of observation as one walks or drives around. The second case is the arbitrary motion of an object com-posed of flat facets or flat surfaces.

If you followed the instructions for experiencing the KDE, you already know that the transformations of the shadow cast by a rotating cube provide effective information for perception. There is one further dem-onstration you can perform to see how transformation sequences may influence your perceptions. If you look at the cube in Figure 3–5 for a few moments, you will experience a reversal of perspective. The face of the cube marked with the "X" can be seen as either the front face or the rear face. After looking at the cube for a while, you will notice that the two perspective orientations alternate, and you can somehow cause the perspective to reverse when you want it to.

In a similar fashion, you can reverse the perspective of the cube's shadow on the wall. If you reverse the perspective of the cube and then rotate it, a strange thing will occur. For the original situation with the cube seen in its correct perspective, the transformation sequence will specify the rotation of a rigid object. However, if you reverse the perspec-tive of the cube, the transformation sequence is no longer the correct one. As long as the perspective is reversed, you will see a strange elastic motion, in which the object seems to be stretching and contracting while it is rotating. For the object seen from that perspective, the transforma-tion sequence does not specify rigid object motion, and so elastic defor-mations are seen.

This demonstration indicates that we are sensitive to the sequence of transformations, and that the transformations undergone by an object affect our perceptions. Farber (1972) found that adult observers are very sensitive to changes in the transformation sequence. He has shown that magnifying an object while it is rotating results in specific alterations of the transformation sequence. These alterations should theoretically result in the perception of a nonrigid object. In fact, adult subjects did report elastic deformations of the rotating object even under fairly slight magnification (1.8x). This result indicates that the sequence of transformations is effective information for the perception of rigid motion and layout. You can observe the effect that Farber studied by viewing your rotating cube through a telescope or binoculars.

The development of the ability to use motion-carried information for the perception of layout has not been systematically studied. The data we have, however, suggest that children are able to use transformation sequence information but that they are less sensitive than adults to distortions of the transformation sequence. When an object rotates, its projected shape goes through a number of regular changes. In spite of these changes, there are characteristics of the object that remain invariant over the rotation. For example, as the object rotates it undergoes the same pattern of projective transformations over and over, with a cyclic regularity. Each side of the object reappears with every 360 degrees of rotation.

Levine (1972) studied whether children were able to detect changes in the rotation of an object that did not conform to this cyclical repetition of the sequence. Using motion picture animation, a film was made in which an rhomboid slowly rotated. When elementary school children were shown this film, they were all able to describe correctly what was depicted. In one experiment, one side of the object was marked with a black square. After every 360 degrees of rotation, the square could be seen again. Then at one point the square did not appear, but a circle was seen in its place. Even first-graders noticed this change and were able to describe what was wrong with the film. Consequently, by the first grade, children know one simple fact about rotational transformations: they do not affect the form of objects.

In a second phase of the experiment, the object rotated with one of its sides marked with a square. At one point, the square began to appear after every 540 degrees of rotation rather than after every 360 degrees. Thus, although a regular cyclic sequence was present, the cycle was wrong. First-graders were unable to notice anything unusual about this sequence, but third-graders and adults responded to the anomaly.

In a third variation, the shape of the back side of the object was continuously varied, so that a transformation sequence was present but was never repeated. To adults, the object appeared to develop holes and grow limbs in an anomalous way, but children did not notice the lack of a cyclic pattern to the transformations.

These results indicate that children are able to use motion-carried information by the time they are in elementary school, but that the ability to detect anomalies in the transformation sequence develops over several years. Further research of this sort will provide more knowledge about the developmental effectiveness of motion-carried information and the interrelationships between different aspects of layout perception.

SUMMARY

The ability to determine the layout of the environment is an essential perceptual capacity. However, no single mechanism underlies spatial layout perception. Instead, different kinds of information specify different aspects of layout and, as a result, different abilities develop at different times. Although infants have the ability to discriminate between different slants when several forms of information are available, the ability to use texture gradient information takes several years to develop and improves into adulthood. In addition, it has been shown that children are not able to use all forms of gradient information available. Compression gradients, for example, are relatively ineffective.

Within a few months after birth, children are able to perceive the sizes of objects in the environment. This early ability improves over the course of development. Theoretically, size perception has two bases: the "calculation" of size from known distance and the use of relative size information from the horizon or from textures. Both of these sources of information seem to underlie developmental improvements in size perception. Although improvements are well documented, the exact developmental course of size perception is not known, due to the large number of factors that influence a child's behavior in the testing situation.

Although there is evidence that neonates are able to perceive motion, there is still little known about the development of this ability. Further investigation of motion perception and the use of motion-carried information may be especially important because such information potentially specifies many aspects of layout. We know that children are able to use the transformation sequences in motion-carried information by the time they are in elementary school, and with age and experience they become more sensitive to violations in the transformation sequence.

Chapter 4

THE DEVELOPMENT OF VISUALLY GUIDED BEHAVIOR

The preceding chapters have shown that visual information exists which precisely specifies spatial layout. Neonates are able to pick up at least some of this information, such as motion perspective and looming, for example. Other types of spatial information can be picked up at least within a few weeks after birth. These perceptual abilities provide a basis for accurately guiding locomotion and spatial behavior as well as for avoiding potentially dangerous events such as impending collision.

These facts give us the basis for our next question concerning the development of visually guided behavior: How modifiable is the relationship between visual perception and motor behavior? Further, is the ability to use visual information to guide behavior an inborn one, or are certain kinds of experience necessary for an infant to learn to coordinate his actions with vision? Some very primitive—and survival-oriented—kinds of abilities may well be prewired. For example, a rudimentary ability to use motion perspective information to avoid collision with an object appears very early, and optical magnification elicits a reflexlike avoidance response even from one-week-old infants. Thus, as we discussed earlier, it would make a great deal of sense if looming avoidance ability were prewired rather than learned, since in an animal's normal environment, the rapid, symmetrical expansion of an object's contours occurs only under potentially dangerous conditions, and even one-trial learning would not save the animal who failed to avoid a predator on the first trial.

With other kinds of perceptual ability, there is less need for early capabilities. Since children cannot locomote for several months after birth, the early occurrence of spatial vision necessary to guide locomotion would have little value. There is a period of several weeks to several months in which spatial vision may develop and be coordinated with behavior. The question is whether experience does, in fact, shape and modify the relationship between perception and behavior.

If a child learns to guide his behavior with visual information, the type of learning that occurs is different from that of "standard" learning situations, such as conditioning and discrimination learning. The ability to discriminate depth cannot be based on punishing or rewarding consequences of locomotion. As we have seen, a child need not be rewarded for choosing the shallow side of a visual cliff before he responds consistently. Some kind of experience may, however, be necessary for a child to respond accurately to visual information—necessary, that is, to affect sensorimotor development. As Gibson (1969) suggests, the visual system may become more precise in differentiating the information that specifies different layouts. As a corollary, certain kinds of experiences may be necessary to reveal the relationship between spatial behavior and vision—that is, to modify behavior as a result of visual information.

If the correspondence between spatial information and behavior is built into an organism, it should be possible to perform accurate, visually guided acts without ever having previous visual experience. If the visual-motor wiring is innately organized so that a spot of light on a certain place on the retina specifies that a certain movement is necessary to reach an object, experience will not affect sensorimotor development. If, on the other hand, the relationship between vision and action is modifiable, specific kinds of experiences will help an infant bring vision and spatial behavior into correspondence.

In principle, it would be easy to perform an experiment to determine which of these alternatives is true. We could raise one group of children in a normal visual environment and, following a suggestion made by Mark Twain, raise a second group in closed pickle barrels. After a few weeks or months, we would test the perceptual abilities of both groups (for example, on the visual cliff) to see what effect experience had. If both groups performed equally well, it would suggest that experience does not affect cliff performance. If the pickle barrel group performed poorly on the visual cliff (for example, not distinguishing between the deep and the shallow sides), we could conclude that total visual deprivation impairs performance, and that some kind of experience is necessary for normal visual-motor development to occur.

Clearly, there are ethical proscriptions against performing the pickle barrel experiment with children. Such experiments have been done with animals, however. Although animal experiments do not directly tell us anything about human development, they do provide evidence that supports the logic of the hypothesis being tested. If other mammals or other primates are affected by visual deprivation, the *possibility* that humans are also affected by deprivation is strengthened.

THE EFFECTS OF LIGHT DEPRIVATION
ON PERCEPTUAL DEVELOPMENT

Must animals learn to guide their behavior visually? One of the early experiments that addressed this question was done by Riesen (1947). He eliminated all opportunities for visual experience by rearing two chimpanzees in total darkness until they were sixteen months old. At this point, they were brought into the light for periodic observations and then returned to the dark room. At twenty-one months of age, the animals were brought permanently into the normal light. Severe, striking deficits were observed. Upon being brought into the light, "the two animals were, in effect, blind" (Riesen 1947, p. 107). For example, the female chimpanzee first blinked her eyes to a threatened blow on the fifth day after being removed from the dark room, but a consistent blink to an approaching object did not appear until forty-eight days of experience in light. The first reaching responses were grossly inaccurate. These remarkable deficiencies led Riesen to conclude that visual ability was not innate, but required a period of "long apprenticeship" in using the eyes.

It also appears that the severity of perceptual impairment is related to the length of the light deprivation period. Fantz (1965a) subjected eleven infant rhesus monkeys to various amounts of visual deprivation. Several days after birth, the infants were placed in a light proof room with their mothers. The infants remained in the dark room for deprivation periods ranging from three days to twenty weeks. Except for occasional, brief test periods in the light, these infants had no exposure to light throughout deprivation. After deprivation, the monkeys were housed in a normally lighted "nursery" and tested daily on a variety of tasks. Fantz expected that these animals would suffer severe perceptual deficits after dark rearing but was most interested in how much time would be required before visual abilities recovered to approximately normal levels.

Results on the test tasks were quite straightforward. On the visual cliff task, one month or less of deprivation had a minimal effect on performance. After three or four days of visual experience in the nursery, all the subjects showed distinct preferences for the shallow side. The subjects deprived of light for two months or longer never showed recovery of depth perception. Although they were tested daily for seven to ten weeks after deprivation, they failed to show a preference for the shallow side of the cliff and testing was discontinued. The behavior of animals deprived of light for one or two months fell between these extremes. Clearly, deprivation severely affects visual cliff performance. Furthermore, the impairment caused by severe deprivation may not be reversible.

On locomotion and localization tests, deprivation resulted in less of an impairment. At the end of dark rearing, the subjects collided with obstacles and inaccurately reached for the nursery bottle. However, performance improved with experience. The animals deprived from three days to eleven weeks developed normal locomotion and localization ability after about a week of nursery experience.

Impairment of the perceptual system as a result of light deprivation is not restricted to primates. Walk and Gibson (1961) reared kittens in the dark from the time the animals were five days old (before their eyes opened) until they were twenty-six days old. After this deprivation period, the subjects were given six trials on the visual cliff. There was no evidence that these animals were able to distinguish between the two depths. As documented in Table 4–1, dark-reared kittens showed no preference for the shallow side of the cliff, whereas light-reared kittens never selected the deep side. After the deprivation period, the kittens were kept in a normally lighted room and given two trials per day on the visual cliff for fifteen days. Cliff performance improved over the first week of experience with light, until there was a normal preference for the shallow side (see Figure 4–1).

Although there are some species differences (dark-reared rats do not show impaired cliff performance, for example), dark rearing results in profound disturbances of perceptual abilities. It would seem at first that space perception abilities are learned, and that these abilities improve with accumulated practice. We could argue that dark rearing effectively prevents any opportunity for visual learning, the lack of this learning results in impaired perception, and as opportunities for learning are provided, perceptual abilities improve to normal levels. For a time, these results were taken as evidence that space perception is learned. However, the situation is not this simple.

One assumption underlying these early studies is that dark rearing merely halts normal development. It has since been found, however, that deprivation of light does not simply halt development and hold it at some stable, early level; instead, deprivation results in physical deterioration of the visual system. These degenerative effects occur at many

Table 4–1.

Visual Cliff Performance of Dark- and Light-Reared Kittens

Rearing Condition	Descents to Shallow Side (percent)	Descents to Deep Side (percent)	No Preference (percent)
Reared in the dark	31.5	35.2	33.3
Reared in the light	86.0	0.0	14.0

Source: Adapted from R. D. Walk and E. J. Gibson, "A Comparative and Analytical Study of Visual Depth Perception," *Psychological Monographs* 75 (1961).

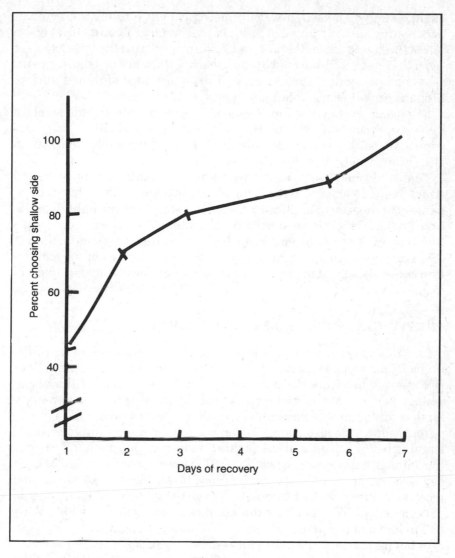

Figure 4–1

Recovery of depth discrimination following a period of light deprivation. (After Walk and Gibson, 1961.)

points in the visual system. At the retinal level, lengthy deprivation (one and one-half to two and one-half years) in chimpanzees results in almost a complete absence of retinal ganglion cells (Chow, Riesen, and Newell 1957). In cats, a short deprivation period (fourteen weeks) results in significant changes in the thickness of the retinal layer containing ganglionic dendrites and in the density of the optic tract (Weiskrantz

1958). Even when such gross morphological changes are not evident, dark rearing has been found to result in biochemical abnormalities of the retina (Brattgard 1952; Riesen 1966). It is apparent that the physiology of the retina is severely affected by dark rearing. Absence of ganglion cells, reduction of dendritic processes, and disappearance of retinal nucleo-proteins can all result from light deprivation.

Degenerative effects of deprivation also occur at more central levels of the visual system. Wiesel and Hubel (1963) found the activity of lateral geniculate cells was considerably diminished. Monocular deprivation also resulted in cortical dysfunctions.

These physiological disruptions demonstrate a degeneration of neural structures that exist at birth. The physical deterioration that accompanies dark rearing complicates the interpretation of the light depriva-tion studies. Deficiencies in perceptual-motor abilities could have been the result of physical degeneration, lack of learning, or a combination of these factors. Since exposure to light is necessary for the normal matura-tion of the visual system, total deprivation does not isolate the effects of experience.

THE EFFECTS OF PARTIAL LIGHT DEPRIVATION

Learning may be necessary in perceptual development even in the normally developed visual system. A certain amount of exposure to light is necessary to assure the proper physical development of the visual system; beyond that, particular kinds of experiences may be necessary for the development of perceptual abilities. Modified deprivation proce-dures that provide visual stimulation without an opportunity for visual learning have been used to assess this possibility. One method provides the animals with some restricted visual experience for a period of each day. For example, diffusers can be placed over the eyes so the animal receives diffuse light that stimulates the visual system, but it receives no patterned light. To experience this condition, you could cut a Ping-Pong ball in half and fasten half over each of your eyes. Light will reach your eyes but pattern vision will be blocked. What you see is similar to a very thick, heavy fog that has no form and has indeterminate depth. Under such conditions, some neural deterioration occurs in cats, but it is sub-stantially less than that which occurs as a result of dark rearing (Weis-krantz 1958; Wiesel and Hubel 1963). Furthermore, there are a number of interesting results involving the motor behavior of subjects given diffuse light experience that are not easily explained in relation to de-generation.

One of the studies suggesting that lack of visual experience affects visual-motor coordination was performed by Riesen and Aarons (1959). After rearing kittens in total darkness from birth to sixteen weeks of age, they gave different groups various kinds of visual experiences. The first group was given diffuse light exposure (which prevented pattern vision) for one hour per day while restrained in holders that prevented movement. Group 2 was restrained in holders but given normal visual experience for one hour per day. Group 3 was given normal visual-motor experience while unrestrained for one hour per day. A control group lived in cages outside the darkroom and received normal visual stimulation throughout the day. Subjects were then given discrimination training in which they learned to respond differentially to a moving versus a stable pattern (a cross).

The animals that were either deprived of patterned vision or restrained during patterned light experience (groups 1 and 2) were unable to solve the discrimination. The unrestrained groups (group 3 and control) had no difficulty with the problem. In addition, the restrained animals revealed a general disorientation of visual-motor coordination: they had difficulty guiding their locomotion in the test apparatus. After entering the incorrect alley, some of the subjects would attempt to correct their choice but would turn in the wrong direction, return to the incorrect alley, and attempt to repeat the attempts at correction. This suggests that the deprivation conditions for groups 1 and 2 adversely affected the ability to guide locomotor behavior accurately or discriminate motion. These results cannot simply be due to a lack of experience with moving objects. Group 2 was allowed to see moving objects during its exposure period and still was unable to solve the discrimination problem. Some other factor common to the experience of groups 1 and 2 must have been the cause of the discrimination difficulties.

The suggestion that visual-motor behavior is affected by experience in rearing is supported by other studies. Riesen and Mellinger (1956) found that their animals were unable to perform successfully on tests involving visual placing, obstacle avoidance, or jumping down from a six-inch-high platform. Riesen, Kurke, and Mellinger (1953) report that their kittens did not seem to use vision to find food and bumped into objects when walking around a lighted room. The implication of these results is that animals deprived of visual-motor experience were unable to use visual information to guide their behavior.

If this conclusion is correct, it offers an interpretation of the Riesen and Aarons results. In this experiment, animals restrained during visual exposure had difficulty with the motion discrimination problem. Since movement was restricted, they could not generate the array changes of motion parallax and motion perspective that occur as one normally moves around. In their first experiences with self-produced array changes in the test situation, the kittens may not have been able to distinguish between array motion caused by their own walking around and actual motion of an object in the test apparatus. The results do not indicate that the rearing conditions affected the ability to perceive motion; rather, the ability to discriminate objective motion from self-produced movement was affected. We should expect, therefore, no performance deficits if the animals were tested in a situation that did not allow locomotion and consequent self-produced movement.

Meyers (1964) reasoned in this way and suggested that a nonlocomotor testing procedure be used. He essentially replicated a portion of the Riesen and Aarons study with a different test procedure. In discrimination learning, the animals were placed in a hammocklike sling and required to learn to flex a rear leg in order to avoid shock when one of the stimuli was presented. Meyers's animals did not show any impairment of discrimination performance as a result of the rearing condition. Considered together, the Riesen and Aarons study and the Meyers study indicate that restricted rearing affects the ability to use motion-carried information in locomotion but does not affect the ability to discriminate between a moving and a stable object. Deprivation of visual experience, then, has a marked effect on the ability to use visual information to guide spatial behavior.

There are few data concerning the effect of restricted perceptual experience on human visual-motor development. However, the data that exist indicate that children are similarly affected by visual deprivation. A child born with cataracts, for example, would receive visual experience similar to Riesen and Aarons's cats reared in diffuse light, since when cataracts form, the lens of the eye is clouded and only diffuse light reaches the retina. The lens can be surgically removed, however, and eyeglasses prescribed to allow vision. London (1960) summarized a Russian report by Pokrovskii of the postoperative behavior of children born with cataracts. One child was ten years old at the time of surgery; the age of the other is not given. After removal of the cataracts, "The children were unable by vision alone to determine distance or, more exactly, the distance of nearest objects. When walking, they collided with these objects" (London 1960, p. 479).

A girl blinded at age five, whose sight was restored at age nine, was unable to reach for or grasp objects accurately even when they were very near. When walking about her room, she stumbled and knocked against things. After two weeks, these deficits disappeared. Another girl blinded at three years of age regained her sight at eight years. She showed the same deficits, but progress toward normal vision was at a much slower rate. We can conclude that limiting visual experience to diffuse light impairs visually guided locomotion in children as in animals.

To summarize briefly, restricted rearing results in substantial perceptual-motor impairment. These deficits are not simply the result of visual deprivation. When animals were given normal pattern vision experience but were restrained so that their movements were limited, deficits in visually guided behavior were found. The ability to determine the position of an object and walk to it was somehow impaired, even though all the animals had pattern vision experience. This clearly suggests that the mere opportunity to view a normal environment is not sufficient for the development of perceptual-motor abilities. Some crucial factor was missing in the experience of these animals.

THE ROLE OF SELF-PRODUCED MOVEMENT

Held and Hein (1963) suggested that this crucial experiential factor was the opportunity to view the changes that occur in the optic array as the animal moves around. Since the kittens used in the Riesen et al. study and the Meyers experiment were restrained, they could not see the effects of their own movements on the visual array. Any changes that occurred during the period of exposure were independent of the animals' behavior. Held and Hein suggested that the variations in stimulation that occur with movement will affect perceptual development when the movements are produced by the subject. The opportunity to see stimulus changes that are not self-produced will not be sufficient for the development of visually guided behavior.

To test these hypotheses, Held and Hein reared ten pairs of kittens in total darkness. Eight of the pairs were reared in darkness from birth until one member of a pair was large enough to move around in the training apparatus. Two pairs were reared in darkness but given three hours per day of visual experience while restrained to prevent movement. Each pair was divided into a passive and an active subject and placed in the test apparatus. In the apparatus shown in Figure 4−2, the active animal was strapped on one side and the passive one was placed in the gondola and held by a body clamp and neck yoke. As the active kitten moved in the apparatus, its movements were transferred by the mechanical arrangement to the passive kitten's gondola. As the active kitten turned, the gondola was turned; as it walked around, the gondola was swept around duplicating the active kitten's motion. Each pair was given three hours of experience per day in this apparatus and then returned to the lightless cages. After training, both members were given six test trials on the visual cliff. The next day, six more trials on the cliff were administered. After the second day of testing, the passive kitten was put into a continuously illuminated room for forty-eight hours and then retested on the cliff.

The important aspect of this experiment is that both members of each pair received *almost* identical experience. Both the active and the passive kitten in each pair were reared in the dark for the same amount of time; both received the same kind and amount of visual experience; and both were tested in the same way. The main difference between these two animals was that one of them (the active one) produced changes in the visual array, whereas the other (the passive one) only observed these changes. The results of the experiment were striking. Every one of the active kittens selected the shallow side of the cliff on every one of the

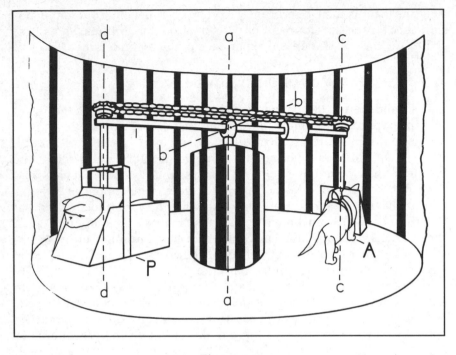

Figure 4–2

The kitten carousel. The mechanical arrangement transfers the active cat's movement to the passive cat, thus equalizing array motion experience. (From Held and Hein, 1963. Copyright © 1963 by the American Psychological Association. Reprinted by permission.)

twelve trials. None of the passive kittens showed any ability to distinguish the shallow from the deep side. In addition, the passive kittens did not show paw placing or blinking to an approaching object. However, after forty-eight hours of unrestricted experience in the lighted room, the passive kittens performed normally on all tasks.

Hein, Held, and Gower (1970) repeated the kitten carousel experiment using each kitten as its own control. Each kitten had one eye open during active (self-produced) movement and the other eye open during passive movement. Each eye received virtually identical stimulation—one when the kitten moved actively, the other when the kitten was moved passively. The animals performed normally on the cliff when the active eye was open but were unable to perform adequately using the passive eye.

One explanation for these results (Gibson 1969) is that the passive kittens' behavior was affected by the nature of their experiences. The active kittens learned that their actions controlled their experience. It might follow that the passive kittens learned there was nothing they could do to affect the environment; that is, they learned that they were helpless. A similar statement could be made about the kittens in the Hein, Held, and Gower experiment. With one eye open, the kittens learned that there was a relationship between their behavior and their visual experience; with the other eye open, they learned that they were helpless. There is no direct evidence to prove that this helplessness theory is correct. But, as we shall see, postulating different kinds of active learning and passive learning helps to explain a puzzling aspect of the kitten carousel data.

Self-Produced Movement and Visual Information

Held and Hein (1963) suggested that the opportunity to see the consequences of self-produced movement affects the development of visually guided behavior. To explain further why the results of active and passive training differed so dramatically and to analyze the role of active movement in visual-motor development, we must first consider the effect of movement on the stimulus information for layout. We know that motion parallax and motion perspective are two important kinds of information in cliff and looming avoidance situations. When an observer moves his head, the retinal position of objects changes in a regular way. When, as a result of this head movement, the image of an object sweeps over the retina, the object is not seen to move in the world but rather is seen to remain stable, and the array motion specifies its distance from the observer. A similar motion of an object in the array when not accompanied by observer movement specifies that the object itself is moving in the world.

Consequently, a basic ability that an animal must have to be able to use motion parallax information is the ability to distinguish between array motions that result from its own movement and array motions that result from movement of the environment. That is, it must be able to distinguish between changes that specify distance and those that specify that an object is moving. On the basis of the experiments done by Riesen and Aarons (1959) and Meyers (1964), we can see that this is precisely what restrictively reared kittens cannot do. Meyers found that his kittens could easily distinguish between moving and stationary objects when they were held stationary. Yet, Riesen and Aarons's kittens could not easily make this discrimination when they were moving. The animals could not distinguish between object motion and array motion produced by their own movement. We should expect, therefore, that these animals would be deficient in the use of motion parallax information.

The failure of the passive kittens in Held and Hein's experiment to avoid the deep side of the visual cliff can be explained in relation to this ability to use stimulus information. Two aspects of information processing are necessary for veridical perception of the world. First is the ability to register variables of stimulation such as motion; second is the presence of mechanisms that relate stimulation to some condition in the world. In the context of motion parallax and depth, an animal must be able to see the relative motion of objects in the array and pick up the differential velocities at which things move. In addition, an animal must have a mechanism for relating these motions to distance. This relationship between motion parallax and distance apparently does not exist in the passively reared kittens. Distance and parallax need to be related or calibrated.

Once the relationship between parallax and distance is established, each degree of parallactic motion is related to a distance. Such a relationship must exist before the deep side of the cliff is avoided. Before calibration of motion parallax and distance can occur, the animal must distinguish between array changes caused by the actual movement of an object and array changes caused by the animal's own movement.

In the kitten carousel experiment (Held and Hein 1963), certain movements on the part of the active kitten always resulted in certain visual changes. The visual system could learn that these visual changes resulted from self-produced movements. With the passive kittens, however, since there was no relation between their movements and array changes, such learning and calibration of the system could not occur. If self-produced movements of the passive kittens could not be related to distance, motion parallax would not specify distance, and cliff performance would be impaired. After an opportunity to generate their own movements and observe the visual consequences of motion, the system could be calibrated, and normal performance could recover. This is, of course, what was found.

A similar argument could explain the effects of restricted rearing on locomotion. Several investigators have reported that after restricted rearing or total deprivation, their animals were unable to locomote smoothly. The animals could not avoid obstacles and often bumped into objects in their path. As discussed earlier, motion perspective provides sufficient effective information for locomoting and avoiding obstacles.

The flow field that arises in motion perspective potentially specifies object location and distance. Furthermore, the regularity or irregularity of flow indicates whether objects in the environment are moving. The deprivation studies suggest, however, that the visual-motor systems must be calibrated before accurate visually guided behavior can occur. Subjects without previous experience with the array changes that occur in self-movement cannot use motion perspective information to guide locomotion.

Array motion and distance must be related for motion parallax to specify object location. If the system that relates distance and array motion does not function properly, object location is not specified. Therefore, experimental conditions that influence the action of this mechanism should impair tasks requiring the use of motion parallax or motion perspective information (tasks such as the visual cliff and obstacle avoidance).

The other results of the Held and Hein experiment cannot be explained in this way. The passive kittens were also found to be deficient on tests of paw placing and blinking at an approaching object. It is not at all clear why passive rearing and the lack of self-produced movement should affect looming avoidance ability. The stimulus information that specifies impending collision is a symmetrical pattern of optical expansion. Whether this expansion pattern is the result of object motion or self-produced movement should be irrelevant. In other words, regardless of whether the organism is rapidly moving toward an object or an object is rapidly moving toward the organism, a dangerous situation results, and the animal should make avoidance responses. A restrictively reared animal may not be able to distinguish between its own movement and that of an object, but in either case a collision is specified by the expansion pattern and avoidance should occur.

The suggestion that the ability to use looming information to avoid impending collision is not dependent on experience with self-produced movement is further supported by Hein, Gower, and Diamond (1970). Kittens were restrictively reared and tested for visual cliff responses and looming avoidance ability. At the end of the deprivation period, none of the kittens could distinguish deep and shallow sides of the visual cliff, but they all showed a triggered placing response. This clearly indicates that experience is not necessary for the development of the placing response to impending collision. It appears, then, that neither self-produced movement nor patterned light experience is necessary for the development of the response to collision. The impairment of looming avoidance ability, which was observed in the Held and Hein experiment, may not have resulted from a disturbance of initial development but rather from a degeneration or deterioration of an existing ability.

Many animals, including cats and monkeys and human infants, possess looming avoidance capability very early in life. Since self-produced movement does not affect the availability of looming information, a plausible explanation of Held and Hein's results is that the training conditions had a negative influence on looming avoidance. The conclusion that passive training suppressed existing looming avoidance ability is further supported by some results of Held (reported in Held 1970). Passive kittens were switched to the active side of the apparatus after thirty-three hours of passive experience. These animals took significantly longer to establish placing responses than did actively reared kittens of the same age. These results certainly indicate that suppression of looming avoidance occurs as a result of restricted rearing.

Should we conclude, then, that the entire behavioral deficit exhibited by the passively transported kittens was the result of a suppression of existing ability, rather than a retardation in development of a new ability? Unfortunately, the evidence that we have at the present time does not answer this question. On the one hand, we know that two forms of information are involved in visual cliff and looming avoidance tasks. It is possible that restricted rearing could disrupt the early development of the use of these sources of information. On the other hand, passive training in the carousel may adversely affect the maintenance of existing abilities. Animals may be able to use motion-carried information early in life, but the absence of active movement may result in a deterioration of this ability. Denying the passively trained kittens the opportunity to maintain a calibration of the system may have damaged normal abilities.

These alternatives provide several possible explanations of the effects of restricted rearing. The first explanation could be applied to the results described above. That is, lacking specific experience, the passive animals' performance remains at a stable level, while the active group develops specific visual-motor coordinations. The active animals could retain abilities present initially, whereas the abilities of the passive animals deteriorate. Or, both these alternatives may be true: the performance of the active kittens improves while that of the passive kittens deteriorates. Or, because of the light deprivation, the performance of both active and passive kittens deteriorates, but the passive kittens' performance deteriorates more.

To understand the relationship between specific kinds of experience and the development of visually guided behavior, we need to separate these alternatives. Unfortunately, we cannot yet do this. The basic problem encountered is methodological. We are asking a question about the absolute levels of performance of the two groups of subjects. How does active experience facilitate performance and passive experience impair it? The studies done so far have been addressed to questions of relative performance: Is there an overall difference between the two groups? Consequently, these studies provide no indication of how the groups would do in absolute terms. This problem is not insurmountable; it simply requires a slightly different experimental design for future research.

Solomon and Lessac (1968) have specified in detail the control procedures necessary to evaluate the effects of restricted rearing. To determine whether experience facilitates or disrupts performance, one group would be pretested on paw placing, then given active or passive experience, then posttested on paw placing. Comparison of the pretest and posttest results would give some indication of the effect of the active and passive training. Because it is possible that the pretest itself might affect performance in some way, a second group would receive no pretest, then be given an active or passive experience, and finally a posttest. (This latter is the group used by Held and Hein.) To evaluate the effect of pretest and training further, a third group would receive a pretest, no active or passive training, followed by a posttest. And, to evaluate the changes that occur in the absence of any experience, a fourth group would receive no pretest, no training, and a posttest. This design is summarized in Table 4–2.

Use of such a design would allow us to directly evaluate the facilitation and disruption of performance due to active and passive rearing. Unfortunately, these procedures have not been used to evaluate the per-

Table 4–2.

A Solomon-Lessac Design for a Deprivation Study.
Litter-mates would be assigned across groups.

Manipulation	Experimental		Control	
	Group 1	Group 2	Group 3	Group 4
Given pretest	Yes	No	Yes	No
Given experimental treatment	Yes	Yes	No	No
Given posttest	Yes	Yes	Yes	Yes

Source: Adapted from R. L. Solomon and M. S. Lessac, "A Control Group Design for Experimental Studies of Developmental Processes," *Psychological Bulletin* 70 (1968): 145–50.

ceptual effects of active and passive training, and we cannot now determine whether passive experience affects the initial development of visual-motor ability or the maintenance of existing abilities. Regardless of the final outcome of this question, however, it is clear that self-produced movement has an important function in the processes responsible for developing visually guided behavior.

THE ROLE OF OTHER FORMS OF STIMULATION

Let us now consider the argument that stimulation from self-produced movement is a *necessary* condition for the development of visually guided behavior. We know that the emphatic form of the statement must be false—such stimulation is not necessary for *all* types of information pickup. Impending collision is perceived and responded to even though the subject has had no experience with patterned light or with reafferent stimulation. However, the use of other kinds of information may depend on specific forms of previous experience. It seems clear that active or passive rearing does affect the use of motion parallax information in guiding behavior. It is necessary that an organism distinguish between object motion in the array and self-produced motion. The important question is whether stimulation from self-produced movement provides the *only* means by which this distinction can be made. Other stimulation could possibly provide the information needed.

Howard and Templeton (1966) suggest that the experiment of Held and Hein did not provide an adequate test of the sufficiency of different forms of stimulation because adequate sources of other stimulation were not given to the passive subjects. They suggest that the results of passive rearing might have been different if other stimulation had been provided. For example, adequate stimulation for visual-motor calibration could have been provided if objects were positioned in the alleyway so that the passive kittens occasionally bumped into them. The stimulation resulting from this bumping would reveal that the animal was itself moving. A second suggestion was to pull the passive kitten and its gondola over an edge or down a set of steps. The visual stimulation combined with the tactile and vestibular stimulation that would result from these events could provide adequate information about self-movement.

In principle, at least, the correlated sensory input that may be necessary for visual-motor calibration can be provided in many ways. Self-produced movement may not be the only means of providing appropriate stimulation. Further experiments should be done to determine whether external stimulation would result in normal development of the passive kitten. In any case, present evidence does not prove that self-produced movement is a necessary condition of visual-motor development. It may be sufficient for the maintenance of coordination, but the carousel experiments do not demonstrate that it is a necessary condition of initial development.

Eye-Limb Coordination

Experience with patterned light stimulation is not necessary for the development of paw placing (looming avoidance) in kittens. However, this conclusion applies only to the elicited, or triggered, placing response. These animals are able to respond to an impending collision, but this response consists only of a reflexlike extension of the limbs. Kittens reared in diffuse light or in normal light while restrained (so that little movement is possible) all showed visually triggered extension of the front legs when they were brought toward a surface (Hein, Gower, and Diamond 1970). This extension is not precisely guided, however. For guided placing to occur (in which the limbs are "aimed" at a solid portion of a surface), certain visual-motor experience is required.

Hein and Held (1967) gave kittens six hours per day of free movement in an illuminated and patterned environment. During this period, the kittens wore opaque "collars" that prevented them from seeing their limbs and bodies. After this exposure, the animals were tested for placing responses on a slotted surface (see Figure 4–3) consisting of 2.5 cm prongs separated by 7.5 cm spaces. All the kittens gave a triggered placing response to a solid surface, but when tested on the slotted surface they did not place their paws appropriately. Half of the extensions hit the prongs and half hit the spaces in between. Eighteen hours of unrestricted visual experience were required before they accurately guided their paws to the prongs rather than to the slots. It appears that kittens must have an opportunity to learn where their limbs are. Without visual exposure to the limbs, their positions cannot be coordinated with visual information for position.

A similar conclusion holds for monkeys (Held and Bauer 1967). When stump-tailed macaques were deprived of the sight of their limbs for thirty-four days, guided reaching was strongly affected. After deprivation, a subject initially reached toward an object with groping motions, which became progressively smoother and more accurate with experi-

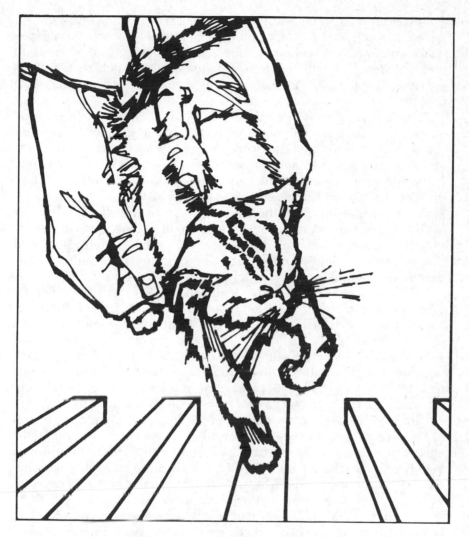

Figure 4–3

Kitten demonstrating paw placement on a slotted surface.

ence. A significant facet of the monkeys' behavior in the initial portions of testing involved prolonged hand watching. With one hand released, the monkey first began to reach for an object, but as soon as his hand came into view the reaching stopped and the monkey watched his hand as it moved. This visual pursuit of the hand was very prolonged, compared with pursuit of other moving objects that he saw. After twenty hours of training, accurate visually guided reaching occurred with one hand. Then the other hand was tested. Attempts at reaching with the untrained hand were awkward, and when the hand came into view, extensive hand watching occurred. If both hands were exposed, accurate reaching occurred only with the hand that had twenty hours of practice.

A crucial aspect of these results is their similarity to those of the kittens raised with collars that obstructed vision of their bodies. In both cases, visual guidance does not occur unless the animal has had a chance to view the limb that will be used. Experience with watching the limbs provides an opportunity for matching the seen position of an object with the felt position of the limb.

These studies demonstrate that specific kinds of experience are required for visual-motor coordination to be established. Cats and monkeys must learn the visual consequences of their own movements, and they must learn also to calibrate the felt position of limbs and body parts with visual position. The calibration that occurs in the development of visually guided behavior is extremely specific to the particular kinds of experiences given the animal. We have already seen that the calibration that occurs under active movement in the kitten carousel is specific to the eye that received reafferent stimulation (Hein, Held, and Gower 1970). Calibration effects are also specific to the limb that was used in the training condition (Held and Bauer 1967).

Hein and Diamond (1971b) have also found that visually guided responses are restricted to the limb that the animal observed in training. Kittens were reared wearing lightweight plastic cones around their front legs. One of the cones was transparent, one was opaque. Animals that were allowed a binocular view of the one limb in the transparent cone were able to guide that limb on a visual placing test. The slotted surface used by Hein and Held (1967) was used to assess placing, and the observable limb was correctly guided to the prongs on virtually every trial. The limb in the opaque cone, unseen by the animal, could not be guided. In the placing test, it contacted a prong on less than half of the trials. Other kittens were reared wearing the leg cones, but with vision allowed to only one eye. These kittens could guide the limb to the prongs using the eye that had seen the limb but not with the eye that had been covered. The development of visual-motor coordination was highly specific to the eye-limb combination that had been exposed during training. The lack of transfer between eyes or between limbs suggests that each facet of visual-motor coordination can be acquired separately. This does not necessarily mean that the position of each limb and the visual input from each eye are normally independently calibrated, but rather that under deprivation conditions, visual-motor coordination may be highly specific.

The extreme dependence of visual-motor coordination on the conditions of experience has been further shown by Hein and Diamond (1971a). Kittens were allowed free locomotion under conditions of very dim light. Under such dim lighting, only the scotopic (rod) system of the eye is operative. Thus, the rod system was allowed experience but the cone (photopic) system was not. The animals were then tested on guided placing and obstacle avoidance under both photopic and scotopic levels of illumination. In dim light, when the rod system was working, the kittens exhibited guided placing and easily avoided obstacles in their path. In bright light, when the cone system was operating, the kittens could not guide paw placing and could not avoid obstacles. In another experiment, each kitten was used as its own control. It was allowed free locomotion under low light levels and was restrained (but was given normal visual experience) under higher levels of illumination. These kittens demonstrated accurate visually guided behavior on all tests in dim light but were unable to perform successfully in brighter light. These results further show the extreme dependence of visual-motor coordination on exposure conditions. Differential stimulation of the rod and cone systems leads to differential visual-motor learning.

RESEARCH WITH INFANTS

For obvious ethical reasons, there have been few attempts to extend this research to children. However, there are some instances in which normally sighted infants have been reared under restricted institutional conditions. Although under institutional conditions infants are not subjected to purposeful sensory deprivation, in some cases visual stimulation is restricted by reduced opportunities for the child to cause changes in his visual array. For example, children may be kept in cribs that have the sides covered with white sheeting. Toys and play equipment are limited. In some respects, this bland visual environment combined with the restrictions on movement are similar to the rearing conditions in the studies we have just discussed.

Most of the investigations of the effects of restricted rearing under institutional conditions have not been concerned with the effects of visual experience on the development of human perceptual abilities. For the most part, deprivation effects have been assessed in relation to the development of emotionality, intelligence, or gross motor abilities (see Bronfenbrenner 1968; Casler 1968; O'Connor 1968). Although we would expect the nature of environmental stimulation and the conditions of visual experience to affect visual-motor development, these aspects of development have not been the primary concern of the previous human deprivation research.

An important exception to this generalization, however, is the series of long-term studies of visual-motor development carried out by White and his collaborators (White and Held 1966; White, Castle, and Held 1964; White 1971). Rather than working within the previous framework of personality development and deprivation effects, White suggested that the notions developed in the course of the stimulus deprivation studies with animals might be applicable to visual-motor development in children. Quite clearly, human infants cannot be subjected to severe deprivation of visual stimulation for the sake of determining the effects of experience on development. However, if development is affected by exposure history, manipulation of the environment should affect the

course of development. Since the normal environment of institutionalized children is in some sense restricted, perhaps the development
of these children could be affected by enriching their experience.
Results of this kind would certainly provide corroborative evidence
about the plasticity of visual-motor development and significantly
expand our ideas about the effects of experience on development.

This basic notion forms the primary rationale of White's study. To
provide normative data on these institutionally reared children, the development of attention and visual-motor coordination was observed
from birth to several months of age. During the first month of life, White's
subjects were visually alert for only abour 5 percent of each day, and

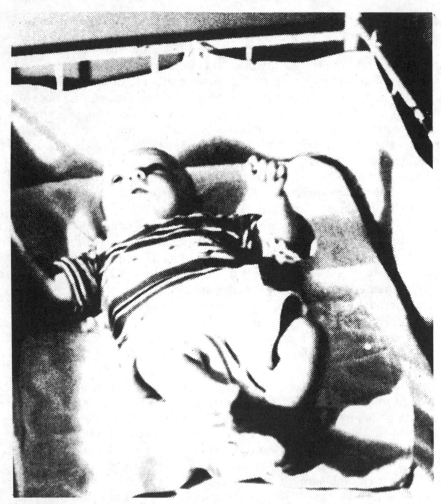

Figure 4–4

Normal environment of the institutionalized children in White's experiments.
(From White, 1971. Reprinted by permission of author.)

there was little development of visual-motor coordination. After this period, changes in visual-motor activities were observed. At an average age of forty-nine days, the children began to spend a great deal of time watching their hands. Hand watching is apparently a very pleasing activity for infants; White reports that they spent literally dozens of hours watching their hands during the third month of life. In addition, during the third month, tactile exploration of objects with the open hand began. This suggests that learning the visual position of the hands takes place quite early.

The development of visually directed reaching follows a very regular chronological progression. Infants were shown a brightly colored, red and orange feathery object. This target was brought within five inches of the child, and his attempts at reaching for the target were observed. At first the target was merely looked at. However, at about two months of age, the child began to swipe at the target with his closed fist. No attempts to grasp the target were made, but accurate striking of the target was common. The next phase of visual guidance occurred soon after swiping and indicates the beginning of fine visual-motor coordination. The open hand was raised to the general area of the target and slowly brought toward it as the child looked back and forth between the target and his hand. Hand position and location seem to be related to some degree at this point, and the repeated glances between target and hand provide comparison of their locations that may result in further refinement of the calibration between visual and motor systems.

Activities that may provide important information for the coordination of vision and touch continue through the third and fourth months. By this time, the infant's hands grasp each other while hand watching occurs. This activity provides a kind of double stimulation, since the movement of one hand is felt by the other as well as being seen. By the fourth or fifth month, the visual-motor systems appear to be integrated. Rapid and direct reaching coupled with accurate grasping of the target occurs. Adultlike guided reaching appears by five months of age. The course of the development of visually guided reaching in human infants has a number of clear parallels with the development of reaching in visually restricted monkeys (Held and Bauer 1967). In both cases, prolonged hand watching plays a large role in the initial visual localization of the limb. Successive comparisons of the visual position of the target and the hand occur, and coordination improves as the opportunity for visual-motor calibration increases.

After White had gathered this normative data on the development of visual-motor coordination, the visual environment of the infants was systematically altered to determine whether the kind of stimulation influenced the development of guided reaching. The results of the animal deprivation studies demonstrate that the nature of the visual environment and the opportunity to view self-produced changes in stimulation are important for development. Since White's institutionalized infants were reared in a bland environment with their movement restricted by the soft mattresses used in the cribs, the course of their development may have been affected. To test this hypothesis, the children's experience was enriched. Each infant received twenty minutes of extra handling per day. The children were also placed in a prone position (on their stomachs) for fifteen minutes per day with the crib liners removed. As they moved their heads and bodies they could see the visual changes that occurred. In addition, multicolored complex forms were hung over the cribs, and multicolored sheets and bumpers replaced the white ones normally used.

Under these enriched conditions, several changes were observed in the course of hand-eye coordination. It seems that the early stages of hand-eye coordination occurred slightly later under the enrichment conditions than under the usual institutional conditions. Early hand watching was much less frequently observed in the enrichment condition. White notes that the hands were first observed by the children as they contacted the objects that were hung over the crib. Compared to the other institutionalized children, hand watching in the enriched environment group was delayed for about twelve days. In addition, the onset of swiping at a target was also delayed somewhat, but only by about five days (an insignificant difference). Although these early aspects of reaching seem to be delayed as a result of the enrichment of the environment, later aspects of reaching were greatly facilitated. Well-directed, accurate reaching for a target occurred about forty-five days earlier in the enriched group than in the control group.

A second modification of the infants' environment also affected the course of eye-hand coordination. In this modified condition, the handling, prone placement, printed sheets and bumpers, and so forth were omitted. In this condition, the only change made was that two pacifiers were mounted on the crib rails and made to stand out by encircling them with red and white patterns. In this modified enrichment condition, virtually all aspects of eye-hand coordination were accelerated relative to the controls. Not only did hand watching and swiping occur earlier, but the onset of accurate reaching also was accelerated.

A third modification of experience entailed having the children wear red-and-white striped mittens. In this condition, colored sheets and bumpers and prone placement were also included in the enrichment. The addition of mittens to the enrichment condition resulted in earlier occurrence of hand watching. The total enrichment experienced by this group was related to the development of eye-hand coordination. Several measures disclosed that the experimental manipulation significantly altered the course of development.

White's results show a definite relationship between visual rearing conditions and the development of at least one aspect of visual-motor coordination. The calibration of the visual and motor systems involved in directed reaching was substantially accelerated by a change in the nature of the environmental conditions. The changes that White observed in the course of development are particularly striking when one realizes that the environmental modifications made in the enrichment condition were quite modest compared with the play, handling, and movement that generally occur in the environment of a home-reared child. The experimental group children were given only twenty minutes a day of handling and fifteen minutes a day in a prone position. Yet even under this slight improvement in the environment, development was substantially facilitated.

White's studies provide some insight into the effects of experience on development. In addition to their value in more fully describing the nature of development, they also suggest some specific alterations in rearing conditions for institutionalized children. Further investigation of the development of visually guided behavior may suggest other means of enriching an infant's environment. The animal deprivation studies suggest many hypotheses about the kinds of effects that may occur. Although it would be useful to determine the effects of self-produced movement on human development, for example, restricting children's experience to assess this effect is, of course, unacceptable. There are, however, acceptable experimental techniques using human subjects, which provide considerable information about the calibration of visual-motor systems and which have important implications for the development of visually guided behavior. These procedures will be discussed in Chapter Five.

SUMMARY

The results of the studies investigating the effects of restricted rearing conditions on the development of visually guided behavior lead to several conclusions that may be generalized over a wide variety of stimulus situations and subject species. Since we will be referring to these facts in the next chapter, let us review them briefly before continuing.

First, total deprivation of light results in physical degeneration of the visual system. The degenerative effects include morphological and biochemical deterioration of the retina, morphological deterioration of the lateral geniculate, and functional changes in the striate cortex. The degree of degeneration is directly related to the amount of light deprivation. Exposure to a lighted environment is a necessary condition for the physical maturation and continued function of the visual system.

Next, we saw that guided behavior is impaired if a subject does not have the opportunity to see the visual changes that result from its own motion. This impairment consists of an inability to locomote accurately, inability to avoid obstacles, and inability to guide reaching or placement of the limbs. Impairment occurs if only diffuse light is provided or if normal pattern vision is allowed without the opportunity to move around in the environment. It follows that the opportunity to view the visual effects of self-produced movement provides an adequate basis for the development of guided behavior. Such experience is sufficient to enable the subject to calibrate the visual system with the motor response system. Although self-produced movement provides an adequate basis for this calibration, it may not be a necessary condition for it. Theoretically, at least, other kinds of stimulation may also reveal the difference between self-movement and object movement and thus provide a basis for visual-motor calibration.

When this coordination is established, it can be highly specific to the conditions of experience. There is virtually no interocular equivalence on spatial guidance tasks if only one eye is given appropriate experience. Only the exposed eye can direct locomotion, placing, reaching, and obstacle avoidance. Similarly, the development of visually guided reaching occurs when the subject has had an opportunity to view its limb during reaching. Without this experience, reaching is crude and imprecise. With increasing experience in watching the limb, reaching becomes more accurate. However, there is no intermanual equivalence after training. Only the limb seen in training can be accurately guided. The calibration of the seen and felt positions of the limb is restricted to the conditions of training.

Further, the specificity of visual-motor calibration extends to the scotopic and photopic systems. If learning occurs when only the rods are operating, only rod vision can direct spatial behavior; coordination with the cone system is absent. This further demonstrates the lack of equivalence of different portions of the perceptual system in guiding behavior and the specific relationship between calibration of the system and training conditions.

Finally, research with institutionalized human infants indicates that enrichment of the environment affects the course of hand-eye coordination. Allowing increased mobility and increased visual experience accelerates development. The developmental course of hand watching, swiping, and guided reaching exhibits a number of parallels between the development of institutionalized children and visually restricted animals.

Chapter 5

CONTROL OF VISUALLY GUIDED BEHAVIOR

It is difficult to determine the effects of visual deprivation on children. Although the little data we have on behavior after surgically alleviated blindness or institutional rearing suggest that deficits similar to those observed in animals would occur, there has been no direct experimentation. Fortunately for the children involved, there are few cases of early occurring blindness. Consequently, the direct extension of notions concerning the calibration of the visual-motor system to human development cannot be made. There are, however, experimental phenomena that retain the essential aspects of the research described in the previous four chapters, and these have been used extensively with human adults.

In the deprivation research, there appear to be several crucial conditions that nearly all of the studies conducted with animals meet. First, the subjects selected are assumed to have an uncalibrated visual-motor system. Then, particular kinds of visual experience are either provided or withheld depending on the requirements of the research, and after some period of time various tests of visually guided behavior are administered. These conditions are met by procedures that are involved in the study of adaptation to optical distortion. The general procedure in adaptation studies involves placing an optical device before the eyes that results in a transformation of the visual stimulation entering the eye. For example, one such device used extensively is the wedge prism. An effect of viewing the world through wedge prisms is that all objects are displaced—they appear to be in a different place than their actual location. Since the light entering a prism is bent toward the base, objects viewed through a prism appear to be displaced in the direction of the apex of the prism.

The main interest in such experiments is that wearing prisms essentially changes the relationship between the visual and motor systems. An adult subject is able to localize objects in the world accurately on the basis of vision alone. It presents no problem to ask a subject to reach for an object, walk between obstacles, or walk across a room and stop at a particular spot. Spatial behavior is closely related to, and accurately guided by, visual information. When a subject begins to wear prisms, this relationship between vision and motor behavior changes. For example, if a person wears prisms that displace the array by 10 degrees, objects that appear to be straight ahead are actually 10 degrees to the side; conversely, objects that appear to be off to the side by 10 degrees will actually be straight ahead. As a result, when an individual rapidly reaches for something that appears straight ahead, he misses its actual location. Since things are not where they appear to be, the subject wearing prisms (unless he is careful) may bump into objects, crash into doorways and walls, or fall down stairs. In many respects, his inaccurate localization and locomotion resemble the behavior of young children and visually deprived animals.

Literature in the area of prism adaptation is extensive; it is impossible here to review more than a small sample of it. However, there are many clear similarities between the development of spatially guided behaviors and the recalibration of the visual-motor system that occurs as a consequence of prism wearing. It can be argued that the mechanisms governing these two processes are quite similar. Thus, let us begin by describing briefly the phenomenon of perceptual adaptation and exploring the similarities between the results of prism adaptation and spatial guidance development. (The reader who would like to explore this phenomenon further is advised to consult the summaries of Howard and Templeton 1966; Rock 1966; Epstein 1967; and Gibson 1969.)

Since there are a large number of different optical transformations that can be imposed, many different training procedures, and many different ways of testing adaptation, an idealized example will be used to illustrate some of the basic aspects of adaptation experiments. Consider an experimental situation in which a subject is asked to wear wedge prisms. If we were to do an actual experiment, we would first attempt to measure the initial accuracy of reaching without prisms. One way to do this is to ask the subject to reach toward or point to a target under test conditions that prevent him from seeing his hand. (This prevents him from correcting any errors by visually guiding his hand.) Prism spectacles would then be placed in front of his eyes with the instructions to wear them during his waking hours for the next few hours, days, or weeks and to return to the laboratory at periodic intervals for retesting. If we were to follow this procedure, we would find that the subject would indeed adapt to the distorting effects of the prisms; his performance would improve as he wore the prism spectacles for longer and longer periods of time. In fact, this direct method of measuring adaptation is rarely used.

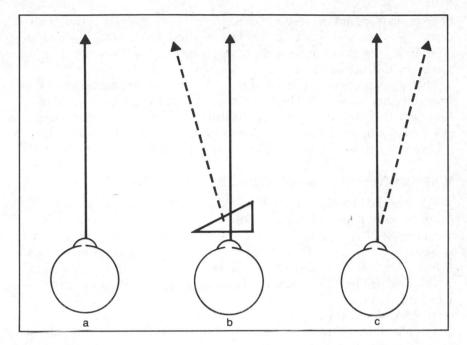

Figure 5-1

Under normal circumstances, a subject will point directly toward an object that is straight ahead (a). Wearing base-right prisms, the apparent location of the object is shifted and a subject will point to the left (b). After adaptation has occurred and the prisms are removed, the subject will point to the right of the actual location demonstrating an aftereffect (c).

One reason is that the reduction in error might not indicate a restoration of visual-motor coordination; instead, the subject may have learned consciously to correct his reaching. He may have noticed that he is always three inches in error when he reaches for objects, so he learns to reach three inches to the right of where things seem to be.

Consider what would happen, however, if a new visual-motor coordination had been learned, and the apparent location of objects and the position of the hand were recalibrated. With this new calibration, the subject would reach toward an object without error. An object seen off to one side and an arm movement directly ahead would match, and no errors would occur. Now, what would happen when the prisms were removed? Since the system had been recalibrated so that an object displaced by the prisms to the left was localized as straight ahead, without the prisms that object should appear shifted to the right. A subject who had adapted to the prisms should make reaching errors to the right when he is not wearing them. This aftereffect of adaptation is most often used to measure the degree of adaptation that has occurred. The greater the amount of adaptation that has occurred, the greater the aftereffect will be. Testing adaptation by measuring the aftereffect, we can reveal changes that are not the result of deliberate correction. If only deliberate correction occurred, there would be no aftereffect. Since there is an aftereffect, the change in accuracy of reaching must be the result of a new visual-motor coordination.

That adaptation occurs to rearranged eye-hand coordination indicates one similarity between the results of restricted rearing and prism adaptation. In both cases, the initial relationship between the visual and motor systems is inappropriate, impairment of spatial behavior is observed, and coordination is learned after some degree of experience.

VISUAL CONTROL AND CONTROL SYSTEMS THEORY

Some might imagine that behavioral similarities among young children, visually deprived animals, and human adults are due simply to coincidence, that these similarities reveal more about the psychologist's imagination than about the actual functioning of the perceptual system. If this were true, it would have numerous restrictive implications for developmental psychology, for it would mean that infant research related only to infants, deprivation research related only to deprived cats or monkeys, and prism adaptation related only to human adults. No general laws would exist, and knowledge gained in one area would be inapplicable to the others.

This is not the case, however. Similarities among these different organisms at different developmental levels are the result of basic underlying similarities. These similarities can best be understood within the context of *control systems theory*, a sophisticated engineering theory concerned with the regulation of activity that has only recently been applied to psychology (Powers 1973).

Since the concept of *system* in conventional usage has become general and vague (economic systems, social systems, The System), we will begin with a few definitions and concepts. A *system* is a set of mechanisms related in such a way as to function as an integrated unit. A *control system*, then, is a set of mechanisms that are related so as to direct or regulate itself or another system. Since visual guidance implies the active regulation or control of behavior, we will be most concerned with active regulating systems.

Two kinds of control systems can be distinguished, based on how the system reacts to its input and output. The first control system (depicted in Figure 5–2) is an *open-loop system*, in which the output never influences the input. Such a system was postulated by early perceptual and learning psychologists. The organism receives some input (stimulus) that is associated with some output (response), so that each pattern of retinal stimulation elicits a response. Perceptual change, learning, and development, then, consist of building up associations between certain inputs and outputs. The basic characteristics of an open-loop system are that the input is not affected by the output it elicits,

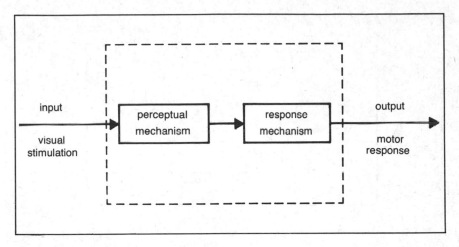

Figure 5–2

Schematic diagram of an open-loop control system in which a response cannot affect input. (After Mittelstaedt, 1962.)

and its accuracy is determined by the input-output relationships (associations). There are circumstances in which human behavior can be made to operate under the control of an open-loop system. For example, if you close your eyes and reach for an object across a desk, your behavior could be described as a reaching response elicited by the prior stimulus of seeing the object. Your accuracy would depend in part on how often you had previously reached for that object in the same way. Of course, if your hand goes off in slightly the wrong direction, there is no way to correct your reaching because the response does not affect the stimulus.

The second kind of control system (depicted in Figure 5–3) is a *closed-loop* or *feedback system*. In such a system, the output influences the input. A cause-and-effect relationship exists between the output and input so that the behavior of the system is a joint function of both the output and the input. An example of the operation of such a system can again be drawn from hand-eye coordination in reaching for an object on a desk. In performing such a task, the goal is not simply to make a response in the direction of the object, it is specifically to reduce or minimize the discrepancy between the seen position of the object and the seen (or felt) position of your hand.

How a feedback system works can be seen by analyzing your behavior according to the schematic diagram in Figure 5–3. One basic input into the hand-eye system is visual stimulation that the perceptual mechanisms can use to determine the position of the object. The output of this perceptual mechanism is fed into a comparison mechanism (comparator) that also receives information about the seen (or felt) position of the hand. The position of the object and the hand are subtracted, and this comparison results in an error or activating signal that operates

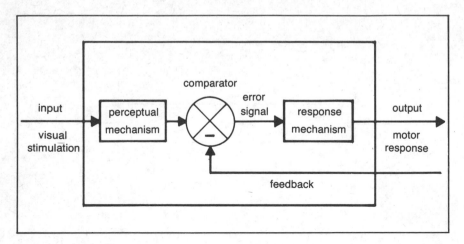

Figure 5–3

Schematic diagram of a closed-loop control system in which a response does affect input. (After Mittelstaedt, 1962.)

the response mechanism and causes a motor response. As a result of this movement, the position of the hand changes as does the feedback to the comparator. As this feedback changes, the error or activating signal is affected, and the response mechanism changes the motor response. This active correction continues until the hand and object position match, at which point there is no longer an error signal and responding stops. Because feedback in such a system is continuous, the reaching response can be continuously corrected. If, at first, your hand moves in slightly the wrong direction, its position can be corrected until it reaches the object.

Based on this description, it might seem that much human and animal behavior is governed by some form of feedback control system. Whenever we walk, run, drive, reach—in fact, when we engage in almost any perceptually guided behavior—our responses are determined by what we perceive. Yet, each movement that we make alters, in some way, the nature of stimulation, which in turn affects the response. Our perceptions are dependent on our actions, and our motor behavior can be guided; this implies that a feedback mechanism underlies our perceptual motor abilities.

We need not rely on our intuitions, however, to conclude that feedback mechanisms underlie visually guided behavior. Mittelstaedt (1964) has described four methods that can be used in experiments or demonstrations to show that feedback affects behavior:

1. Reversing the sign of the feedback information
2. Disturbing the input to the system
3. Examining reaction times
4. Opening the feedback loop

Reversing the Sign of Feedback

In the simple feedback system diagrammed in Figure 5–3, the comparator receives an input from the perceptual system and the feedback signal is subtracted (hence, negative feedback) from this input to give an error or activating signal to the response mechanism. In other words, the activating signal equals the perceptual input minus the feedback signal. If, in some way, it were possible to reverse the sign of the feedback signal so that the activating signal equals perceptual input plus feedback, an overly large response would occur and errors would result.

We can reverse the sign of feedback in humans by requiring them to perform while wearing prisms or mirrors in front of their eyes which invert right and left. Under such conditions, subjects will make errors when asked to point to a target without being able to see their hand. If they are to perform a more complex visual-motor task such as tracing a drawing that can only be seen in a mirror, their responses oscillate around the correct path until they learn to correct for the mirror inversion.

Disturbing the Input to the System

Since one of the prime capabilities of a feedback system is the modification of behavior to correct for imposed disturbances in the system, one should expect that imposing perceptual distortion should not affect accuracy, at least under some conditions. One form of disturbance that can be easily introduced occurs when laterally displacing prism spectacles are worn. With these eyeglasses, the entire world is displaced some amount from its original position. If, under these circumstances, a person *slowly* points toward a target, he can see both the target and his hand and minimize the distance between them. In other words, he can accurately respond even with the prismatic disturbance, because the feedback system allows a continuous correction to minimize error.

Examining Reaction Times

One key to the correction of responses, which can occur under induced distortions, is that the response must be made fairly slowly. A specific characteristic of the feedback loop underlies this requirement, and an examination of response accuracy when a subject responds at different speeds reveals the action of a feedback loop. Because feedback must enter the system, be compared with an input, generate an error signal, and activate the response mechanism, correction of a response would take at least as much time as necessary to operate the feedback loop once. Consequently, any response that took less time to perform than the time needed by the feedback loop could not be governed by feedback.

In the prism wearing case described above, if the subject can respond slowly, the feedback loop can operate to guide and correct the pointing response. If we ask a person wearing prism spectacles to point to a target as fast as he can move his hand, the response can be performed in less time than is required to correct any errors. With such rapid movements, the response will be completed before any correction can take place, and errors will result. Consequently, a comparison of accuracy as a function of different response times indicates whether a feedback system controls that response and can also indicate how complex that mechanism is.

Opening the Feedback Loop

If a control system depends on feedback to regulate a response, an easy way to demonstrate this is to open the loop, or prevent any feedback from occurring. Obviously, one way that this could be done for any visually guided task is to close your eyes, thus eliminating visual feedback. This is a rather trivial example, but the principle is an important one, and we will refer to it later. Any method that denies feedback to the subject should increase error if a control system underlies the behavior.

A Simple Demonstration of Control Principles

The ideas underlying control theory may at first seem unfamiliar and difficult to understand. A simple experiment will help illustrate many of the principles (Powers 1973). You need two rubber bands knotted together and a sheet of paper with an "X" marked on it. Place the knotted rubber bands on the paper and put one finger into one of the loops. This illustrates a simple control system. You can see the position of the X, the position of the knot, and move the rubber band so as to place the knot over the X. Your job as a control system is to keep the knot over the X, or to minimize the discrepancy between the position of the knot and the position of the X.

Have another person put his finger into the other rubber band loop and act as an experimenter investigating your control system. He can introduce disturbances by pulling or moving his end of the rubber bands, thus moving the knot away from the X. Since you can sense the discrepancy between the position of the knot and the X, you can respond so as to minimize that discrepancy. If the experimenter moves slowly (perhaps one inch per second), you should be able to control the position of the knot relative to the X rather easily.

Completing the feedback loop and making corrections in your control system will take some amount of time. You can demonstrate the time necessary for your control system to operate by having the experimenter introduce his disturbances at a faster rate. At this rapid rate, you will be unable to maintain control of the knot's position because the amount of time required for the control system to operate is greater than the amount of time required for the compensating response.

You can also demonstrate the effect of reversing the sign of feedback with this simple experiment. At one side of the sheet of paper, prop up a mirror and have someone hold a sheet of cardboard between your eyes and the knot and X, so that you cannot see the knot and X directly, but can see them in the mirror. Now have the experimenter introduce a series of disturbances into the system by moving his end of the rubber bands. The first thing you should notice is that your control actions are now in the wrong direction. They tend to increase error rather than decrease it. Second, notice that if the disturbances are made very slowly, you can still control the position of the knot relative to the X. You are able to compensate for the reversal of feedback.

Notice also that as the experimenter makes his disturbances more quickly, it becomes harder to control the knot's position. As the speed of the disturbances increases, your ability to control breaks down sooner with feedback reversed through the mirror than with direct observation of the knot and X. Comparing your reaction times in these two conditions shows that your control system requires more time, or extra compensation, in the reversed feedback condition.

CONTROL SYSTEMS IN ADAPTATION AND DEVELOPMENT

Much guided behavior can be characterized using the principles of control systems theory developed above. In addition, psychologically interesting problems in adaptation and development involve changes in the control system. For example, it was pointed out that a subject wearing prisms becomes more accurate in guiding his behavior, and further, that the relationship between perception and motor abilities somehow changes. We could say that changes occur in the feedback loop so that when the prisms are removed, an aftereffect is found. The control system is altered so that a new visual-motor coordination is learned. In development also, the system controlling visually guided behavior must change with experience so that specific visual-motor coordinations are learned.

We can see immediately that there is an important difference between the learning processes occurring in adaptation and those occurring in development. In adaptation, an existing control system must be reorganized; in development, a new control system must be organized and refined. In spite of this difference, we can pose an important question for the study of perceptual development: How similar are the control systems that underlie coordination in development and adaptation? Are they similar enough to allow us to apply principles learned through studying adaptation to development?

A definite answer to this question is beyond the scope of this book, for it relies on a more sophisticated mathematical description of control theory than would suit our purposes. We can, however, outline the nature of this solution and discuss the data that bear on it. Both the preceding and the following sections of this chapter present a qualitative description of feedback notions using simple block diagrams (see Figure 5–3, for example) and verbal descriptions. A more precise way of describing control systems and feedback is to use mathematical equations that provide a detailed account of the system's error correction over time. These equations are called the *system transfer function* and, in principle, can be written for any system.

In mathematical terms, asking how similar are the control systems underlying adaptation and development is equivalent to asking how similar the transfer equations that describe the action of the control systems are. Although we cannot write and directly compare the equations for different systems (often because enough data are not yet available), we can formulate a partial, qualitative answer based on the data now available.

There are three possible alternatives. First, the systems that underlie both development and adaptation may be identical: they consist of the same processes, and the equations that describe them are the same in all respects. Second, the systems might be homologous: the principles governing operation of the two are similar, and the mathematical description of the systems are of the same form, but not identical. Third, the systems might be analogous: there are similarities between the two, but these similarities are not the result of any similarity of process, and the laws governing the two systems would be dissimilar.

Of these three alternatives, we can immediately rule out the speculation that the systems governing adaptation and development are identical. Although feedback and control systems underlie both development of visually guided behavior and perceptual adaptation, the systems are different, at least in some respects. One of the most obvious differences lies in the systems' responses over time. The first of these differences is the time required to organize or reorganize control loops to coordinate behavior. In adaptation studies of rearranged hand-eye coordination (for example, Harris 1965), adaptation or reorganization takes place fairly rapidly and is complete after a few hours or a few days. In initial development, however, the organization and coordination of the system takes several weeks or months (White 1971).

A second difference between the control systems in adults and children can be seen in a simple examination of reaction times, which you can verify for yourself. If a large ball is tossed to an adult over a distance of six feet, it presents no problem for that person to perceive the changes in the ball's location and bring his hands together at the appropriate instant to catch it. This simple act indicates that the reaction time of the control system in this case is less than the amount of time taken for the ball to travel six feet. Anyone who has spent time playing with a young child, however, knows that his behavior is different. If a ball is tossed to a two- or three-year-old, he can track the ball visually and will make an attempt to catch it. Most often, however, his hands will come together slightly too late, and the ball will bounce off his chest or fall through his hands before he brings them together. This activity demonstrates that the reaction time of the child's control system is longer than the time needed for the ball to travel six feet. You may demonstrate further that the child's problem lies in the reaction time of the control system by trying the same demonstration with a balloon, which moves more slowly. In this case, the response will generally not occur too late.

This simple demonstration shows that the control system's response over time differs for an adult and for a child. Since only one difference need be shown to demonstrate that two things are not identical, these differences in reaction time and organization time prove that the functions describing control systems in organization and reorganization or in children and adults are not identical. The specific relationship between these control systems can be further examined on a qualitative level by comparing the results of studies in the areas of restricted rearing, early development, and perceptual adaptation.

ORGANIZATION AND REORGANIZATION OF VISUAL-MOTOR COORDINATION

In comparing development and adaptation a complication arises. Although the previous section on control theory discussed visual guidance as if a single system underlies coordination, this is not strictly true. In fact, the system that guides visual-motor behavior can be broken down into a number of different subsystems, each of which is itself a control system. For example, in hand-eye coordination we can separate out several subsystems—one that controls eye position relative to head position, one that controls head position relative to body position, and one that controls hand position relative to body position. These subsystems combined give a larger-order system of hand-eye control. In comparing the organization and reorganization of coordination to determine the nature of the relationship between adaptation and development, we can look for similarities and differences in the total system as well as in its subparts. One important aspect of the total system involves locomotion and self-produced movement.

Array Motion and Self-Produced Movement

A direct conclusion that can be drawn from the literature on restricted rearing of animals is that depriving the animal of the opportunity to move around while looking at the environment affects its ability to locomote, localize objects, and perceive depth. Further, it is clear that a portion of this deficit is due to an inability to distinguish between object motion and motions in the array caused by self-movement (Meyers 1964). We also know from the kitten carousel experiments that this deficit is not due only to the restriction on self-motion but also to the restricted ability to experience the consequences of responding. Active kittens received feedback in the apparatus and were able to perceive depth on the cliff. The passive kittens, although they could move in the gondola, received visual stimulation that was independent of their own movement. Without this feedback, the system controlling depth perception and action could not be correctly organized.

A control system that may be implicated in the development of spatial layout perception and coordination is the efferent copy model described by Mittelstaedt (1962) and shown in Figure 5–4. Using this model, let us begin by talking about the *response effector mechanism*. This response effector issues an order or *efferent command* to the muscles to act; a copy of this command is made and stored. The visual consequences of this response (visual feedback or *reafference*) can be picked up and compared to the efferent copy. If the change in visual stimulation was the result of the response, the reafference and efferent copy should match, indicating that the array changes were the result of self-movement.

Since the information for distance that is contained in motion parallax is specified by the relationship between self-movement and array motion, such a feedback loop could provide the preliminary information needed for the use of motion parallax. If an animal had been deprived of opportunities for self-produced movement, the appropriate comparison between efferent copy and reafference could not be established, and depth perception based on motion parallax should be impaired. This is exactly what has been found in the kitten carousel experiments.

If a feedback-comparison system underlies the general ability to distinguish between array motions that are self-produced and those that are

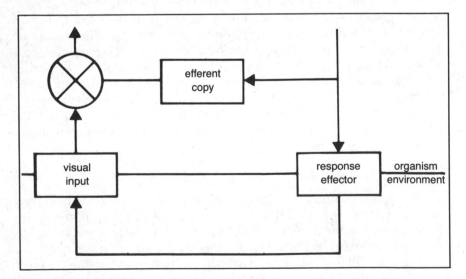

Figure 5–4

A control system in which feedback is provided by efferent copy. (After Mittelstaedt, 1962.)

not, evidence for the existence of such a system should be found in other situations. Also, if the mechanisms underlying organization and reorganization of visual-motor coordination are similar, evidence of such similarity should be found in adaptation studies. If the relationship between array motion and observer motion is changed, will adaptation and reorganization occur?

Minification is an optical transformation that affects the extent of array motion. If one looks through the wrong end of a telescope, all objects appear to be farther away than they really are. This effect occurs because the minification alters the texture gradient of surfaces and because the parallactic motions of objects are reduced. The parallactic motion of an object seen through a minifying optical system is only a fraction of its normal value. If adaptation to minification were to occur, there would necessarily be a change in the mechanism relating observer movement and array movement. Wallach and Kravitz (1965a, 1965b) have found that such a change does occur as a result of experience with altered array motion. They used an apparatus that allowed them to manipulate the amount of target movement occurring as a result of head movement. In the first portion of the experiment, subjects' judgments of "normal" parallactic movement were recorded. Subjects were asked while moving their heads to indicate when the array displacement of the target indicated that it was stationary. At the point that the subject indicated this, we can assume that the subject's head motion and the array motion matched, so that motion was cancelled out and the target was seen as in a constant position. The subjects were then given experience with the altered head motion–array motion relationship through a minifying device, and position constancy was measured a second time. Evidence was found of a significant recalibration of the motion system. After the experience with altered parallax, subjects' estimates of target stability were substantially changed. A new head movement–array movement relationship indicated target stability.

Based on these data that the calibration between head motion and array motion can be affected by experience with minification, we should expect that judgments of distance based on motion parallax information should also be affected. This is also a clear implication of the deprivation studies, since cliff avoidance is affected by restricted rearing. There is evidence that adults use the relationship between head movement and array motion in distance judgments based on motion parallax. Johansson (1973) had subjects judge absolute distance in centimeters of a pattern of small lights in a totally dark apparatus. Since binocular vision, texture gradients, and other sources of distance information were not present, the only way that accurate judgments could be made was to compare the extent of head motion with the extent of array motion in order to use motion parallax as information for the judgments. Johansson's data demonstrate an extremely high level of accuracy, thus indicating that such comparisons were made. In the context of adaptation, however, it is not known whether visual-motor recalibration would affect distance estimation based on motion-carried information. Further research on the effects of adaptation to minification will no doubt provide an answer to this question.

Other Forms of Feedback

The restricted rearing studies discussed in Chapter Four reveal that actively moving animals showed accurate visually guided behavior, whereas passively moved animals did not. An explanation of this finding can be offered in the context of the feedback model depicted in Figure 5–4. If the crucial portion of the system is the comparison between efferent copy and reafferent stimulation, such a comparison process could not be established in the absence of an efferent copy. Since the existence of the efferent copy depends on the initiation of motor commands, and passive movement occurs without such efference, no efferent copy would be formed and no comparison could take place.

If important similarities exist between the adaptation and development of control systems, one should expect that active, self-produced movement would similarly affect adaptation. Do such similarities exist? Held and Gottlieb (1958) examined this question by first asking subjects to mark the location of several targets (the intersections of the lines in Figure 5–5) without being able to see the positions of their arms. They then looked at their arms through a prism that shifted its apparent location. This adaptation phase took place under one of three conditions. (1) The subject watched while he actively moved his arm. (2) The subject watched while his arm was passively moved by the experimenter. (3) The subject looked at his stationary arm. After three minutes of looking at the arm, the prism was removed and the subject marked the target locations a second time. As shown in Figure 5–5, the static condition resulted in no adaptation; the passive condition resulted in slight change; but the active movement led to a pronounced, significant adaptation effect even though a very brief exposure time was used. Similar results have been reported by Pick and Hay (1965).

In a further experiment that was more closely analogous to the Held and Hein kitten carousel experiment, Held and Bossom (1961) measured adaptation effects under two exposure conditions. In one, the prism-wearing subjects were allowed active movement as they walked around outdoors. In the second condition, they sat in wheelchairs and were wheeled around the same route as taken by the active subjects. In this experiment, eye-body coordination was assessed rather than eye-hand coordination. Subjects were tested in an apparatus in which they were to position their body so that a visual target appeared straight ahead. As in the preceding study, the active subjects showed significant (occasionally 100 percent) adaptation, whereas the passive subjects showed relatively little adaptation.

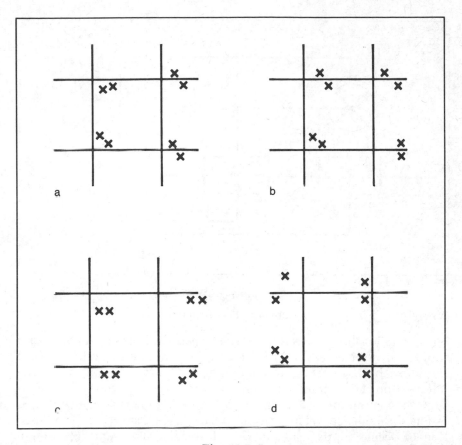

Figure 5-5

Idealized representation of the results of Held and Gottlieb (1958). The X indicates the approximate area in which target markings occurred; (a) before wearing prisms, (b) after wearing prisms with no hand movement, (c) after wearing
prisms with passive hand movement, (d) after wearing prisms with active hand
movement. Condition *d* results in significant adaptation. (After Held and
Gottlieb, 1958.)

These experiments show that in adaptation as well as in initial development, self-produced movement is a sufficient basis for changes in
accuracy of visually guided behavior. Is such stimulation a necessary
condition of change? In the realm of the restricted rearing studies, there
is no direct evidence that bears on this question.

The studies of Held and Gottlieb, and of Held and Bossom, however,
suggest that reafference-efferent copy matches may not be necessary for
adaptation to occur. In both of these studies, some adaptation was found
in the passive conditions. Thus, some other source of feedback may be
sufficient for adaptation. One kind of feedback system that does not
require efferent copy comparisons has been suggested by Mittelstaedt
(1962) and is diagrammed in Figure 5-6. In this system, the loop consists

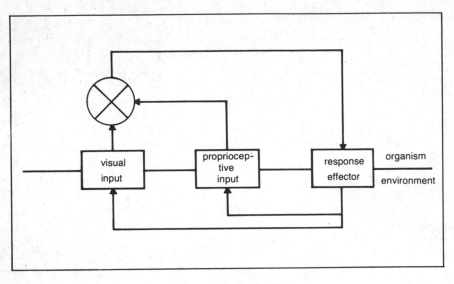

Figure 5–6

A control system in which proprioception provides feedback.

of the relationship between the visual (seen) and proprioceptive (felt) inputs. In normal reaching, for example, the control system would minimize the discrepancy between the seen position of an object and the felt position of the hand. In development or adaptation, the system relating vision and proprioception would be organized or reorganized.

There is evidence that proprioceptive feedback is sufficient for adaptation to occur in prism adaptation. Howard, Craske, and Templeton (1965) had their subjects look through an optical device that displaced objects to the left. With the subject's head held stationary, a rod was brought forward until it touched the subject in the middle of the lips. Since the rod appeared as if it would hit to the left of the mouth, this contact informed the subject that the rod was not where it appeared. After twenty trials, subjects demonstrated a significant adaptation effect. Since the subject's head was restrained during adaptation and the experimenter controlled the rod, only tactile feedback was available. Yet these subjects did show an adaptation to the optical distortion. A similar group, which had the same experience except that the rod did not actually touch them, showed no adaptation.

Using a different procedure, Wallach, Kravitz, and Lindauer (1963) also demonstrated that reafferent stimulation is not necessary for adaptation to occur. Their subjects wore a base-right prism (objects shifted to the left) while looking down at their feet for ten minutes. During this exposure, a subject was told not to move his feet, and his head was held rigidly by a bite-board. The discrepancy between the visual position of the subject's feet and where he felt them to be provides no reafferent stimulation as long as the legs are not moved, yet in this experiment the proprioceptive feedback resulted in a significant degree of adaptation. In both of these experiments, adaptation occurred under conditions in which the subject remained passive and no reafferent stimulation was available. Wallach and Kravitz (1965b) also found adaptation in their position constancy experiment when subjects were given passive experience. If sufficient proprioceptive stimulation is provided, adaptation still results even in the absence of self-produced movement.

CHANGES IN CONTROL SYSTEMS

To this point, we have spoken in general terms of the control of the visual and motor systems that are necessary for accurate visually guided behavior. How does control change? What is altered as a result of the adaptation experience? There are two alternatives. First, the change could be in the linkage between visual information and the comparator. Retinal locations that specify a particular location in space before adaptation may come to indicate a new direction after adaptation. An object in the center of the array may come to look as if it were off to the side. Data in support of such a theory (for example, Kohler 1964) are not conclusive, and some controversy exists concerning whether such visual changes are possible.

A second alternative is that visual changes are not involved, but that either proprioceptive or efferent copy changes occur. During the adaptation period, the subject sees his hand in one place but feels it in another. The resolution of this conflict could take place if the hand came to feel as if it were in a different location—the location where it is seen. Adaptation may consist simply of a change in the felt position of the hand. The most direct evidence for this change in the position sense of the hand comes from a series of studies measuring adaptation effects in the absence of visual information. Suppose a subject adapts while looking through prisms at one of his hands. If adaptation results in a change of the felt position of the hand, this altered position should be evident in a number of tasks. When the subject is blindfolded and asked to point to the source of a sound, he makes sizable errors. Since the felt position of the hand has changed, his pointing is inaccurate. If the unadapted hand is used, there are no errors since its felt position is unchanged (Harris 1963). Similarly, if the subject is asked to estimate the distance between his two hands after adaptation, he is in error since the felt position of one hand has changed.

If adaptation were solely a visual phenomenon, these effects should not be observed. If vision adapts, there should be no errors in pointing to sounds or estimating the distance between hands while blindfolded. These results indicate that the substantial change occurring in the course of adaptation is learning a new felt position of the hand. In relation to the feedback model diagrammed in Figure 5–6, the action of the proprioception mechanism has changed adaptation so that it sends a different signal to the comparator.

In light of this proprioceptive change, several interesting parallels can be drawn between experiments in adaptation, restricted rearing, and development. In adaptation, the control system governing hand-eye coordination is reorganized by proprioceptive change. Of course, if the feedback loop were opened, one would expect that limb-eye coordination would be affected. This is exactly what happens in both monkeys and cats. When the animal subjects of Held and Bauer (1967) and of Hein and Diamond (1971b) were deprived of the sight of their limbs, reaching or guided movements of the limb were very inaccurate.

In addition, across many situations the organization and reorganization of control systems for eye-limb coordination takes place under conditions that allow comparison of visual and proprioceptive inputs. Thus, the adult subjects of Held and Gottlieb (1958) adapt under conditions in which they can observe the position and action of their hands. The monkeys used by Held and Bauer learn to reach accurately for a target only after prolonged hand watching. The kittens used by Hein and Diamond can accurately guide only the limb that was seen during early experience. And, White's human infants show pronounced hand watching in the early stages of the development of hand-eye coordination.

One further aspect of Harris's results has implications for the general system discussed here. Harris found that after prism displacement, a new felt position of the hand was learned, but the two hands were not equivalent in their ability to reach accurately toward a target. Little intermanual transfer was observed. Similarly, with the monkeys little intermanual transfer was found, and the animals could accurately guide only the hand that had been observed (Held and Bauer 1967). Kittens could guide one paw but not the other (Hein and Diamond 1971b). Human infants also do not show intermanual equivalence. Each hand operates accurately only on one side of the body's midline (Bruner 1969). This pattern of results suggests that in each of these separate cases, the position of the limbs must be learned more or less independently, and that a separate input from each limb exists in the control system.

Harris has argued that the notion underlying change in the felt position of the hand can be extended to cover a wide variety of adaptation phenomena. If we assume that the position sense of other parts of the body can be altered in adaptation, much of the adaptation literature can be explained according to changes in position sense. For example, the adaptation to the changed relationship between head motion and array motion found by Wallach and Kravitz (1965a, 1965b) could occur if the felt position of the head during movement were altered. If, as a result of adaptation, a head movement of a certain magnitude came to feel as if it were a larger movement, then the results obtained would flow simply from this proprioceptive alteration. Harris has argued further that changes in visual-motor coordination that occur in adaptation are primarily the result of changes in the sensed position of the body. He summarized a large body of data, and his explanation is remarkably comprehensive in the huge amount of data it can explain.

Examining the development of visual-motor coordination in the context of a control system that compares proprioceptive (or efferent) information with visual input reveals a number of similarities in system organization. As we have seen, the variables that influence behavior and their effects are similar in young children, deprived kittens, deprived monkeys, and human adults. Furthermore, even a simple qualitative control theory provides a means for understanding these similarities and integrating a great deal of data.

Other similarities in system organization are revealed if we consider the organization of subsystems involved in visual-motor coordination. Hein and Diamond (1971a) found that kittens reared in dim light were able to control their behavior visually under dim light when the scotopic (rod) system was working, but not under bright light when the photopic (cone) system was operating. These results suggest that there are separate inputs into the control system from the rod and cone systems of the eye, and that each must be calibrated more or less independently of the other. A similar independence has been found in human adaptation studies.

In a study akin to that of Hein and Diamond, Graybiel and Held (1970) conducted adaptation periods under photopic and scotopic conditions, using the Held and Gottlieb testing procedure. The results indicated specific effects depending on the type of exposure and the test. Although adaptation occurred under both lighting conditions, there were significant differences between transfer conditions. Under scotopic exposure, there was a high degree of transfer to photopic test. Transfer from photopic exposure to scotopic test, however, was significantly reduced.

There are differences between these two sets of results. Kittens showed no scotopic-photopic transfer, whereas human adults showed large scotopic-photopic transfer, but little photopic-scotopic transfer. This difference in stimulus relevance between animal and human studies may reflect species differences rather than differences in control organization. Although cats have cone receptors in the eye, they appear to rely very little on color vision. For example, it is very difficult to teach a cat color discrimination even though it has the sensory receptors necessary for such discrimination. The transfer differences, then, may reflect differences only in the utilization of photopic vision in cats and humans. Further research on restricted rearing of primates (whose photopic vision is known to be similar to that of humans) may clarify this point. The important fact, however, is that in both cases, there is a dissociation between the rod and cone components of the control system.

A second parallel in subsystem organization may also be drawn from the deprivation and adaptation research. In the restricted rearing studies with animals, none of the investigators found evidence of interocular equivalence after visual-motor experience. In both kittens and monkeys, coordination is specific to the eye that receives the experience. Such a finding is not common to the human adaptation literature. In fact, Hajos and Ritter (1965); Pick, Hay, and Willoughby (1966); and Foley and Miyanishi (1969) found virtually complete interocular transfer in different adaptation experiments.

Some evidence indicates, however, that under some circumstances, eye-specific effects can be found in human adults. Foley (1974) conducted an experiment in which the subject's two eyes were differentially adapted. For example, one eye might look through a prism that displaced objects to the right, while the other eye looked through a prism that displaced objects to the left. Foley found adaptation effects that were specific to the kind of visual distortion each eye was exposed to. She points out that such results may be explained in the context of a control system that maintains independent processing of the information registered by the two eyes. Thus, it appears that both the deprivation and adaptation research suggest that separate inputs from each eye enter the visual-motor control system.

Discussion of a qualitative control system that can guide visual-motor behavior and a comparison of relevant data (see Table 5–1) suggest a tentative conclusion about the relationship between adaptation and visual-motor development. We cannot say that the two phenomena are governed by identical laws, since the correspondence between the two is not close enough. However, this comparison suggests that the general principles underlying the two are the same. When quantitative models replace qualitative ones, specific details such as the value of certain parameters and the weighting of certain variables will no doubt be different, but the form of the functions relating components of the systems will be the same.

The relationship between these two situations allows us to draw some conclusions about the nature of visual-motor development. For example, the heavy bias in favor of visual information over proprioception in the adaptation experiments suggests that a similar bias exists in development. The classical theory of visual development—that vision comes into correspondence with tactile or proprioceptive information—must be false. Existing evidence shows that vision is the primary sense modality, and that coordination changes that occur are mainly the result of calibrating tactile sense information to the visually specified percept. The extensive hand watching observed in infants can easily be interpreted in this vein. By watching his hands, the infant learns the position of his limbs and comes to relate proprioceptive information concerning visual location. Proprioception is altered to correspond to vision. This primacy of vision also suggests that the ability to pick up visual information exists before the ability to use that information to guide behavior. If motor behavior must be brought into corre-

Table 5–1.

Summary Comparison of Development and Adaptation Studies

Observed Effects	Development	Adaptation
Increased coordination with experience	Yes (Fantz 1965a; Held and Bauer 1967; White 1971)	Yes (Ebenholtz 1966; Hay and Pick 1966)
Sufficiency of self-produced movement	Yes (Held and Hein 1963; Riesen and Aarons 1959)	Yes (Held and Gottlieb 1958; Pick and Hay 1965; Held and Bossom 1961)
Necessity of self-produced movement	Unknown	No (Howard, Craske, and Templeton 1965; Wallach, Kravitz, and Lindauer 1963; Wallach and Kravitz 1965a, 1965b)
Altered head movement–body movement relation	Yes (Held and Hein 1963; Hein, Held, and Gower 1970)	Yes (Wallach and Kravitz 1965a, 1965b)
Calibration of motion parallax and depth	Yes (Held and Hein 1963; Hein, Held, and Gower 1970)	Unknown
Intermanual equivalence	No (Hein and Diamond 1971b; Held and Bauer 1967; Bruner 1969)	No (Harris 1963; Hamilton 1964)
Photopic-scotopic equivalence	Unknown	Yes—however, little (Graybiel and Held 1970)
Scotopic-photopic equivalence	No (Hein and Diamond 1971a)	Yes—nearly complete (Graybiel and Held 1970)
Interocular equivalence	No (Riesen, Kurke, and Mellinger 1953; Hein, Held, and Gower 1970; Hein and Diamond 1971b)	No (Foley 1974) Yes (Hajos and Ritter 1965; Pick, Hay, and Willoughby 1966; Foley and Miyanishi 1969)

spondence with vision, perceptual abilities must exist before calibration can occur.

In addition, we know that adaptation can result in changes in the perceived relationship between self-movement and array motion. Since layout is specified by information (such as motion parallax) that is conveyed by the relationship between self-movement and array motion, some aspects of the development of spatial layout perception may be a function of the development of this feedback system. That is, the perception of layout may involve a calibration of the visual-motor system.

The experimental work in the restricted rearing of animals in addition to the work on adaptation effects in humans suggest that the relationship between physical growth and perception may be important in development, since several physical changes that occur in growth have implications for the development and calibration of perceptual systems. In particular, many of these changes could be closely related to depth and distance perception. As growth proceeds, changes such as the increased distance between the eyes, increased strength and extent of head and body movements, and increased height would affect the use of binocular disparity, motion parallax, and texture gradient information. To develop or maintain accurate perception of distance over these body changes, the perceptual system must be continually recalibrated to maintain appropriate stimulus-specific correlations. No experimental work on the influence of growth on perception has been done. However, the experiments in adaptation and animal rearing suggest a number of specific hypotheses related to the development of distance perception abilities.

A further growth change that may be inherent in the development of perceptual abilities is related to changes that occur in body proportion. For example, as the limbs lengthen, the relationship between vision and proprioception changes. To maintain accurate visual-motor coordination, the felt position of the limb must undergo a change, just as it does in adaptation studies. The apparent awkwardness and coordination difficulties that are said to accompany rapid growth spurts in children may be directly related to the fact that visual-motor calibration is changed, and a new calibration must be learned. The adaptation studies also suggest a number of specific hypotheses concerning the kinds of experiences that may be sufficient for such recalibration to occur.

Because the principles that govern the establishment of visual-motor calibration in prism adaptation experiments cannot be said to be identical to those governing development, adaptation results cannot be directly used as explanations of developmental phenomena. However, the apparent homology between these processes generates a number of testable hypotheses about the course of development. The sample presented above is just a small portion of those that may be relevant to the study of development. Although little research has been done exploring the course of visual-motor development in relation to the adaptation literature, this area promises to be a fruitful one for developmental psychology.

SUMMARY

It is impossible to extrapolate the results of animal research to humans directly. There have been experimental procedures used with human adults, however, that suggest similarities in the principles that govern visual-motor coordination in animals and humans. These procedures involve the use of an optical device, such as a prism, that alters the apparent location of things. Individuals wearing prisms first show substantial error in visually guiding behavior, but then coordination improves. The reason for such changes is that a new relationship between the visual position of an object and behavior must be learned.

The similarities between learning a visual-motor coordination in development and relearning one in adaptation can be understood in the context of control systems theory. This theory distinguishes between an open-loop system in which an individual's action has little influence on sensory input and comparison, and a closed-loop system in which continuous feedback from the senses allows comparisons that guide responses to be made. For accurately guided behavior to occur, accurate feedback comparisons must be established, and there are several demonstrations that such comparisons operate in guiding much of human and animal behaviors.

There is an important difference between the learning processes occurring in adaptation and in development. In adaptation, an existing system must be reorganized; in development a new system must be initially organized and refined. There are, nevertheless, reasons for suggesting that basic principles are similar. Examination of numerous experiments suggest that adaptation and development are comparable processes with similar manipulations of experience often resulting in similar phenomena.

Chapter 6

PATTERN PERCEPTION: PROCESSES AND EARLY DEVELOPMENT

Thus far, our discussion has centered on the perception of spatial layout and the kinds of experiences necessary to use spatial information to guide behavior. Although the ability to pick up and use spatial information certainly involves the most significant perceptual systems, it is only one of the abilities necessary for visual perception. In his or her interactions with the environment, an individual must know not only the distance, size, and orientation of an object but must also be able to identify what that object is. A perceptual system that could tell you where an object was but not specify that it was a tiger, for example, would not contribute much to your survival. Even the simplest organism that relies on sight must be able to distinguish between foods and predators. What is it? is as important a question as Where is it? Human beings must be able to distinguish among different objects (people, cars, buildings), as well as among different representations (pictures of people and so forth) and different symbols (letters, numbers, words). The development of the perceptual interaction with the environment, then, involves pattern perception as well as spatial perception.

DIFFERENCES BETWEEN SPATIAL AND PATTERN PERCEPTION

Distinguishing between two different kinds of perception—*where* it is as opposed to *what* it is—is necessary because these two aspects differ in the kinds of mechanisms involved. Different kinds of information and different processing mechanisms are brought into play in spatial and pattern perception.

It has also been suggested by Schneider (1967, 1969), based on work with hamsters, that the perception of space or of patterns differs in the neural mechanisms involved in each. Schneider found that removing a portion of the brain called the superior colliculus abolished the animals' ability to orient to a stimulus or to locate food visually and severely impaired the ability to make visually guided responses to objects. However, these hamsters were able to learn pattern discrimination problems with no difficulty, even though visually guided localization was completely absent.

Hamsters with lesions of the visual cortex, in contrast, showed quite different deficits. Although their abilities to orient to a visual stimulus and visually guide locomotion were unimpaired, pattern perception abilities were severely disrupted. For example, most of the animals were unable to learn a discrimination between horizontal and vertical stripes, or between stripes and dots. To Schneider, these results suggested that different physiological systems may be involved in localization and visual discrimination. Schneider argues that the ability to localize an object requires the operation of lower level (subcortical) mechanisms, whereas discrimination involves areas in the visual cortex. These experiments provide the clearest example of the dissociation between the two mechanisms of perception. Unfortunately, however, it is not certain that such strict segregation of visual function occurs in other animals.

Vastola (1968) discussed a number of other studies on the localization of visual functioning that do not indicate strict differential location of these functions in the visual system to the same extent as does Schneider's work. To cite just two examples, cortical lesions in the monkey affect localization ability as well as pattern discrimination ability, and collicular lesions in cats seem to result in a permanent impairment of the ability to recognize familiar objects. Thus, it appears that cortical and subcortical mechanisms may be involved in both localizing and discriminating, at least in certain animals.

Since these two functions are integrated in the visual system of higher animals, the interrelationships between them may, indeed, be complex. It may be too optimistic to hope that functional differences in perception are directly related to structural location. Furthermore, spatial location is multiply determined, involving many different kinds of information. Even hamsters with subcortical lesions possess some spatial localization abilities (as demonstrated in visual cliff performance) at normal levels (Keselica and Rosinski 1976). In spite of these complications, however, there seem to be differences in the physiological mechanisms underlying spatial and pattern vision. For example, subcortical mechanisms may play a crucial role in relating vision and body movements (Trevarthen 1968). The overlap between cortical and subcortical mechanisms is yet to be totally determined, but the distinction between two modes of vision is still a useful one.

There are functional reasons for drawing a distinction between two modes of vision (Held 1968). Behaviors that are dependent either on localization or on pattern perception abilities are affected differently by manipulations of experience. For example, in relation to the visual deprivation paradigm discussed in Chapter Three, many studies have found that deficits of visually guided behavior are relatively severe compared to impairment of pattern perception. While working with monkeys, Fantz (1965a) found that the amount of visual experience necessary for the development of preferences on the visual cliff was directly related to the amount of visual deprivation that the subjects had undergone. The longer the animals had been reared in the dark, the longer it took for recovery of depth perception on the cliff. No such relationship was found, however, in tests of pattern perception and object recognition. Performance on these tests was not consistently related to length of deprivation. Similar results have been reported for cats as well. Restricted rearing conditions that are sufficient to produce visual-motor deficits result in little impairment of form perception (Held 1968).

Adaptation to optical transformation also reveals differences between a wide ranging *ambient mode* of vision used in locomotion and a more restricted *focal mode* used in pattern perception. When laterally displacing prism spectacles are worn, the prisms change not only the apparent locations of objects but also the shapes of those objects; straight lines seen through prisms seem curved and undergo rubbery deformations as the subject moves his head. Long-term experiments in adaptation show that adaptation to such curvature is not complete even after fifty days of exposure (Kohler 1964). Adaptation of visually guided behavior, however, occurs very quickly. Such adaptation may be nearly complete after a few hours. These results suggest that different processes are involved in visual-motor calibration and pattern perception. Ambient vision is easily modifiable, and the relationship between vision and action is quickly reestablished after disruption. Focal vision is less modifiable. No close relationship between deprivation and recovery of form perception has been found, and it is difficult to adapt to distortions of shape. These two modes of visual processing are functionally quite distinct.

Focal and ambient modes of vision can also be distinguished on the basis of the information and perceptual processing involved in each. In relation to spatial perception, it is appropriate to speak of a specific relationship between information and perception. Perhaps for biological reasons, certain types of information have come to specify directly the arrangement, orientation, size, and distance of objects in the environment. The perception of patterns cannot be conceptualized in this way. A simple, direct relationship does not exist between stimulus information and the resulting percept. In all aspects of perception, stimulation must be analyzed and information extracted. In pattern perception, a process of memory comparison and categorization is involved in addition to an analysis of perceptual information. That is, stimulus information for different patterns must be stored, organized, and compared to incoming stimulation to distinguish similarities and differences among patterns. The nature of this process of comparison can be illustrated through three aspects of pattern perception: discrimination, recognition, and identification.

TYPES OF PATTERN PERCEPTION

Discrimination

Consider the simplest type of pattern perception ability. You are presented with two patterns simultaneously and must determine whether they are the same or different. In such a task, a minimum requirement is that you compare, more or less systematically, portions of the two patterns. If all the aspects of the two are the same, the patterns are identical; if a difference is found, then they are not identical. The notion of discrimination as used here refers to this comparison between physically present patterns. In such a discrimination, few demands are made on one's memory for a pattern. Since both patterns are present at the same time, one must remember aspects of a pattern only as long as it takes to look from one to the other—roughly less than a quarter of a second. Since there is such a small memory component in discrimination, errors or difficulties in discriminating patterns are primarily the result of inappropriate comparisons. If certain comparisons are not made, or subtle features are not noticed, errors may result. Moreover, since discrimination is a simple task, we should expect that it would be found early in development.

Recognition

Now consider a more difficult task. You are given a pattern and asked whether you have seen it before. In recognition as in discrimination, a set of comparisons is necessary, but in this case the comparison must be between a pattern that is present and the representation of a pattern that is stored in memory. The first presentation of a pattern may allow it to be stored in memory. When the pattern is presented a second time, it can be categorized as having been seen before—if its characteristics match those stored in memory. In such a recognition task, more demand is placed on memory ability than in a discrimination task. A stored representation of a pattern must be retained throughout the interval between the two presentations of the pattern. Consequently, failures of recognition may be due to either failure to store the appropriate aspect of the pattern or failure to make the comparisons necessary to distinguish between different patterns. In the first case, when a pattern is presented, all of its important characteristics may not be stored. Later, a similar pattern that differs in ways that are not represented in memory will be falsely recognized. As a corollary, if the memory representation is inaccurate, the pattern may not match its memory representation and will not be recognized when it is presented a second time. In the second case, even if the memory of a pattern is totally accurate, failures of recognition may occur if insufficient or inappropriate comparisons are made, just as in discrimination. Since the minimal aspects of recognition are more complex than those of discrimination, recognition ability may develop later than discrimination. As a child's ability to store patterns improves, recognition ability may improve.

Identification

Although the activity that underlies identification has some things in common with discrimination and recognition, it involves a higher level of cognitive activity. To be identified, a pattern must be compared with some stored representation, but the process does not end with a simple match or mismatch between the two. To result in identification, the comparison must be detailed enough to assign the pattern to a conceptual category. In an identification task, we must not only be able to say that a pattern has been seen before, we must also be able to assign it to a specific category (for example, "dog"). Consequently, in addition to the factors that affect discrimination and recognition, identification is also affected by the nature of the concepts that we possess. For example, consider a child whose conceptual classes differ from those of an adult: she calls all furry animals "doggie." Suppose she sees the family pet, a Great Dane, walking with a Manx cat. She will certainly be able to tell that the two animals are different. She will also be able to recognize the Great Dane as something that she has seen before. But since she assigns both to the same category (that is, all furry animals are "doggie"), the cat will be misidentified as a "doggie." Since identification requires an established relationship between perceptual data and cognitive classes, its development should take considerably longer than that of discrimination or recognition and be closely tied to the development and elaboration of concepts.

Specifying these three perceptual processes—discrimination, recognition, and identification—also defines their hierarchical nature. Clearly, a child could discriminate between two patterns without knowing whether they had been seen before. Similarly, a pattern could be recognized without knowing what it was. Each level in this hierarchy requires the prior existence of abilities at a lower level. To recognize a pattern, the comparison ability of discrimination is necessary. There exists some evidence concerning this hierarchical arrangement. If the identification of a pattern requires the ability to match the pattern against a stored representation and assign it to a category, identification should affect recognition memory. Such effects have been found. Kurtz and Hovland (1953) and Rosinski (1970) have shown that requiring children to identify a pattern facilitates subsequent recognition of that pattern.

Although this description allows us to differentiate among three different aspects of pattern perception, some overlap between categories is apparent. Increasing the time between comparisons changes a discrimination task into recognition. If a sufficiently long time elapses between presentation of the first stimulus and the second, memory matching must be involved. Similarly, a task can be seen as either recognition or identification depending on the conceptual classes that we use. If we are willing to say that a person in a recognition task categorizes a pattern as either an old one or a new one, then recognition can be viewed as a primitive form of identification. In spite of this difficulty, the distinctions among discrimination, recognition, and identification will prove useful in the following discussion of pattern perception.

MODELS OF PATTERN PERCEPTION

A representation process and a comparison process are two vital aspects of pattern perception. A description of pattern perception, then requires an answer to two questions: What is represented in memory? and What is the nature of the comparison process? In other words, we must discover what information enables us to distinguish among patterns and how this information is used by the perceptual system. Two general theoretical models have been developed to answer these questions.

Template Matching

The first class of models, called *template matching models*, suggests that recognition and identification involve comparing a pattern with a global representation of the pattern—a *template*. This template consists of a replica of the pattern, perhaps like an image of the pattern. Recognition consists of matching an input against a set of templates. Each pattern that can be recognized must have a stored template. A physical analogy can be used to demonstrate how this process could work. A pattern (say, a letter) is presented to a person, and that pattern is superimposed on a template consisting of a set of grooves cut in a board. If the letter exactly matches the set of grooves, it is recognized; if it does not match, a different template is tried.

We can see without any experimentation that such a simple model cannot explain our pattern perception abilities. We know that a pattern can be recognized even if its size is changed or if it is in a new orientation. Although F, F, F, F, Ⅎ, and Ⅎ are seen as the same letter, any of these changes would disrupt the match between a pattern and its template. Figure 6–1 demonstrates how these mismatches would occur. To overcome this problem, the pattern must be changed in some way so that it can be compared to the set of templates. The pattern could, for example, be centered, expanded, or contracted so that size is constant, and then rotated so that the major axis corresponds to that of the templates.

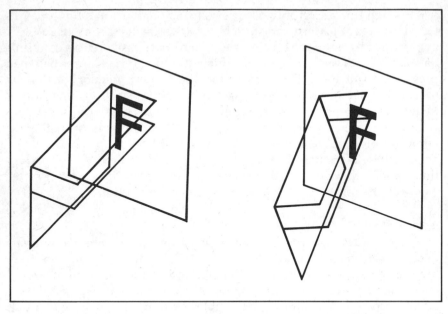

Figure 6–1

Two ways in which a pattern could fail to match its template.

However, even if such a scheme were developed, template matching theories would still have difficulty accounting for pattern perception. By far the most serious objection to a template notion involves the problem of accounting for errors. Since a stimulus either matches or does not match a template, no errors of recognition should occur. Similarly, since each pattern has its own template, there is no way that similar patterns could be confused. If the entire pattern must match a template for recognition to occur, two slightly different patterns (like O and Q) should never be confused. Our everyday experience tells us this is not the case. The only way out of this problem is to assume that complete congruence between the stimulus and its representation need not exist. If some details of the pattern are missing, and some parts of the stimulus match the representation, a pattern can be falsely recognized and erroneously assigned to a category.

Feature Testing

The notion that only certain parts of a pattern are matched against a memory representation is the defining characteristic of feature testing theories. The theory of feature testing assumes that a set of pattern features or attributes is stored, and the stimulus is compared to this set of features. Since many patterns may be constructed of the same general features, it is unnecessary to have a separate representation for each pattern to be recognized. A pattern is analyzed into features, and these features are compared to the stored set. Depending on which features are present, the input is classified. Selfridge (1959) suggested such a model, called Pandemonium, for pattern recognition. At an early level, the pattern is broken down into its components by a set of feature analyzers (called "demons" by Selfridge). Each analyzer looks for a certain feature in the pattern—perhaps a straight line, a curve, or a particular kind of angle. The presence of these features is signaled to a second set of analyzers called "cognitive demons," each of which is responsible for one pattern. As appropriate features are discovered, the cognitive demon calls out; as more of its features are found, it begins to scream louder. Finally, a decision is made about which pattern is present based on which cognitive demon screams loudest. If the feature analyzers find straight lines and angles (as illustrated in Figure 6–2) the demons for A, I, and E might begin shouting. Since more features would be found by the E demon, it would yell loudest and the pattern would be seen as an E.

An alternative procedure that could describe feature testing would organize feature tests so that not all tests would have to be made for pattern recognition (see Figure 6–3). For example, we might first test a letter for the presence of any curved lines. If the answer to this test is that there are no curved lines in the pattern, then letters B, C, D, G, J, O, P, Q, R, S, and U are eliminated. We might then test for right angles. If some are present, letters A, I, K, M, N, V, W, X, Y, and Z are eliminated. Continuing such a series of tests would enable us to eliminate other letters until only the right one remained.

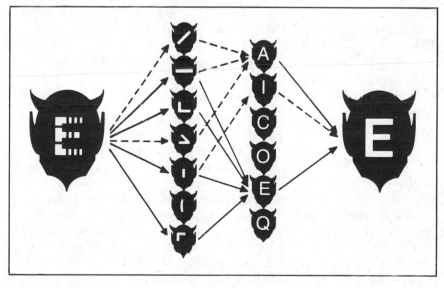

Figure 6–2

A representation of Selfridge's feature model of pattern perception.

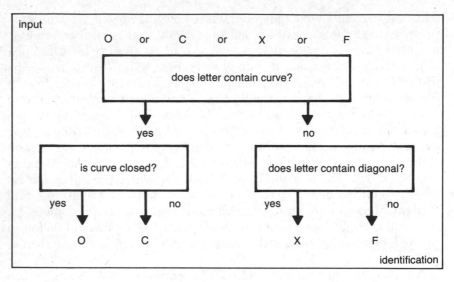

Figure 6–3

A simple hierarchical model of feature testing for a small set of letters. Each feature test would reduce the number of possible alternatives by one-half.

Either of these feature testing schemes is able to account for errors. If some of the feature tests are omitted, the pattern will be misclassified. In the second model, one mistake in a test will send us off in the wrong direction. Since similar patterns share a number of features (and therefore require more tests to distinguish them than do dissimilar patterns), they should be more easily confused than dissimilar patterns. In addition, since more feature tests must be made to distinguish similar patterns, it should take longer to differentiate such patterns. As we shall see, experimental data supports these notions about feature testing.

INFORMATION FOR PATTERN PERCEPTION

These two models of feature testing suggest what kinds of processes might occur in a feature testing system for pattern perception. They do not tell us what features are used or even whether human pattern perception is based on specific features. These are basic difficulties involved in feature testing theories of pattern perception. No theory defines the features that are actually used in the test process, and we have little idea of what these features might actually be.

Some psychologists have attempted to specify what features might be used on the basis of the neurophysiology of the visual system. Studies of the horseshoe crab, the frog, and the cat have revealed that their nervous systems are organized in such a way that only certain stimulus features cause specific neural cells to respond. Some cells in frogs and cats (Hartline 1938; Kuffler 1953) increase their rates of responding when a circular area of the retina is stimulated. This circular area is surrounded by an area that decreases the cells' rate of firing when stimulated. Thus, the receptive field for this cell is made of two concentric areas—an *on-center* and an *off-surround*. Other cells have "on" and "off" receptive fields that may be related to feature processing in pattern perception. In one arrangement, a spot of light anywhere along a line causes the cell to fire. On either side of this line are two areas that decrease the cell's rate of response if stimulated. The cell responds maximally to a slit of light that is aligned appropriately. Rotating the slit decreases the cell's response. A different organization would act as a line detector. Other cells respond maximally to a line of a specific length. Still others are most sensitive to the presence of specific angles (Hubel and Wiesel 1965).

With a little imagination, one can see how these neural detectors could act as feature analyzers in pattern perception. The detector cells analyze a pattern and signal the presence of certain features, just as Selfridge's feature demons do. Other neural cells may play the role of cognitive demons and "listen" to the feature detectors for specific sets of features. If the detector cells signal a straight line, a curve, and three right angles, the P circuit operates. A decision circuit then signals the presence of a particular pattern.

The similarities between this account of neural feature detectors and Selfridge's account of feature analysis in pattern perception are intriguing. Perhaps in the future, psychologists and physiologists will spell out the connections between neural feature detectors and the psychology of pattern perception. At present, however, any relationship between these neural feature detectors and pattern perception is purely speculative. We are not sure that the line and angle detectors found in the nervous system are, in fact, the building blocks of pattern perception. Nor do we know if these detectors are connected in a way that would put feature results together.

Another possible analysis procedure is also based on the neural pathways in the visual system. Kabrisky, Tallman, Day, and Radoy (1970) have suggested a complex integration scheme for pattern processing. In this model, a complex pattern is analyzed into mathematically simpler components, *harmonics*. Although in theory, an infinite number of harmonics might be necessary to describe a complex pattern completely, an adequate description can result from a small set of components. Kabrisky's work has led to the development of a pattern-identifying computer that analyzes a pattern into four components. These four components are then matched against a master pattern, and on the basis of this comparison the test pattern is categorized. Considerable success in identifying patterns has been achieved using even this small set of components.

Identification of a pattern seems to be invariant over a large number of changes. For example, changes in size, proportion, and location of the pattern do not impair identification. Even significantly degrading the pattern does not eliminate accurate identification, yet this model is far from being a complete success, since it does not approach the capabilities of the human perceiver. The model designed by Kabrisky et al. does suggest, however, that our pattern perception may involve highly complex analysis mechanisms far more sophisticated than the addition of simple line, angle, or curve detectors.

Even after a description of the analysis mechanism is made, it must be combined with the psychology of visual stimulation and patterns. In the context of space perception, we argued that there is a direct relationship between visual information and what that information specifies. Under normal conditions, texture gradients, for example, are uniquely related to distances and slants in the world. Such informational specificity may also exist for some object and pattern displays. Faces, for example, may be recognized and identified on the basis of a set of features that are specific to each individual. Such features as distance between the eyes, nose and lip proportions, and so forth may provide information for perception of faces or facial displays like photographs and line drawings. The notion of stimulus information cannot be directly and simply extended to other aspects of pattern perception.

An important argument against a direct relation between feature information and patterns has been developed by Neisser (1967) and by Kolers and Perkins (1969). Most patterns that we deal with involve what Neisser calls "ill-defined categories." That is, there are no necessary or sufficient conditions that a pattern must meet to be correctly perceived. Many patterns are categorized in the same way because of arbitrary definition rather than physical similarity. The patterns A and a are the same letter, although they are not physically similar. Consider the patterns in Figure 6–4. What unique features do these patterns share that allows us to see them as representations of the same letter? Kolers and Perkins argue that there may be none.

> Any letter of the English alphabet can be printed in an infinite number of ways. Any set of rules established to define a letter in terms of its geometry of hooks, bars, arches, loops, and the like can be violated easily and the letter still be recognized. . . . It is within reason to conjecture that no deterministic principles can be established to define individually printed or written characters unambiguously. . . . hence, lists of "distinctive features" based on geometry cannot by themselves account for performance. What S uses as a clue to a letter's recognition may have little direct relation to the formally specifiable feature of its geometry. (Kolers and Perkins 1969, p. 279)

This view is impossible to prove conclusively since it is possible that a set of features exists, although it has escaped the notice of psychologists. Research evidence suggests, however, that unique sets of features for

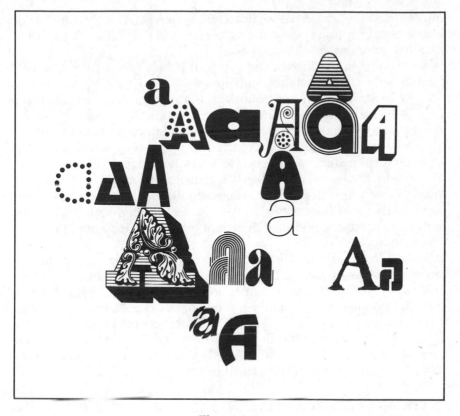

Figure 6–4

Various ways of printing the same letter. Do they have any features in common?

patterns in the same category do not exist. Within any small class of patterns (for example, Roman capital letters), a set of features that uniquely describe each letter can be defined. These features are not the same over classes. Different features distinguish handwritten letters, and still other features distinguish among lower-case letters. Such distinctions suggest that different physical characteristics of patterns may be specific to one set of patterns but not to another.

To use a feature processing approach, then, a perceiver must know which class of patterns is being seen to determine which physical characteristics function as information features—that is, the pattern class must first be known before pattern features can be defined. This appears to be the case in adult pattern perception. The time taken to identify a pattern is long if the subject does not know which class of patterns will be presented, since the pattern class must be determined before feature analysis can proceed. If a subject expects Roman capital letters, for example, then this set of features can be used in perception. But, if either handwritten or Roman capital letters may be presented, the subject must first determine which class is presented and which set of feature tests is appropriate before he can analyze the pattern. This added step takes more time.

An experiment by Bruner and Minturn (1955) further demonstrates that the subject's expectation influences how physical characteristics shall be defined in terms of features. If the pattern 13 is presented to a subject, identification will depend on the pattern class that he expects. For example, if the subject expects to see a letter, the pattern will be perceived as a B. If a number is expected, however, a 13 will be seen. The same physical pattern can function as two different feature sets depending on which analysis the subject is prepared to make. These results indicate that a direct relationship between physical characteristics and pattern categories does not exist. At least for artificial patterns such as letters and numbers, information cannot be defined according to physical stimulation alone.

The preceding discussion touches on some of the problems encountered in explaining pattern perception capacities. The information and processes involved in pattern perception are not well understood. However, developmental psychology has begun to describe the characteristics of pattern perception in children. The aspects of patterns that children can perceive and the processes involved in perception can be discussed under our general categories of pattern perception: discrimination, recognition, and identification.

PATTERN PERCEPTION IN INFANTS

Discrimination

Only recently have developmental psychologists been able to discover some of the characteristics of the infant's perceptual system. Methodological problems prevented early psychologists from assessing infants' capacities. Since infants can make few responses, there seemed to be few ways to determine perceptual abilities. One of the first methodological advances was made by Robert Fantz, when he refined the visual preference technique (described in Chapter One) and applied it to infants. Until that time, little was known about infants' pattern perception, and no data existed for children under two months old. The early studies generally explored infants' basic perceptual capacities. Fantz's preference technique, however, proved to be a simple means of directly assessing infants' abilities to perceive patterns, as follows: if two patterns are presented and the infant prefers to look at one more than the other, he must be able to discriminate between the two patterns.

In one of the early preference studies, Fantz (1958) observed the looking behavior of infants under fourteen months of age. The stimulus pairs depicted in Figure 6–5 were shown to the infants for a total of one minute. The majority of the children showed a preference (inferred from differential fixation times) for the red and white checkerboard over the

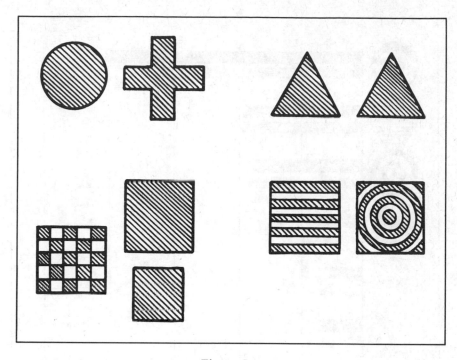

Figure 6–5

Stimuli used in Fantz's early work on infant discrimination. (From Fantz, 1958. Reprinted by permission.)

red square, and for the bull's-eye pattern over the stripes. When the members of a pair differed only in form (circle versus cross), no preferences were observed. Of course, when the two members of a pair were identical (two red triangles), no differences in fixation occurred. Even the youngest children were able to discriminate between grossly different patterns.

A further study was conducted to determine whether young infants (two to three months old) were capable of discriminating between patterns. In this study, Fantz (1961) determined preference for pairs of six different patterns: a schematic face, concentric circles, a section of newsprint, a white disc, a fluorescent yellow disc, and a dark red disc. The results in Figure 6–6 show roughly twice as much visual fixation of the patterns as to the plainly colored discs. As can be seen from the figure, even children a few weeks old were able to discriminate different patterns. Furthermore, the differences in fixation time among the stimuli demonstrate that visual responses were related to pattern rather than to the effect of color or brightness. Some ability to discriminate patterns is clearly present in early infancy.

Many of the early preference studies were directed simply at determining whether infants possessed *any* pattern perception ability. Because of the broad scope of the research, the particular stimuli used were

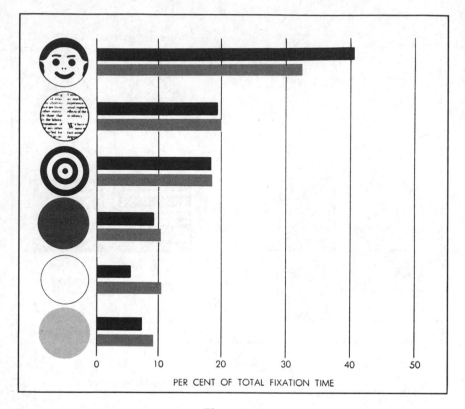

PER CENT OF TOTAL FIXATION TIME

Figure 6–6

Visual preferences of younger and older infants for various stimuli. The black bars represent the data from 2–3 month olds, the gray bars from infants more than 3 months old. (From R. L. Fantz, "The Origin of Form Perception." Copyright © 1961 by Scientific American, Inc. All rights reserved.)

of little importance. Stimuli were often selected intuitively—the experimenter simply guessed at what stimuli might be discriminable to a child. For example, the kinds of displays presented in early experiments ranged from geometric forms to such diverse patterns as checkerboards to objects such as plastic fruit, a light switch plate, wire mesh, and even Egyptian art. Although the use of such varied displays demonstrated that infants were able to perceive differences between patterns, little could be said about the basis for such discrimination since one could not determine the specific features used by an infant's perceptual system, due to the fact that the displays differed in so many ways. Later preference studies attempted to select stimuli so that the specific features or attributes that form the basis of discrimination could be discovered.

Curved versus Straight Contours. Among the most obvious differences that may exist among patterns is the presence or form of contours. Kessen, Salapatek, and Haith (1972) found that newborn infants could distinguish the presence of sharp black-white contours. Further, when the edge was aligned vertically, the infants' scanning was drawn to it. Kessen et al. suggest that babies may be able to detect all edges but are visually attracted to vertical ones.

In addition to knowing that infants can perceive contours, we also know that they can discriminate between straight and curved edges. In his first infant preference study, Fantz (1958) mapped the developmental course of the ability to distinguish between stimuli by measuring relative preference of a bull's-eye pattern and a set of stripes. Prior to eight weeks of age, most of the infants tested showed a slight preference for the stripes, which was then followed by a marked, consistent preference for the bull's-eye. A further investigation by Fantz and Nevis (1967) confirmed the preference for the bull's-eye in infants over six weeks old.

Of course, the bull's-eye and stripes differed from one another in a number of ways, and it might be that discrimination was based on one of these other factors. Symmetry, concentricity, connected versus unconnected lines, and amount of contour may all be the actual basis of discrimination. To assess these alternatives, Fantz and Nevis (1967), Fantz and Miranda (1975), and Fantz (1972) ran experiments varying the nature of the stimuli. The patterns tried were a bull's-eye versus stripes (both drawn with discontinuous line segments), curved versus straight bars, a clover leaf versus concentric squares, circles versus rectangles—and infants consistently preferred the curved patterns to the straight ones. Fantz and Miranda (1975) found a strong preference for curved over straight patterns even in newborns.

Other work by Fantz (1972) strengthened the suggestion that curvature is a discriminable feature for infants. Curved and straight lines of various widths were presented to infants shortly after birth. The brightness of the patterns was varied to determine at what point infants would first be able to detect the lines. Infants were able to detect the curved lines before they were able to detect the straight lines of the same width. Like results over several studies demonstrate that some stimulus feature involving curvilinearity is an important aspect of infants' discrimination ability; that is, curvature can be used by infants to distinguish between two patterns. Also, the infant's perceptual system seems more sensitive to curved than to straight contours.

Complexity. The stimulus differences between displays that were used in the early studies of infant preference do not lend themselves to an exact description of pattern features. It was possible, however, to infer some stimulus differences that were related to discrimination and preference. To begin with, many of the pattern pairs seemed to differ in complexity. For example, when a plain form is paired with an illustration from a magazine, one stimulus can be described as more complex than the other. Although it would be difficult to specify the basis on which we make this judgment, this description is clearly a meaningful one for adults. Perhaps the notion of complexity might underlie infant perceptual abilities.

Impetus for this line of reasoning was first given by a study performed by Berlyne (1958). When three- to nine-month-old infants were shown pairs of stimuli—one rated as complex and one rated as simple—the infants more often looked first at the complex one. Some aspect of the two patterns that was related to complexity seemed to influence visual preference. In further investigations, checkerboard patterns were used to determine the effects of complexity on infant discrimination. Brennan, Ames, and Moore (1966) defined complexity as the number of elements in a checkerboard, and presented infants with checkerboard patterns varying in size (2 × 2, 8 × 8, 24 × 24). Three-week-old infants preferred to look at the 2 × 2 pattern and could not distinguish the 24 × 24 pattern from a gray surface. Eight-week-olds preferred the 8 × 8 pattern, while fourteen-week-old infants preferred the 24 × 24 pattern.

Defining complexity in other ways also leads to the conclusion that it was a relevant variable in infant research. Hershenson, Munsinger, and Kessen (1965) used forms that had different numbers of bends or corners in the outer contour. Stimuli with five, ten, or twenty bends were used. Two- to four-day-old infants were able to discriminate among these forms and showed a preference for the one that possessed ten bends over the other stimuli. Testing older infants (nine months to forty-one months) with these stimuli, Munsinger and Weir (1967) found that the more complex stimulus was consistently preferred to the less complex.

It would seem from these studies that some variable, which we may call "complexity," influences infants' discrimination and pattern preference. The effect of complexity may be spurious, however. It is possible that the results obtained by the investigators cited above had nothing to do with stimulus complexity. Although the displays can be ordered on the basis of a concept of complexity, this ordering may have little to do with the actual means by which the infants were discriminating among patterns. This difficulty is the result of the inferred notion of complexity, which is at the base of this research. It is certainly true that 24 × 24 checkerboards are somehow more complex than 2 × 2 checkerboards; it is also true that infants can discriminate between these two patterns. The conclusion that the discrimination is based on the infants' pickup of complexity is not warranted, however.

In all studies varying complexity, the stimuli also varied in several other ways. For example, checkerboards that differ in complexity also differ in the size of the elements, the area of the elements, the number of angles, the amount of contour, and the number of elements. Any one or a combination of these factors could determine infant discrimination and preference. Adult ratings of complexity are determined by a combination of four different variables (Stenson 1966). Complexity, therefore,

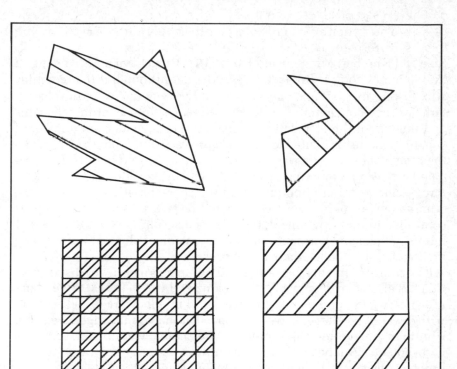

Figure 6–7

Patterns of the type used in the investigation of complexity as a determinant of infant preferences.

may not reflect an attribute or feature that is important in infant perception but rather a conceptual framework that adults have for dealing with a conglomeration of different features or attributes. Infants may discriminate on the basis of these individual features rather than on the basis of rated complexity.

A study by Karmel (1969), in which he used patterns made of squares that were arranged either to form a checkerboard or arranged randomly on a surface, supports the suggestion that infant perception is based on individual features. Adults rated the complexity of these patterns and measured the amount of contour in each directly. As might be expected, Karmel found that infants were able to discriminate among these patterns. By varying complexity and contour length, the effectiveness of these two factors could be assessed. Although the data are rather involved, it seems that the amount of contour present in a display is a more efficient way of describing the basis of discrimination than is rated complexity. The notion of complexity had relatively little bearing on the infants' performance.

Size and Number. Miranda and Fantz (1971) also have pointed out that the notion of complexity lacks a specific definition, and that complex stimuli vary from simple ones in a number of ways. Two of the characteristics they concentrated on were differences in size of the elements and number of the elements in a display. The size and the number of square elements presented to infants were varied independently. When the number of elements was controlled, three-day-old infants discriminated between patterns on the basis of element size. Element size, therefore, seems to be an important stimulus characteristic for pattern discrimination even in neonates. When the size of the elements was controlled in this experiment, the infants discriminated on the basis of number of elements present. The apprehension of element number as a distinguishing characteristic of patterns, then, also occurs in infants.

The ability of infants to use size and number as a basis for discrimination has also been demonstrated by Fantz and Fagan (1975). Five-, ten-, fifteen-, twenty-, and twenty-five-week-old infants were tested. Stimuli with fewer large elements were preferred at the younger age levels, but stimuli having an increased number of elements were preferred by the older infants. Analysis of the data showed a straightforward effect of these two features on the infants' preference responses.

The results of experiments dealing with contour length, size, and number indicate that these features may provide a better description of the perceptual basis of pattern discrimination than does the notion of complexity. Specific physical differences between patterns affect discrimination and preference. The concept of complexity can, no doubt, be separated into other features that influence discrimination and that can be specified more exactly than complexity.

Recognition

The preference studies discussed thus far clearly show that the ability to discriminate among patterns is present shortly after birth. Human infants show an early capacity to compare and distinguish patterns containing feature differences. As was pointed out, however, preference data imply only that infants possess the ability to compare feature differences. No inference can be drawn about the nature of the comparison process or about the perceptual organization of features.

The ability to recognize a pattern, however, presupposes not only a process of comparison but also the storage of an organized feature testing scheme. An examination of children's recognition ability will give us some insight into the development of feature organization. To demonstrate recognition of a pattern, there must be evidence of the ability to store features in memory. That is, a child must be able to respond to a pattern on the basis of his or her past experience or familiarity with that pattern.

To determine whether infants were able to store pattern features, Fantz (1964) investigated the influence of familiarity on preference. Infants from one month to six months of age were given ten successive exposures to pairs of patterns. Six color photographs and five black and white photographs were used as stimuli. One of the photographs served as a familiarization pattern; it was presented for one minute, ten times in succession. During each exposure, the photo was paired with a different one of the other ten photos. Fantz's main interest was whether preference for the constant pattern would change as a result of its increasing familiarity. The results were clear. The youngest group of infants (under two months) showed no change in their preference for the constant pattern over the familiar one. Ten exposures to one pattern did not influence their preference for that pattern. Each of the groups over two months showed decreasing preference for the constant pattern over the ten trials. At the end of the familiarization trials, virtually all infants over two months old showed a marked preference for the novel pattern of the pair. The fact that such novelty preferences developed demonstrates that experience with a pattern results in storage of some of the features of the pattern. Furthermore, this experiment suggests that storage capacities influence preference at least by the second month.

Although this study shows that infants over two months of age are able to store some features of a visual pattern for later recognition, little is known about the kinds of feature differences that infants can remember. Since Fantz did not specify what his photographic stimuli were, there is no way of determining the features that were retained in memory.

Other experiments have replicated the preference for novelty that Fantz observed and have isolated some general pattern characteristics that can be retained by an infant. Saayman, Ames, and Moffett (1964) studied the recognition ability of three- to four-month-olds using a procedure that was similar to that of Fantz. A pair of stimuli was presented in a preference apparatus to assess initial looking behavior to these stimuli; then one of the patterns was presented alone for 4½ minutes in a familiarization period. After this period, two 30-second test trials were conducted to determine the effect of familiarization on preference behavior. Since the Saayman et al. paradigm is similar to Fantz's, we would expect that the infants would show recognition of the familiar pattern— that is, they would prefer to look at the novel pattern in testing. Indeed, this result was obtained.

An interesting aspect of the Saayman et al. data, however, concerns the general aspects of the patterns that could be recognized. In one condition, the stimuli used differed in both form and color (red cross versus black circle). In a second condition, the patterns differed only in form; and in a third condition, they differed only in color. In all three conditions, there was a decline in the amount of time spent looking at the familiar stimulus. Since this habituation occurred, some memory of the pattern attribute must have developed over the familiarization period. When the stimuli differed in both form and color, there was a substantial increase in the time spent looking at the unfamiliar stimulus. These results show that some aspect of color and form can be retained in memory by infants. Furthermore, as the test stimuli are made increasingly different, the more easily the familiar stimulus is recognized. Although both form and color influenced behavior during the familiarization period, the combination of form and color resulted in a preference for novelty.

The direct conclusion from these studies is that infants possess an ability to recognize patterns within the first six months of life. This conclusion has been further supported by Fagan (1970), who suggested also that there may be a long-term memory component to this recognition ability. Since the Fantz and the Saayman et al. experiments tested children shortly after the familiarization period, it is unclear how long the effect of familiarity would last. Although recognition memory is present, it may last only a short time.

Fagan tested the preference for novelty in a complex experiment that involved the recombination of stimuli into new pairs over several days. Although there was a significant preference for the novel stimulus of a pair on the first day of the experiment, this novelty preference disappeared by the third day. One way to explain this change in response is to suggest that continued exposure to the same three stimuli over the three-day test period resulted in the children's becoming familiar with all of the test designs. Since there was no difference in novelty after three days, no preference was found. This explanation assumes that the children were able to remember the stimulus designs over the whole period of the experiment. Further experiments by Fagan (1970, 1971, 1973) verified that the ability to recognize a pattern persisted over time. Recognition ability was found to remain stable over intervals ranging from several minutes to two weeks.

In a further study, Fagan (1974) isolated some factors that influenced infants' pattern recognition. Infants five to six months old were able to recognize a photograph of a face after a three-hour delay between presentation and testing. If, after presentation of the original stimulus, the infant was immediately shown an inverted photo of a different face, recognition of the original photo after a three-hour delay was not found. Fagan suggests that a limitation on infant recognition and a cause of forgetting is due to diverting the child's attention to similar material.

Infants under six months old clearly possess a recognition memory for patterns. Little is known about the specific features held in memory over the interval between familiarization and testing. Some features of the pattern must be stored. We might expect that the features that preference studies have found to be easily discriminable for infants would be those that are easiest to retain for recognition. Consequently, recognition measures may offer an effective means of converging on the basic features of infant perception.

Identification

Practically nothing is known about infants' ability to identify patterns—that is, to categorize them. The major difficulty in determining categorization ability is developing response measures that allow an experimenter to infer that a class or category underlies an infant's performance. The few indicators we have of infant ability are indirect. One of these indicators is early language development. Before age two, a child may learn dozens or hundreds of different names for objects and patterns in his environment (Dale 1976). Furthermore, these names are not simply responses that are given to specific, individual members of a class; rather, considerable generalization and overgeneralization occurs. A year-old child who is able to label a ball can apply that label to identify many different members of its class. If the child has never seen a beach ball, it is still identifiable by him as a ball. Objects are categorized on the basis of common attributes, even if the specific instance of the concept has never been encountered. Overgeneralization shows that the name is being used to identify a class of objects rather than a single member of the class.

Although it is clear that some identification and classification must be occurring by the time a child begins to use language, it is difficult to demonstrate whether identification occurs before the onset of language. Logically, this must be the case. Since a word is simply a label for some semantic category, the category must exist before a label can be learned for it. Fagan (1973) has suggested that the categorization necessary for identification may occur early in infancy and assumed that class concepts are formed by abstracting common features of a group of objects. As a result of this abstraction process, novel (previously unencountered) patterns that share the features of the class can be categorized. Once this class membership is established, recognition of patterns in the class will be easier than recognition of patterns not in the class. Fagan has found that upright faces (one class) are more easily recognized by six-month-olds than are inverted faces (a different class). He has also found that six-month-old infants familiarized on faces can recognize the faces in photographs. These data may indicate that classification and abstraction of common features does occur in young infants.

Other evidence for early identification in infants can be drawn from a phenomenon that occurs in socialization. Within the first few months of life, a child is able to categorize people on the basis of whether they are familiar or are strangers. We know this by observing an infant's reaction to his mother as opposed to his reaction to a strange woman. When confronted with an unfamiliar person, an infant may show signs of anxiety and fear. The presence of his mother, in contrast, exerts a reassuring and calming influence on the child. Stranger anxiety usually begins when the child is seven or eight months old, following the onset of the first specific attachment.

It is no coincidence, of course, that stranger anxiety develops at the same time or slightly after the ability to recognize faces. To be able to distinguish a stranger from its mother, the infant must have some recognition ability. As pointed out earlier in this chapter, recognition may be a primitive form of categorization since it enables a child to distinguish between familiar and unfamiliar things, which is what must exist for stranger anxiety to manifest itself.

SUMMARY

Based on physiological studies with animals and behavioral studies of human perception, we know that there are substantial differences between the processes involved in spatial perception and pattern perception. The ability to perceive patterns in a meaningful way requires that the individual first be able to make a set of comparisons among patterns as in discrimination, or between a pattern and some memory representation as in recognition. Then an assignment to some conceptual category can be made through identification. Research in models of pattern perception reveals that the information necessary for pattern perception involves combinations of features that can define a pattern.

Infants possess the ability to distinguish between different patterns from birth. The perceptual basis of this ability has not been totally determined yet, but several stimulus features are clearly important. Curvature and contour length can be used to distinguish patterns even by newborns. The size and number of elements that make up a pattern are two other features that seem to play a role in infant pattern discrimination. These features all affect preference and distinguish patterns that differ in complexity. Although ratings of complexity influence infant preference and discrimination, complexity is not a single stimulus feature but is a combination of characteristics such as size, number, and contour length, which can be dissociated into components that affect discrimination.

The ability to recognize patterns begins during the first six months of life. At least by two months of age, a child is able to store some pattern features in memory and compare this stored set to a physically present pattern. This ability develops rapidly so that by the age of six months, a child is capable of recognizing complex objects such as faces and can store for several hours the features of a face that he has seen only once before.

The capacity for recognition implies some crude form of identification in that the child can categorize patterns into two groups—familiar and unfamiliar. The phenomenon of stranger anxiety confirms that such categorization can take place by six months. Some of the changes that occur in later identification can be seen in language development. Through the latter half of infancy, the categorization process becomes increasingly refined and differentiated. By the end of his second year, a child may have developed several dozen categories and category labels.

Chapter 7

PATTERN PERCEPTION: FURTHER DEVELOPMENT

Experimental investigations of pattern perception in infancy indicate that some pattern perception abilities exist at birth. Newborn infants can make the comparison of features required for discrimination. Furthermore, the processes for the comparison and storage of features, which are necessary in recognition, develop within the first six months of life. This early occurrence of perceptual ability suggests that the feature analysis process that takes place in perception may be innate. Neural feature analyzers may develop prenatally and reach a sufficient maturational level at birth to allow pattern discrimination. This suggestion, that the ability to perceive patterns may be present from birth, has been made many times throughout the history of developmental psychology.

Until recently, arguments about the basis of early pattern perception were based heavily on speculation, with little experimental evidence. Of course, posing questions about the origins of perception in simple dichotomies must lead to unsatisfactory answers. Perception is not simply either maturationally or experientially determined. Clearly, since normal infants are not born blind, they must have some initial perceptual ability. Consequently, all pattern perception cannot be built from the experiences the child has in the first few hours or days of life. It is equally obvious that development of perceptual abilities cannot be completely independent of a child's experiences. In some way, maturation and experience must combine in the development of pattern perception.

THE NATURE OF EARLY DEVELOPMENT

To determine which abilities change over the course of development, we must first determine which abilities the child first possesses and how these change. We can begin by asking how similar the abilities of a newborn are to our own. Does a child immediately upon birth perceive patterns and forms, or does he or she simply register certain features that the nervous system can detect?

Perception of Form

Studies of infant preferences were designed to determine whether infants were capable of discriminating between different forms. The preference and habituation studies clearly show that infants are able to discriminate and recognize. The question then becomes what we can safely infer about infants' perception from such preferences. To begin with, when a preference is shown, we know that the infant can discriminate between the patterns. Something in one stimulus is seen as different from something in the other. However, we have no idea of what that "something" is. Assume that a group of infants show a consistent preference for a circle over a square. Are they discriminating between a circular form versus a square form, or between curves versus straight lines, or between the presence and absence of angles? Are whole forms or simple features perceived? Hershenson (1967) suggested two ways that one might determine whether an infant is perceiving a form, a stimulus dimension, or a simple feature.

Hershenson's first criterion involves scanning eye movements. If an infant moves his eyes around the entire contour of a form, we might be able to infer that he has perceived the form. This is not a necessary condition for the perception of global form, however. It is well known that a form can be perceived and classified in a shorter time than it takes to make an eye movement. If we show a circle to an adult subject for 60 milliseconds, the subject will see it as a circle and discriminate it from a square shown for an equal amount of time. Yet, an exposure time of 60 milliseconds is insufficient for scanning eye movements. Clearly, then, scanning eye movements are not necessary for the perception of form. As we will discuss later, there are other grounds for knowing that the presence of eye movements is not sufficient criterion for the perception of form.

Second, Hershenson suggests that preference can be ordered along some dimension of form. Consider the circle-triangle discrimination. To determine whether children respond on the basis of form, we might test them with a series of stimuli that are less and less triangular—for example, a triangle rounded to such a degree that it is a closed curve with three foci. If a transitive relationship is observed (that is, A preferred to B, B preferred to C, and A preferred to C), then we may "assert that there is a stimulus dimension which could have generated the response set" (Hershenson 1967, p. 332). The difficulty with this notion, as Hershenson also pointed out, is that we have no a priori notion of what underlies the response. The transitive relationship described above could equally have resulted from the perception of "triangularity," "curved versus straight line," or "angle versus no angle." The presence of a transitive relationship among responses does not assure that the dimension we have selected is the one that the child is using in perception.

The basic difficulty here can be cleared up if the question is rephrased in theoretical terms and analyzed in the context of discrimination. The crucial issue is not whether a form or its components are perceived. We know from other work in pattern perception that the perception of any pattern seems to be based on the analysis of that pattern into its features. In our theoretical terms, the issue is whether the child's perception is based on the pickup of simply a few features in isolation or whether it is based on the pickup and integration of these features into a whole form. That is, is preference based on the perception of a straight line or on the integration of straight lines into a square? Because this question involves whether the features are integrated into some organized structure, the eye movement criterion also is not a sufficient basis for determining form perception. A child may scan the entire contour of a pattern, successively viewing all the features in order, yet not integrate these features over the eye movements.

There is, however, a way to determine whether the preference responses of a child are controlled by simple individual features or by the integration of these features into a form. Two patterns that possess exactly the same features but differ only in the way those features are organized can be presented. If the presence or absence of a feature is all that determines preference, then no differential response should be observed. If, however, not only the features but also their integration is important, preferences should occur. Experiments that fit this strategy have been conducted.

Fantz (1965b) presented schematic faces to infants of various ages. Using the preference procedure, the scrambled and unscrambled faces, illustrated in Figure 7–1, were shown to the infants. Note that both of the patterns contain the same elements, only the arrangement differs. When infants under one month old were tested, no preferences were found. When the patterns contained identical individual elements, their organization did not affect performance. This suggests that young infants discriminate patterns on the basis of simple elements and not on their organized combination. Infants between one and four months old, however, showed a different pattern of response. In children this age, there was a definite preference for the unscrambled face, demonstrating a discrimination of the two patterns that differed in organization.

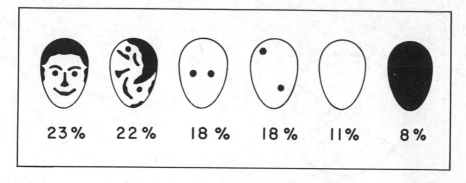

23%   22%   18 %   18%   11%   8%

Figure 7–1

Relative amounts of fixation to targets varying in arrangement of features. (From Fantz, 1965b.)

Using a different measure, Kagan et al. (1966) also found that four-month-olds are able to discriminate between faces that differ only in the scrambling of features. The frequency with which infants smiled at scrambled versus unscrambled faces demonstrated a discrimination of the faces based on organization of the features. It would be tempting to conclude on the basis of these two studies that the perception of infants under one month old is based on the pickup of simple features, whereas the perception of older infants involves the organization of these features into a unit.

Unfortunately, such a conclusion is not justified from this evidence. Because of the problems inherent in the preference procedure, it is possible that the newborn infants could discriminate the patterns on the basis of organization but did not prefer to look at one more than the other. Infants of all ages may discriminate between the scrambled and un-scrambled patterns, but older infants may recognize one as a face and prefer to look at it. Other evidence, however, shows that the differences in preference across age are not an artifact of the method. Infants at the age of four months do seem capable of perceiving a featural organization, whereas younger infants do not have this capability.

Converging evidence for this conclusion can be drawn from a study by Bower (1966). Infants between the ages of eight and twenty weeks were conditioned to make a head-turning response to the pattern shown in Figure 7–2. After a stable response level had been established, transfer testing was initiated. In testing, either the whole figure or its components (b, c, and d in Figure 7–2) were presented for fifteen seconds. The number of responses to these test stimuli was recorded. The rationale behind the experiment is as follows. If the children had seen the pattern in training as a set of separate components (a cross, and a circle, and two dots), then the sum of their responses to these components in isolation should equal the number of responses given to the whole pattern. If, on

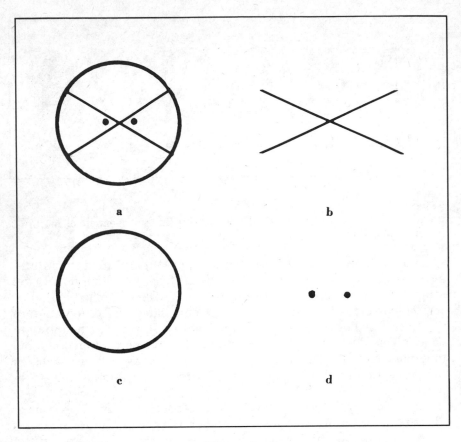

Figure 7–2

Training and test stimuli used by Bower. (After Bower, 1966.)

the other hand, the training pattern is seen as an organized, integrated unit, then the responses to the whole pattern should be different from the responses to the unintegrated isolated parts. Bower found a clear developmental trend. For children eight, twelve, or sixteen weeks old, there was no difference between the number of times they responded to the whole pattern and the sum of the responses to the parts. For twenty-week-old infants, however, there were twice as many responses made to the whole pattern than to the sum of its parts.

For the particular stimuli used in Bower's experiment, the ability to integrate the components into some organized pattern developed between sixteen and twenty weeks of age. At this point in development, the pattern is perceived as an integrated form that is more than a simple set of component features. As in the previous studies, younger infants appear to behave on the basis of a perceptual knowledge of individual features, whereas older infants' behavior is affected by the organization of a set of features into a whole pattern.

Evidence from the study of recognition memory in infants also indicates that the ability to organize features into a pattern develops with age. Fagan (1972) conducted a series of experiments that demonstrate that organized storage occurs with some patterns. Four- to six-month-old infants were shown photographs of faces. After a one-minute familiarization period, a recognition test (preference for novelty) was administered. Four-month-olds showed no ability to recognize the face used in familiarization training. By five to six months of age, however, the results indicated that the face could be recognized. The most interesting aspect of this series of experiments involves infants' recognition of faces presented in an unusual orientation. When upright faces were used, five- to six-month-olds were able to recognize the familiar face. However, when inverted faces were used in familiarization and testing, no evidence of recognition was found. These results show that faces are not recognized on the basis of simple features that are stored independently of one another. Since changing the orientation of the face affects recognition ability, spatial relations among features must be an important structural aspect of the pattern.

This series of experiments points strongly to a dual characterization of pattern perception in infancy. In children less than one month old, discrimination is controlled by the presence or absence of particular elements in the pattern. Organization of these elements does not influence perception. Between two and six months of age, the operation of the perceptual system in discrimination and recognition changes. In this period, the elements of a pattern become organized and integrated. The spatial relations among elements and their configurational structure come to affect perception.

Effects of Maturation and Experience

Some notions about the pattern discrimination mechanisms of newborns have been provided by work on preference and discrimination. For example, Fantz (1972) extended some of his early work on visual acuity and curvature discrimination by examining the preference behavior of premature infants. As in his other experiments, acuity was determined by observing preference for stripes of different widths. In addition, curved versus straight stripes were paired to assess the development of curvature preference. The important difference between this experiment and others is that Fantz was able to include subjects that differed in postmenstrual age at birth (a measure of maturation based on the amount of time since the mother's last menstrual cycle), as well as in postnatal age at the time of testing. The experimental data show that the premature infants demonstrated less of a differential response to the patterns than did full-term infants. This conclusion applies even when the postnatal ages of the two samples of infants was the same. Infants of the same chronological age (and who therefore had equal opportunities for visual experience) performed differently depending on their post-menstrual age.

The results of this study indicate that early discrimination capacities are heavily influenced by maturation of the visual system. The preference responses of the infants, however, were highly similar when the entire sample was regrouped according to their total postmenstrual age; when postmenstrual age was equated, response differences between groups were reduced. Fantz concludes from these data that certain pattern resolution and pattern discrimination capacities are related to age from conception rather than age from birth.

This conclusion is further supported by the results of Fantz and Fagan (1975). In this experiment, infants' preference for size and number of elements as a function of age was investigated. Previous research found that preference for size and number changed with age. In this comparison, the premature and full-term infants were about equal in postnatal age, but the full-term infants were five weeks older postmenstrually. Although the two groups were approximately equal in postnatal age, preference differences were observed. The full-term infants preferred fewer, larger elements, whereas the premature infants preferred more, smaller elements. Thus, the preference for size and number was influenced by postmenstrual age.

This study shows that visual acuity and curvature, size, and number preference are affected by visual maturation. However, this conclusion must be restricted. It would be incorrect to assume that all aspects of pattern perception are simply determined by maturation or that opportunities for visual experience did not affect pattern preference development.

Even in simple discrimination, experience influences performance. Fantz and Nevis (1967) compared home-reared and institutionally reared children. When the preferences of the two groups for concentric versus linear line segments were compared, the developmental functions relating preference and age were virtually the same. Although similar developmental curves were found for both groups (see Figure 7–3), the development of the institutionally-reared children lagged by about two weeks. Although there were many possible differences between these two groups of children, an obvious one is the differential visual experience of both groups. Therefore, even though curvature preferences have a strong maturational basis, development of preference may be affected by the rearing environment.

Kagan (1970, 1972) has suggested how maturational and experiential factors may be related in the early development of pattern perception. We know from data such as that presented in Figure 7–3 that the preference behavior of infants changes. At different ages, infants attend to some patterns more than to others; they seemingly select different kinds of visual experiences. Kagan has suggested that such changes may be determined by the changing characteristics of the child's pattern percep-

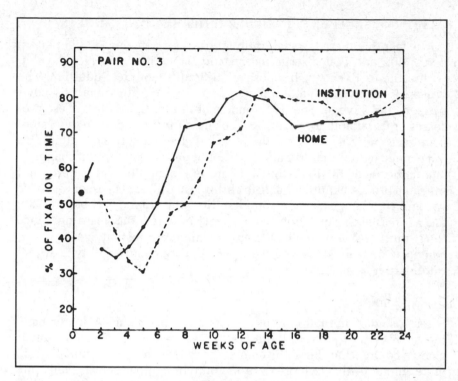

Figure 7–3

Changes in visual preference of home-reared and institutionally-reared children for a concentric over a linear arrangement of line segments. (From Fantz and Nevis, 1967.) Reprinted by permission of the authors and the *Merrill-Palmer Quarterly of Behavior and Development.)*

tion abilities. Over the first few months of life, infants can combine features and the relations between them so as to be able to discriminate and recognize global forms and patterns. Kagan suggests that this integration results in a mental representation of the pattern, called a *schema*. Such schemata underlie recognition ability because whether a pattern is recognized depends on whether it matches a schema for the pattern that the child possesses.

This representation can become more veridical as more experiences are assimilated into it. According to Kagan, maturational processes exist that result in more elaborate schemata being built up. As a schema is developed (such as for a particular pattern), the infant searches for patterns that are discrepant from the established schema. Patterns that differ from the schema elicit greater attention from the child than do totally familiar patterns. Thus, the child selects experiences that allow him to learn the range of differences that exist among patterns and to construct more elaborate representations of the world. At any point, the nature of the schema determines which experiences a child will select, and these experiences affect the further refinement and elaboration of schemata.

PATTERN PERCEPTION IN OLDER CHILDREN AND ADULTS

The fact that there is a maturational basis for some aspects of pattern perception and that discrimination and recognition abilities develop within the first years of life poses a difficult theoretical question. The processes involved in pattern perception involve feature analysis, comparison, and storage. The performance of infants shows that these processes are available to infants. Since the ability to compare and store features is present, and since the physical characteristics of patterns do not change with the child's age, how could pattern perception change in later childhood? In other words, if both the same physical patterns and the same processes are available to children at different ages, how can we account for changes in perceptual ability after infancy? Gibson (1969) has addressed this question in her theory of perceptual learning. Since the stimulation provided by the environment is constant over age, perceptual change must involve changes in the organism's ability to extract information from stimulation.

Discrimination

Because discrimination requires that a subject make comparisons of the features in a pattern, there are at least two ways that perceptual change could occur. First, the comparisons that are made could become more efficient—that is, more features could be compared in a given time. Second, the comparison process could become more systematic—that is, discrimination could proceed from a random comparison of different features to a systematic, pair-by-pair comparison of features. Both of these changes occur in the course of perceptual development.

An experiment by von Mickwitz (1973) shows that feature comparison becomes increasingly efficient in discrimination. She analyzed children's performance according to the amount of time taken to discriminate unfamiliar patterns. Unfamiliar letters were used to test the discrimination ability of elementary school children. Pairs of letters were presented on cards, and the children were asked to sort the cards on the basis of whether the letters were identical or not. In addition, the letters were paired in one of two ways, as shown in Figure 7–4. One group of children sorted letters that differed only in one feature (distinctive feature condition). The other group sorted letters that differed on three or more features (maximal difference condition).

Two findings of this study demonstrate that the comparison process children use in discrimination influences the amount of time taken to differentiate between patterns. First, letter pairs that differed greatly should be easier to discriminate than those that differed only slightly. For a pair of patterns to be seen as the same, all features must be compared and found identical. For a difference between patterns to be seen, only one difference between the two patterns need be found. Since in the maximal difference condition, patterns differed in at least three ways, it

Figure 7–4

Stimuli used in the discrimination experiment of von Mickwitz: Upper letters paired for maximal similarity, lower letters paired for maximal difference. (After von Mickwitz, 1973.)

should be easier to discriminate these patterns from one another than to discriminate the distinctive feature patterns. The results substantiated this hypothesis. Both first- and fifth-grade school children found the maximally different stimuli easier to discriminate than the distinctive feature stimuli.

The amount of time taken to sort the stimuli and the improvement that occurred with practice are significant. The children tested were given twenty-six identical pairs and twenty-six different pairs of letters to sort. The amount of time taken to sort these letters was recorded, and the children were asked to sort through them again. After the second sort, a third sort was asked for. Analysis of the times taken to discriminate the items in a pair showed a substantial effect of practice. The amount of time taken on the first sort was substantially longer than the amount taken on the second sort, which in turn was significantly longer than the time taken on the last sort. The amount of time necessary to discriminate between the pairs of letters decreased even with this small amount of practice. Since the feature comparisons that were necessary in discrimination were the same across the three practice trials, the data indicate that practice affected the amount of time needed to compare each pair of patterns to determine their similarity or difference.

In addition to this improvement in the child's ability to make comparisons within a certain period of time, other changes occur in the course of perceptual development. Gibson, Gibson, Pick, and Osser (1962) have suggested that one such change involves learning the characteristics of a pattern that must remain invariant for similar patterns to be classed as identical. For example, if a child is to determine whether two patterns are identical, feature comparisons must be made. However, certain discrepancies between patterns may be tolerated, and others not. Gibson et al. attempted to determine which feature differences were important in children's discrimination, and how the ability to detect invariant features of patterns changed with age. To do this, they constructed a set of line patterns that could be manipulated in a variety of ways. Twelve such patterns were constructed, and each pattern was accompanied by a set of twelve transformations in which certain features of the original pattern were altered. Figure 7–5 shows the stimuli that were used in the experiment and the transformed stimuli.

In the first three transformations, a line in the original pattern was changed to a curve. In the next five transformations, the original pattern was rotated or reflected. In the next two, the pattern was slanted or tilted. In the last two transformations, lines were added (the pattern was closed) or deleted (a break was introduced into the pattern). The experiment was concerned with how well children could discriminate the original pattern from its various transformations. One of the standard patterns was selected, and subjects were asked to indicate which of the patterns in that row were exactly the same as the standard pattern. Of particular interest are the confusions that the children made between patterns in the transformation group and the standard. Gibson et al. found that the total number of confusions decreased as the subjects' age increased. Younger children made substantially more confusions than did older children. Thus, a developmental trend in children's ability to discriminate between patterns that differed in specifiable ways was observed.

Of even more interest is the relationship between specific kinds of pattern transformations and children's confusions. Not all the transformed patterns were equally confusable. Figure 7–6 shows the differences in errors that subjects made with different transformations. Transformations that involved a slanting or tilting of the pattern (perspective changes) were highly confused with the standard by all the children. Fewest confusions resulted from the introduction of a break or close in the standard. The rotational and reversal transformations and the line-to-curve transformations fell between these two extremes; the number of errors that occurred with these conditions decreased with age of the subjects.

This finer analysis of the confusion errors that were made suggests something about the kinds of changes that occur in the subject as a result of increased experience with patterns. First of all, older children are capable of making more accurate feature comparisons. That is, similar

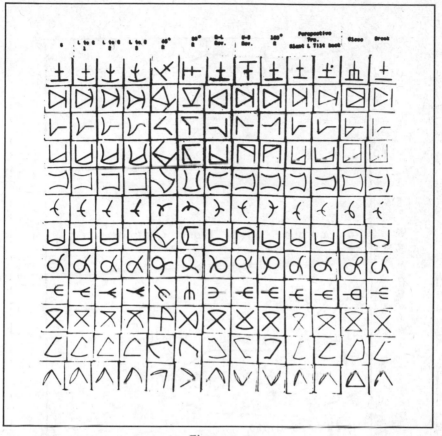

Figure 7–5

Twelve simple patterns and the twelve transformations of each constructed by Gibson, Gibson, Pick, and Osser. (From Gibson, Gibson, Pick, and Osser, 1962. Copyright © 1962 by the American Psychological Association. Reprinted by permission.)

patterns result in fewer confusions with older children than with younger ones. In addition, the reduction in confusion errors is related to the types of transformations that are seen. Gibson et al. explain this relationship by pointing out the connection between these transformations and shape invariance in the world. Stated differently, the child learns which of the transformations do not affect the nature of the pattern and which do. For example, certain transformations such as slanting the pattern do not affect pattern identity. Consequently, stimuli that vary in perspective are not seen to be significantly different from the standard pattern. Other changes in pattern, however, are crucial. Eliminating one component of the pattern, as in the break transform, or adding an extra component, as in the close transform, changes the nature of the pattern. Children are able to detect and compare these important features for discrimination.

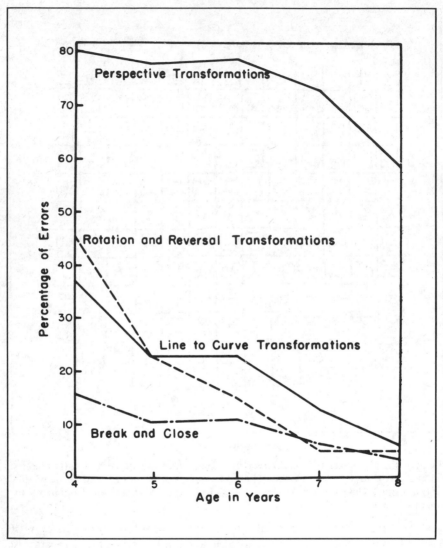

Figure 7–6

Confusion errors for four types of transforms as a function of age. (From Gibson, Gibson, Pick, and Osser, 1962. Copyright © 1962 by the American Psychological Association, Reprinted by permission.)

Other kinds of changes in the patterns are important only within a specific context. For example, a reflection of an object or pattern in the world does not alter its identity with another pattern. A face is still the same face whether it is seen in its true orientation or reflected. Since this transform does not influence pattern identity for objects, young children confuse patterns that vary in these ways. As a child gets older, however, the influence of rotations and reversals becomes more important. In learning to discriminate letters, for example, identity is affected by rotation and reversal. Both of these feature alterations must be attended to in order to distinguish between letters b and d, or p and q. The child's experience with patterns in reading or letter identification results in a change in the kinds of transforms that may be considered to be permissible. As the age of the children increased, the salience of the rotation and reversal transforms increased, and fewer confusions were made among patterns that differed in these ways.

The Gibson et al. study points out that a developmental change that takes place in pattern perception ability is a change in the variations among patterns that are seen to influence identity. As the child gets older, he learns which of the pattern features must remain invariant for pattern identity to exist, and which types of changes do not affect identity. The improvement that takes place in pattern discrimination in later childhood involves two perceptual changes: the abstraction of pattern features that are invariant, and increasing efficiency in making comparisons of features of patterns.

There is yet another way in which discrimination errors can occur and, consequently, a further change that could occur in the development of pattern discrimination. Consider a pair of patterns to be distinguished by the child. Assume that we can specify what the features of the two patterns are, and that in both patterns there are ten potential feature differences (ten ways in which the patterns could be different). Let us take two patterns that are identical on nine of those features and different on only one of them. For a child to make an accurate judgment of the differences in the patterns, all ten features must be compared. If only half of the features are compared, there is a probability that the important feature difference will not be seen, and the patterns will be misperceived as being identical. One way that pattern perception may improve, then, is through an increase in the completeness of the comparisons that are made. There is evidence from several sources indicating that young children do not make a complete set of comparisons in discrimination and that older children and adults do.

One cause of this lack of completeness in feature testing seems to result from a bias in the young child's scanning of some features, but not others. Kerpelman and Pollack (1964) investigated children's ability to determine which of an array of shapes was identical to a standard shape. For four-, five-, and six-year-old children, they found that discrimination was easiest when the shapes differed in features that were at the bottom of the figures. Discrimination was much more difficult if the differences were in the center of the figure or at the top. This result suggests that scanning and comparison of the entire figure does not take place, but that only certain portions of the figures are compared. Similar evidence comes from the context of discrimination learning in children. Discrimination studies have found that children base their discriminations on the portion of the pattern that lies near the bottom. These findings show that not all feature comparisons are made by children in a discrimination task.

A further study by Vurpillot (1968) shows that the scanning and comparison strategies of children in a discrimination task change with age and become more complete and thorough. Vurpillot presented two "houses," each of which had six windows. Children between the ages of 2 and 9½ years were to indicate whether or not the contents of the windows in the two houses were identical. As the children were making these judgments, their eye movements were recorded to determine which portions of the displays they looked at and what comparisons were made. In the experiment the houses could be identical, or there could be one difference, three differences, or five differences between them. For accurate discrimination to occur, each window in one house would have to be scanned and compared to the corresponding window in the other house. Furthermore, if a judgment of difference can be made as soon as one of the feature differences is found, fewer comparisons should need to be made when five differences exist. More comparisons are needed when three differences exist, and still more with only one difference. All windows should be compared to determine if the houses are identical.

The results of the eye movement recordings indicate that the comparisons that young (2 to 4½ years old) children make are incomplete and unsystematic. With increased age, there is a definite change in scanning. For example, the accuracy levels of the youngest group of children were influenced by the number of feature differences that distinguished the two houses. As Figure 7–8 shows, the youngest group was likely to say that the houses were the same without comparing all windows. The accuracy of the oldest group, however, was not affected by the number of differences between the houses. This indicates that their comparisons were based on a more complete comparison of the houses. This conclusion is further supported by an analysis of the number of windows that were looked at in the period before judgment. For accurate judgments of identity to be made, all of the windows had to be scanned. For judgments of difference, the number of comparisons would be influenced by the number of differences that existed between the two displays (for example, fewest comparisons need be made to discriminate the houses that had five differences, since it would be easier to find a difference when five existed). As the second part of Figure 7–8 shows, the young children scanned the same number of windows regardless of the similarity of the houses. For the oldest children, the number of windows that were looked at was related to the number of differences that existed in the displays.

A third change that occurred in the development of scanning and pattern comparison involved the systematic nature of the comparisons. The most efficient strategy for determining the similarity or difference of a pair of houses would be to compare appropriate pairs of windows. For

Figure 7–7

Vurpillot's discrimination stimuli: a pair of identical houses and a pair of different houses. (From Vurpillot, 1968.)

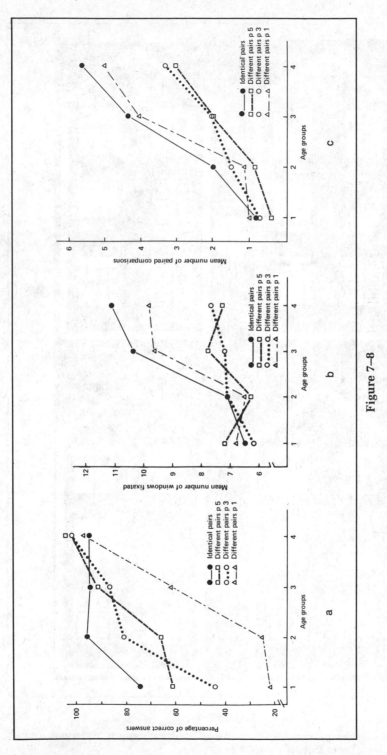

Figure 7–8

Developmental changes in discrimination: (a) percent correct, (b) number of windows fixated, (c) number of paired comparisons. The average ages of the groups were: Group 1, 3.1 years; Group 2, 5.0 years; Group 3, 6.6 years; Group 4, 8.9 years. (From Vurpillot, 1968.)

example, window 1 in one house would be compared with window 1 in the other house, and so on. From the third section of Figure 7–8, we can see that this systematic approach of comparing the displays is almost absent in young children. Regardless of the number of feature differences between patterns, the children below the age of 5½ years made few pair -by-pair comparisons. The oldest subjects were quite systematic in their scanning, and the number of paired comparisons was affected by the differences in the houses. When the houses were identical, the 9-year-olds made the six paired comparisons that would be necessary to determine identity. As the number of differences that existed between the houses increased, fewer paired comparisons were necessary for a difference to be observed and, in fact, fewer were made.

These studies show several changes that occur in the pattern perception processes of children. Although the feature analysis mechanisms that are essential for perception may be present from infancy, children must learn how to use these mechanisms efficiently. Some of the most important things learned in the course of pattern perception development are the ability to determine the invariant features of particular patterns and the permissible transforms of these features that still preserve pattern identity. The ability to make feature comparisons, to scan, and to compare patterns in a complete and systematic way are crucial aspects of development.

The end point of the development of these three discrimination abilities is demonstrated in the performance of adult subjects in simple discrimination tasks. Gould (1967) performed an experiment with adults, which is analogous to the type of study discussed above. A series of patterns was arranged around a single standard pattern in the center of the array. The adults were to indicate which of the patterns in the array were identical to the standard, and Gould recorded their eye movements as they made their comparisons. The scanning and comparisons were all found to be highly efficient and systematic. For example, a pattern in the array that was very different from the standard was looked at very little. The extreme difference that existed enabled the subjects to decide quickly that a pattern was not identical to the standard. As the patterns in the array were more similar to the standard, however, discrimination became more difficult, and a longer time was spent fixating them. These results agree with the developmental trends observed in the childhood studies. As the pattern perception processes of the child improve, the scanning and comparisons that are made become more efficient, and the comparisons made are related to pattern similarity.

Recognition

Since the processes involved in discrimination and recognition are very similar, we should expect that the changes observed in children's discrimination would also be present in recognition performance. That is, since the abstraction of features for recognition and the systematic exploration of a pattern in presentation both play a role in recognition, changes in recognition ability should reflect these factors. In addition, since there is a memory component to recognition performance, recognition may improve in development with the increased ability to store patterns in memory.

The evidence that we have in the development of recognition supports the first of these hypotheses. One of the earliest studies to show that the isolation and extraction of important features played a role in children's recognition performance was conducted by Gibson and Gibson (1955). Spiral patterns were devised to investigate the effect of practice on children's recognition. The different spirals could vary in several ways. For example, the number of coils could be changed, the compression or stretching of the spiral could be altered, and the direction the spiral faced could be varied from card to card.

Subjects were shown a standard pattern and told to remember what that pattern looked like. They were then given a deck of cards, each containing a spiral. The task was to select out of the deck only those cards that exactly matched the standard. To pick out only the cards that matched the standard, the subject would have to know that the standard consisted of four loops that had a specific amount of compression and that faced to the left. If all three of these attributes were not used in recognition, inaccuracies would result. If memory comparison between the standard and each card did not involve these three aspects, many spirals would be classed as the same as the standard. Such results were obtained for children six to eight years old, eight to eleven years old, and adults. Subjects at all ages made errors of recognition that involved incorrectly identifying a pattern as the same as the standard.

For correct recognition to occur, the subjects must refine the set of features used in recognition to include the three critical attributes of the pattern. In testing, it seems there were substantial differences in the way the standard pattern was stored for recognition. For example, the first time adults had to sort through all the cards and select those that matched the standard, they classed three different types of patterns as the same as the standard; eight- to eleven-year-olds classed eight as the same as the standard; and six- to eight-year-olds classed thirteen of the different items as the same as the standard. With experience, however, all subjects were able to restrict their stored set of attributes and become more accurate. After one trial through the deck of cards, the adults were able to recognize the standard and distinguish it from the other spirals. Eight- to eleven-year-olds restricted their set of features to the appropriate ones after 4.7 trials. The youngest children, however, were still confusing four of the classes in recognition after an average of 6.7 trials.

These results indicate two things about the nature of recognition and the changes that occur in recognition with experience. First, as a result of simple experience, the subjects were able to determine what the important attributes of the spirals were and to restrict their testing in recognition to these attributes. As more experience is gained with a set of patterns, the dimensions of difference can be better differentiated. Second, the different rates of improvement with age suggest that this process of differentiation improves with age. Older children and adults are able to pick up the important differences among patterns and use them in recognition much quicker than are young children.

This pattern of results again suggests a dimension of increased efficiency in the development of pattern perception. As an individual gets older and accumulates more experience, his ability to discover the variations among patterns improves. As a result of this improvement, the set of features or attributes that are stored in recognition is refined to the extent that it contains only those aspects of a pattern that are necessary for accurate recognition.

Another aspect of the change in recognition performance that occurs in development involves a change in the way patterns are examined in presentation. As in discrimination, young children seem to go through an incomplete examination of the figure that is to be recognized. When Zaporozhets (1965) monitored eye movements of children as they were learning the shape of a figure, he found large differences in the nature of the exploration that occurred. Figure 7–9 depicts some of these changes. As illustrated, the strategy used by children of various ages differed greatly. In three- and four-year-old children, the scanning movements in exploration were contained within the contours of the form. Eye movements were not numerous, and the duration of fixations between movements was longer than in older children. In children four to five years old, the pattern of movements changed, so that although the eye movements were still mainly within the contours of the figure, there was a greater number of movements. The time per fixation was correspondingly less, and the size dimension of the form seemed to be scanned. By the time children were six to seven years old, their eye movements scanned the outline of the form, tracing its contours.

These eye movement records show that there are different types of scanning strategies used by children at different ages. By themselves, these records do not tell us anything about the recognition capacities of these children. Since eye movements are not a sufficient basis for determining what features of a figure are being processed for subsequent recognition, some other measure of performance is necessary. Zaporozhets supplied this other measure in a recognition test, in which he found a clear relationship between scanning strategy and performance. The youngest children (three to four years old) made large numbers of errors of recognition. Fifty percent of the figures they were presented were inaccurately recognized. For the oldest group of subjects, their error rate was about 2 percent. The obvious implication from these results is that the accuracy of recognition over age is related to the thoroughness with which the pattern is scanned during presentation. Furthermore, scanning behavior changes with age, so that older children are more likely to examine a figure's contours than are younger children.

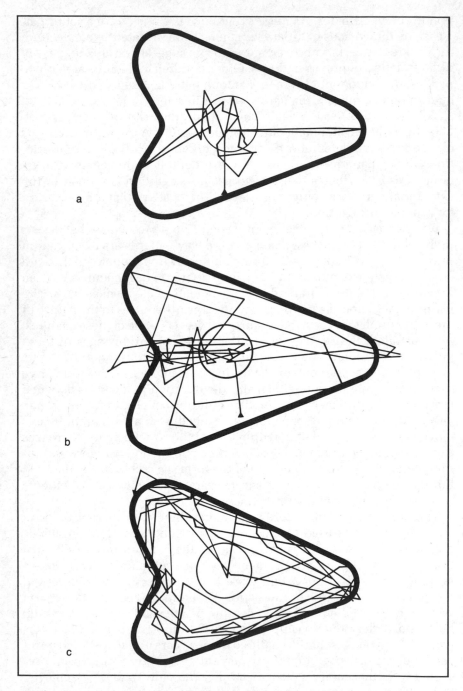

Figure 7–9

Samples of scanning eye movements of: (a) 3 to 4 year olds, (b) 4 to 5 year olds, (c) 6 to 7 year olds. (After Zaporozhets, 1965. Copyright © The Society for Research in Child Development, Inc. Reprinted by permission.)

Both the Gibson and Gibson and the Zaporozhets studies show that there are changes in the way children are able to abstract and examine the features of a pattern prior to recognition. These changes seem to be directly related to the subjects' age at the time of testing and are mirrored in the errors that are made during recognition. A further change that could accompany the changes in recognition performance in children would be increased capacity for retention.

Although we know that infants are able to recognize complex patterns by the time they are six months old, the limits of this ability have not been determined. There are indications, however, that recognition ability changes in slightly older children. Perlmutter and Myers (1974) studied the recognition memory of three- and four-year-olds. The children were shown a set of eighteen common objects and then asked to indicate which objects in a thirty-six-item test series they had just seen. Differences in the performances of the two age groups were found. The three-year-olds were able to recognize 81 percent of the test items, whereas the four-year-olds recognized 92 percent of them. A signal detection analysis revealed that this difference was due to differences in retention ability in the two groups. The capacity of the children to retain the objects in memory had changed.

By the time children are in elementary school, a brief (two-second) presentation of a pattern is sufficient for the recognition of large numbers of patterns. Rosinski (1970) presented first-, third-, and fifth-grade school children with up to ninety-six drawings of familiar objects and animals. In recognition testing, some of the stimuli in the presentation series were paired with new items, which had not been shown to the children. The children's task was to indicate which member of each test pair had been shown to them before. All children were able to do this with high levels of accuracy (about 85 percent). Furthermore, no differences were observed in the accuracy of the different age groups. Performance of first-grade children did not differ from that of the fifth-graders. In addition, the number of items presented in the experiment did not influence accuracy of recognition. At all grade levels, the percentage that was correctly recognized was approximately the same, regardless of whether thirty-two, sixty-four, or ninety-six items were presented. If there is a limit to recognition memory for patterns in children, it is beyond ninety-six items by the time children reach elementary school age.

Whatever recognition limits exist in adults, the number of different patterns that can be recognized is exceedingly high. In one experiment, Conezio, Haber, and Standing (cited in Haber 1970) presented 2,560 different pictures to college students over a four-day period. Recognition testing on this set of pictures revealed high levels of ability. Even though a huge number of pictures had to be remembered, accuracy was found to be about 90 percent. In adults, then, there may be no determinable limit to the number of patterns that can be recognized after a short exposure.

SUMMARY

Evidence from investigations of early pattern perception ability suggests that neonates may possess at least some of the feature analyzing mechanisms necessary for perception. However, these mechanisms appear to be unintegrated in the first few months of life. Several pieces of evidence indicate that specific organization of pattern components does not affect infant behavior until some time between the first and fourth month. Over this period, the organization of a pattern exerts an effect, and the infant is able to discriminate between patterns that are identical except in the structural organization of the components.

The strong maturational basis of early perception is further suggested by an examination of the preference behavior of premature and full-term infants. Visual preferences for particular features and developmental changes in these preferences have been found to be closely related to the postmenstrual age of the child rather than the postnatal age. This fact indicates that the physical maturation of the visual system plays a large role in early visual ability. Kagan has theorized that the changes that occur in infant attention and preference are part of a larger maturational sequence in which the infant comes to organize pattern components into a schema and then searches for experiences that are moderately discrepant from this schema. In this way, particular experiences elaborate and refine the existing schemata.

In older children, perceptual development involves a different set of principles. Although a young child is capable of making feature comparisons in discrimination, as he gets older these comparisons become more efficient. Children learn to make feature comparisons faster, in addition to learning which features of a pattern are crucial and which remain invariant over various transformations of the pattern. A further change that occurs in the development of pattern discrimination is that comparisons between patterns become more systematic with development. Although young children may scan in an almost random fashion, older children make increasingly systematic feature comparisons.

In recognition, it appears that children learn to attend to important aspects of a pattern and become more systematic in exploring novel ones. In addition, it seems that the capacity of the recognition system changes as well. Although we do not know the limits of recognition ability in infants, there are increases in capacity that occur in the preschool years. By the time an individual fully matures, his recognition capacity appears virtually unlimited.

Chapter 8

REPRESENTATIONS AND SYMBOLS

The preceding chapters have described general developmental characteristics of pattern perception. The notion of pattern has been very broadly defined in this context, referring to any two-dimensional display as a pattern. Whether photographs, designs, drawings, or geometric figures were used, studies were related to the general topic of pattern perception. Although such a general view is suitable for discussing the simple processes of discrimination and recognition, we can now present a more complete view that relates pattern perception to other aspects of perception and distinguishes between different aspects of pattern perception.

Patterns are often more than simple stimuli that we discriminate or recognize. As do other aspects of perception, the perception of patterns supplies the observer with knowledge about the world. That is, under some circumstances, patterns provide a source of stimulation that has meaning to an organism. An important distinction in pattern perception relates to the nature of this meaning. We know that some patterns provide stimulation similar to that received from an array generated by objects in the world. Photographs, for instance, can provide the viewer with knowledge about the world because they capture some essential part of the stimulation available from real objects and activities or settings.

Other types of patterns provide a different kind of knowledge. A passage of prose, for example, may give the reader very specific information. Yet, it does this in a way different from the perception of photographs. Knowledge is gained from reading because the reader has learned the arbitrary connections between marks on a page and what those marks mean. This distinction in the relationship between some patterns and their meanings is a way of separating different kinds of pattern perception. In this chapter, we will see that the development of perceptual ability differs depending on the relationship between the pattern and its meaning.

PICTORIAL PERCEPTION

Much of our perceptual experience involves pictures rather than actual things. These representations play a large role in the way we learn about the visual characteristics of many objects: a drawing of part of a town may be used to give travel directions; an advertisement may tell us what a product looks like; a photo of poison ivy may tell us what plants to avoid. The existence and pervasive use of this ability is so common and ordinary as to be almost unremarkable. All of us can look at a flat piece of paper covered with differently colored splotches and see a rolling landscape, or we can look at a pattern of lines on paper and see the face of a friend.

Yet, at one level this ability is rather extraordinary. A black and white photograph of a familiar scene can be recognized and identified instantly. But how is this possible? There are really few similarities between a black and white photo and the object it depicts. Colors are different; brightness relationships are changed; gradations of lighting are often blocked out; no binocular or motion-carried information indicates depth or shape; and the choice of lens or camera adjustment may, in fact, distort the real shape of the object. In spite of this, we perceive what is represented.

There are two vastly different theoretical attempts at explaining how we are able to perceive pictorial material. Each explains a different aspect of our ability to respond to pictures, and each deals with a different aspect of the function of pictures in perception. The first approach can be called a "communications theory of perception." It deals primarily with the fact that pictures have an ability to convey to a viewer an idea, an emotion, or a mood. This ability of pictures to be used as a communications medium has prompted some people (for example, Kepes 1945) to treat pictorial perception as a system of signs and symbols. In this context, perceiving and understanding a picture can be considered in the same way as understanding a language. Certain dimensions of stimulation are given an arbitrary meaning, and perceiving a picture consists of learning what connections between stimulation and meaning are appropriate in a culture.

Just as we must learn the arbitrary meanings that are assigned to sounds in language (*semantics*) and the organization of those sounds into meaningful sentences (*syntax*), so must the semantics and syntax of pictures and graphic design be learned. The development of pictorial perception, then, would consist of learning to interpret a visual display in ways that are consistent with cultural norms. Since different types of graphic design and different schools of art have different rules, effective communication depends on the viewer's knowing the specific conventions being employed.

Anyone familiar with graphic design or with different schools of painting would agree that learning to interpret artistic conventions plays a large role in understanding what is being communicated by a visual display. Many aspects of art (such as the use of symbols in surrealistic art) are unintelligible unless the specific artistic conventions are known. Many types of graphic design use standard symbols for visual communication, such as stick figures for people or word abbreviations on traffic signs. To some extent, it must be true that learning the meaning and permissible organization of artistic symbols is necessary for interpretation and, thus, communication. From the standpoint of perceptual development, however, little is known about the acquisition of this interpretive ability. Although most people do not learn the artistic conventions of a particular school of art until they have attended a fine arts course, this does not mean that the ability to learn is not present earlier.

A second approach to pictorial perception concentrates not on the interpretive and communicative aspects of graphic displays but on their ability to act as surrogates for the perception of the world (Hochberg 1962; Gibson 1966). This "surrogate" view attempts to explain how a picture can result in the perception of an object or of the layout of the world. Since much of the theoretical groundwork for this approach has been discussed in previous sections of this book, we can summarize the approach quite simply. As we have said at length, the ability to perceive objects, events, and the layout of the world is dependent on the pickup of certain kinds of stimulus information and on the stimulus-specific relations that exist between this information and perception. Consequently, the only way a picture could act as a surrogate for perception would be if it projected the same information to the eye as did the original scene. Thus, a picture of a landscape is perceived as a landscape because it projects some of the same information to our eyes as does the original scene.

This surrogate theory of pictorial perception leads to a number of specific perceptual and developmental expectations. First, since the perception of a picture depends on the congruence between the information available in that picture and the information contained in the original array, we should expect that as this congruence increased, perception of the thing represented should be more accurate. And, if the array from the picture closely matched that of the original scene, a picture of a scene should be indistinguishable from the real scene. Second, since a picture acts as a surrogate because of the information it contains, pictorial perception of representations should require no specific learning of symbols or their interpretations. If a child can pick up the information that specifies layout, for example, he or she should be able to do so regardless of whether the information arises from a photo or from the actual scene. Both of these expectations have been supported.

A third implication of this information-based theory of pictorial perception permits us to explain an individual's ability to perceive what is depicted in a representation even though the representation may not be very accurate. The crux of this theory is that the information projected to an eye is the stimulus determiner of perception. As long as appropriate information is picked up, a specific percept will result. This principle has far-reaching significance.

To act as a surrogate for perception, a representation need not provide a faithful reproduction of the original stimulus array. The actual array of light projected from a picture need not be identical or even similar to that projected from the real object for perception to occur. Consider for a moment what might happen if an individual viewed a high fidelity photograph from an appropriate station point. Under these conditions, there would be a great deal of similarity between the array that reached the eye from the photo and the array from the original scene. As the observer moves past the picture, the array reaching his eye would change. If the picture were viewed from a point far to the side, the array would be so distorted (geometrically) that it could never have arisen from the real scene. Yet, despite this distortion, the observer is still able to perceive what is depicted.

A second example illustrates this same point. Line drawings, even distorted ones such as cartoons, are easily recognized and identified. However, there is virtually no correspondence between the stimulus array from a cartoon and that from the real object. The conclusion drawn from these examples is that a point-to-point correspondence between a representation and what it represents is not necessary. As long as a representation provides the appropriate kind of information, a person can perceive what is being depicted. All three of these aspects of the information-based theory of pictorial perception have been supported with experimental evidence. The applicability of this theory can be shown in the pictorial perception of objects, spatial layout, and events.

Perception of Objects in Pictures

There are two important points to consider in examining the development of pictorial perception in children. Both are related to the two theories proposed above, and both involve the origin of pictorial perception ability. First, if the perception of pictures involves the pickup of stimulus information, then we should expect that the ability to perceive objects, layout, and events in pictures should follow the same developmental course as the ability to pick up such information in the real world. If a child is unable to use a particular kind of perceptual information until a given age, he should be unable to do so regardless of whether the information arises from an actual scene or from a picture of that scene.

Second, if pictorial perception simply requires the ability to pick up stimulus information, no specific pictorial training should be needed. When a child is able to pick up information for patterns and objects, he should also be able to do so when the stimulus is a picture. On the other hand, if a specific "language of art" must be learned, perception of representations should depend on the specific kind of training and experience a child is given. (Both these points have been explored in the context of the perception of pictured objects.)

As stated in the earlier discussions of the development of pattern perception, many investigators have used pictures, photographs, and graphic designs to study the perceptual ability of young children. Even neonates seem to respond differentially to pictures. This evidence, however, is not adequate to infer the existence of pictorial perception. Young infants are able to discriminate between two patterns, but can they perceive what is being represented in a picture?

Yonas (1973) examined this question using seven- to eighteen-week-old infants. In a preference situation, the infants viewed either a small bump or a small depression in a surface. After being habituated on one of these objects, their recognition ability was tested using photographs of the objects. If the infants were unable to perceive the objects depicted in the photos, we should expect that they would show no preference for either object in testing. If, on the other hand, they were able to recognize the pictured objects, a preference for the novel object should be observed. Yonas found that the infants preferred the novel object in testing, thus indicating that some degree of pictorial perception ability is present this early in infancy.

Studies by Fagan (1972, 1973) provide other evidence related to this question. Fagan was interested in determining whether four- to five-month-old infants are able to recognize an object in a photograph. Except in testing, the children never saw the picture of the object, they saw only the object. Recognition could occur only if the child were able to see what the photo depicted. Fagan habituated the subjects to a lifelike, three-dimensional mask of a face. In testing, a photo of this mask was paired with one of a group of different face masks (see Figure 8–1). Fagan found that the subjects were able to recognize the face on the basis of the photo.

Apparently, Fagan's choice of subject age in this study was appropriate for determining the initial point at which children are able to perceive representations. It is clear that between age four and five months marks an important point in the development of this ability. At this age, there appears to be a transition in perceptual ability. Some of the children were able to recognize a previously seen object from its representation, but others were not. Four to five months of age, then, may mark an

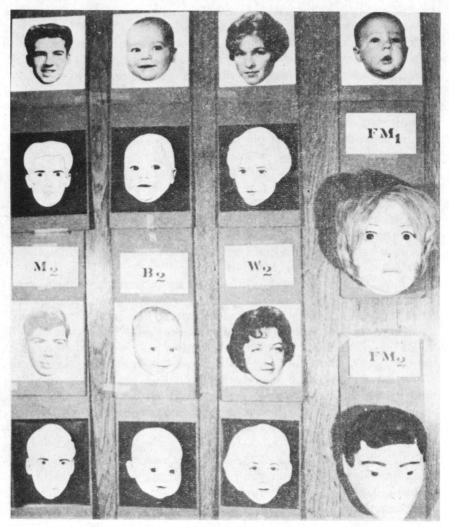

Figure 8–1

Face models and test stimuli used in investigating infants' pictorial recognition ability. (From Fagan, 1972.)

early stage in representational perception, when children are able to pick up pictorial information about some objects.

This conclusion holds only when photographs are used as the representational medium. The ability to perceive faces when represented by line drawings rather than photos appears later. In another study, Fagan examined the ability of four- to five-month-old infants to discriminate line drawings of faces. These drawings consisted of tracings of the photos used in the previous study. None of the infants was able to recognize the line drawings of faces. This result seems to indicate that the pickup of information for line drawings takes longer to develop.

It could be argued that the difference Fagan found between the ability to perceive photos and line drawings was a result of the experience infants had with the two stimuli. A photo is very similar to an actual object: both project somewhat similar arrays to the eye and, consequently, could be expected to give rise to the same percept. A line drawing, on the other hand, is much less true to life. After all, there are few similarities between a drawing and what it represents, since the edges, contours, and boundaries of objects are not marked by heavy black lines. Since a line can represent all of these features of an object, the specific relationship between a line and what it specifies in a drawing might have to be learned. Such a viewpoint is plausible, and if true would argue against the information-based theory of pictorial perception. The argument would show that lines do not provide information but must be interpreted.

An experiment by Hochberg and Brooks (1962) is addressed specifically to the question of whether it is necessary to learn to perceive representations by associating a picture with what it represents. One child was raised with little experience with pictures and no training with pictures. His entire vocabulary was acquired by naming solid objects. He was never told the name of a picture or depicted object, nor was he allowed to view television. In general, pictures and drawings were kept away from him. This absence of training with pictures was maintained until the child was nineteen months old. In subsequent testing, the child was shown photographs and line drawings of familiar objects. With almost all of the stimuli (see Figure 8–2), the child was able to identify both the photographs and the line drawings even though he had never been trained to do so. These results strongly argue against the view that there is a language of pictures that must be learned before representations can be perceived. Since the child in the Hochberg and Brooks experiment never had training in identifying either photographs or line drawings, his ability to do so must have been based on something other than specific learning. The developmental processes involved in initially learning to identify the objects must have transferred to the representations of those objects. In the absence of training, then, information can be picked up from an object or from a photo or drawing that depicts the object.

Perception of Spatial Layout in Pictures

Since the pickup of stimulus information is necessary for perception to be mediated by a picture, visual displays must provide layout information for the perception of space. Because of its nature, a picture or photograph cannot provide any binocular or motion-carried information; only monocular information can be received. Consequently, a child who can use monocular information in perceiving depth should be able to do so regardless of whether the information arises from a picture. Based on these facts, pictures have often been used to determine the

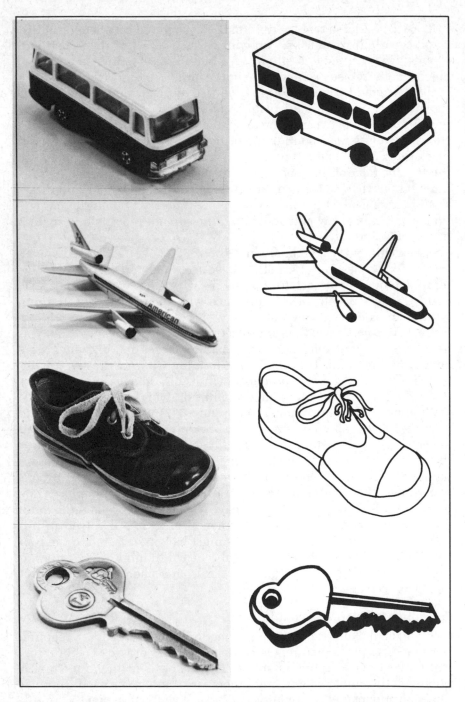

Figure 8–2

Photographs and drawings of the type used by Hochberg and Brooks. (After Hochberg and Brooks, 1962.)

development of monocular depth perception in children. Many of the studies discussed in Chapter Two can be directly related to pictorial perception in children.

From these studies described earlier, it seems that the perception of pictured space develops later than the perception of pictured objects. Space perception in young children cannot be mediated by pictures. You will recall that Bower (1965) trained fifty- to sixty-day-old children to respond to a cube placed three feet away from them. When the size and the distance of the cube were specified by motion parallax, the children responded correctly. However, when the cube was represented by a photograph, the children gave no indication that they were able to perceive size or distance in the picture. Benson and Yonas (1973) have shown that at least by the time a child is three years old, he can correctly perceive size relations in pictures.

The ability to use monocular information available from pictures improves for several years after birth. Wohlwill (1965) asked children to judge the distance of objects based on the texture gradient information present in a photograph. Although first-graders were able to make these judgments, Wohlwill found that the ability to use texture information in pictures improved with age. Similarly, Rosinski and Levine (1976) found that when slanted surfaces were projected on a screen, the children's ability to perceive the slant improved with age. Although first-grade children could use the pictured information for their judgments, accuracy was greater for older children. Both of these studies indicate that the ability to use monocular texture information in pictures develops over several years.

As the ability to use pictorial information for the perception of spatial layout improves, so does the way in which pictures act as surrogates for perception. If the information from a picture is very similar to that of a scene in the world, pictures should be strikingly realistic. Under normal viewing conditions, an individual would never mistake a picture for a real object or layout. Since a picture provides only monocular information, binocular vision and motion parallax would immediately indicate that a flat picture rather than a three-dimensional layout were being seen. However, if the situation is arranged so that no binocular or motion-carried information is available, pictorially mediated perception may be indistinguishable from direct perception. In such a case, the picture may act as a true surrogate for perception.

When adults view a photograph of a room, the spatial layout of objects in the room can easily be perceived. The information generated by the photo is adequate to allow an observer to perform a variety of tasks that are dependent on space perception. For example, if subjects are asked to throw a ball so it will hit a target in the room, their tosses are quite accurate. In performing such an experiment, Smith and Smith (1961) found that their subjects made only very small errors of judgment. After the experiment, the subjects were shown the photographs used and asked if they recognized them. They were also asked whether there was anything unusual about the viewing conditions in the experiment. All of the subjects were able to recognize the photos as pictures of the experimental room, but apparently none realized that he had seen the pictures in the course of the experiment. Further, though the photos were achromatic, none of the subjects noticed anything unusual about what was seen in the experiment or realized that photos had been used in the experiment. The information for distance was so complete that the photos were able to act as complete surrogates for a real array, even to the point that the subjects thought they were looking at a real room rather than a photo.

We can conclude that the ability to perceive objects and space based on photographic representations does not take specific training and follows a course of development similar to that of nonmediated perception. This demonstrates that the pickup ability of stimulus information in pictures is a crucial aspect of pictorial perception. Some kinds of learning may be necessary for the perception of pictures. However, this learning is not specific to pictures but involves the pickup of stimulus information that specifies objects and layout.

Perception of Actions and Events in Pictures

The preceding studies in pictorial perception indicate that children are able to perceive representational photographs and line drawings as depicting actual objects and spatial relations. A question that has only recently been posed in this area is whether children are able to perceive actions and events on the basis of pictorial information. Do dynamic arrays generated by moving pictures provide information for event perception in the way that static arrays depict objects and space?

On intuitive grounds, we might suppose that they do. An artificial array could be constructed to be virtually identical to an array generated by a real event. Since the information contained in these two arrays would be highly similar, they should yield almost equivalent percepts. We might also expect that infants are able to perceive actions and events in moving arrays that are artificially generated. Most parents know that even young infants can be entertained by watching television. Children under a year old often pay close attention to action on a television screen.

Of course, there are several alternatives that could explain this behavior. Patterns on a screen may not be perceived as representations of actual things. Simply the movement of "strange" forms on the screen may be what is attracting the child's attention. Movement of form is an attractive stimulus for an infant. For example, some of the preference studies have used a kaleidoscope pattern to hold infants' attention between test trials. Moving forms on a screen may serve the same function, independent of representation.

One way to determine whether moving pictures are perceived as representing an action or event by children is to determine if characteristics of the action are differentiated. For example, if a child is able to distinguish between the cause of an action and the recipient of that action, he must be perceiving a directed activity.

Golinkoff (1975) has performed one of the earliest studies of this kind. The design and results of the experiment are rather complex, so they will only be briefly summarized here. Essentially, the experiment involved showing movies to infants between fourteen and eighteen months old, and between twenty and twenty-four months old. One sequence, for example, showed a girl pushing a boy; the subjects were shown this sequence six times. Then another sequence was shown, which depicted the boy pushing the girl. Other control conditions were introduced. For example, at one point the change might involve the boy pushing the girl in a new direction. The amount of time the subjects spent looking at the sequences was recorded. The interesting question is whether the children's differential attention was affected by the changes that occurred between the two sequences; in other words, whether they were able to notice and respond to the changes.

Consider two possible ways in which this experiment might have turned out. If the children were unable to perceive the activity occurring on the screen but saw only moving shapes, we should expect that they would respond to differences in position of the shapes or direction of the action, but not to differences in the activity itself. If, in contrast, the subjects could perceive that a specific action was taking place, their responses should indicate that changes in this activity were noticed. The results suggest that this latter alternative is true. For both age groups, the change in activity influenced behavior more than did a simple change in position or direction. These infants were apparently able to differentiate between representations of two similar events—a boy being pushed by a girl and a girl being pushed by a boy. The event itself was perceived, and the children were able to differentiate between the initiator of the action and the recipient of that action.

The studies of Fagan (1972) and of Hochberg and Brooks (1962) show that photos and drawings can act as perceptual surrogates for real objects. Golinkoff's study extends this by showing that infants are able, on the basis of pictorial information, to perceive these objects taking part in specific activities.

Young children are able to perceive objects, spatial relations, and events in pictures because the representations provide appropriate information. When the child learns to use this information under normal circumstances, this ability transfers directly to perception of representations. There are some forms of representation, however, that do not depend on the same information as does perception of the three-dimensional world. In some cases, arbitrary symbols or clues may be used to convey a meaning. Since these symbols are arbitrary, pictures containing them cannot act as surrogates for perception of the world.

Under conditions using arbitrary symbols, we should expect that perception of what is depicted would depend on learning the meaning of the symbols. Friedman and Stevenson (1975) have shown that the ability to understand the use of symbols in pictures changes over development. Consider the problem of depicting motion in a drawing. Since motion occurs over time, a static drawing cannot provide information for movement. Instead, motion must be symbolized. Two common ways to do this are to provide multiple body parts symbolizing successive "snapshots" over time or to extend a group of lines from the subject to indicate that it is moving. (See Figures 8–3a and 8–3b for examples of these two symbols.)

When Friedman and Stevenson presented such drawings to kindergarten and first-grade children and to college-aged adults, they found some interesting differences. Subjects were asked to classify such drawings according to whether the object was moving. For patterns such as those shown in Figure 8–3a, all the children and adults said that the figure was moving. This indicates that by four or five years of age, children have learned the relationship between this symbol and depictions of motion. For the cue in Figure 8–3b, however, there were marked differences. Although the majority of adult subjects classed this drawing as depicting motion, few of the children did so. This particular symbolization is learned at a later age than is the other.

From the available work on children's perception of pictures, we can conclude that a communications theory and a surrogate theory of picture perception explain different aspects of the development of perception. When pictures provide information of the same type that is present in the array from the world, picture perception is based on the development of

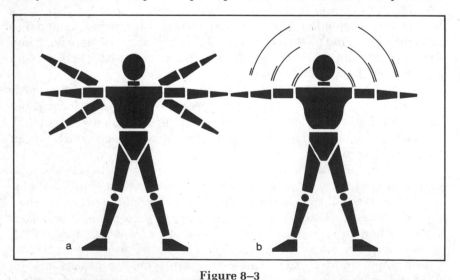

Figure 8–3
Symbolic representations of movement. (After Friedman and Stevenson, 1975.)

the ability to use such information. When a picture uses arbitrary symbols to depict something, picture perception is based on learning the symbolic system.

PATTERN PERCEPTION AND READING

One of the most complex kinds of symbolic learning is learning how to read. Compared to other perceptual tasks that children learn, reading is many times more difficult. The facility for recognizing a set of novel patterns is developed within a few months after birth; gross features can be discriminated and stored even by young children. However, the rudiments of reading take years to learn.

Part of the difficulty in learning to read is the lack of similarity between reading and other pattern perception tasks. A child can judge distances, recognize faces, and locomote using few of the processes essential for reading. After years of being an active independent perceiver, the child is faced with a task unlike any other. Previously, even very different patterns could correctly be judged to be the same. Many changes can be made in the appearance of a person without affecting perception of that person. For example, gross changes in clothes, hair style, eyeglasses, and so forth can all be ignored when recognizing or identifying an individual. Yet, relatively trivial changes in a word or letter completely change pronunciation, meaning, and use. The presence of a single line changes pop to pep, or slam to clam. New pattern features must be attended to.

Another novel aspect of reading compared to other forms of recognition involves the orientation of patterns and components of patterns. With almost all other patterns, orientation is irrelevant. Mother is the same person when seen from the left, right, or front. The family auto is the same car whether seen from the side, front, or rear. In reading, however, a whole set of patterns must be learned that differ mainly in orientation. The orientation of letters and their arrangement into words are the only features that determine whether we have read or written bob, pop, dop, or bop. Clearly, learning to read involves learning a new set of pattern features and a new strategy of attention.

In addition to these relatively obvious perceptual problems, reading also involves a set of complex relationships between perception and other cognitive abilities. For a reader to extract meaning from printed text, he must be able to recognize the words. He must be able to retrieve the meaning of those words from memory and determine how the meanings are modified by context. Further, he must be able to pull out the relationships between words given by syntactic structure and then relate all this to what he already knows about the subject. Each pattern must be related to an acoustic pattern (the pronunciation of the word), a semantic category (the word's meaning), and a syntactic category (the role the word plays in language).

All these different processes required in reading clearly involve several components. Reading involves language, attention, motor ability, various kinds of memory, text organization, and mental imagery. Many of the components are interrelated. As we shall see, the pronounceability of a word influences its perception, as do the meaning and structure of the sentence in which the word appears. In the following discussion, we will concentrate on the perceptual changes that occur in reading and learning to read. Discussions of other aspects of the reading process may be found in Gibson and Levin (1975).

Perception of Letters

A logical place to begin to consider the development of reading skills is with the perception of letters. Western languages are based on alphabetic writing; that is, only a small set of individual patterns is necessary to write any word in a language. This has obvious advantages. Once a small set of letters has been learned, totally new words can be read. Every new word does not have to be learned individually, as in some *ideographic* writing systems. If reading involves putting together different letter units into words, the ability to differentiate these letters must occur first.

Unfortunately, little is known about the ability of very young children to perceive letters. We might infer that the features that distinguish among letters would seem to have some things in common with features of other patterns. Lines, curves, number of elements, all play an important role in making up a letter. We know that even very young infants possess the ability to discriminate among patterns that differ based on these features. It is an intriguing possibility that all the perceptual features necessary for the identification of letters are available to a child long before he begins to read, perhaps even in infancy. Learning to identify letters, then, may involve learning to attend to specific combinations of features that have been discriminable since birth.

We know that children are able to discriminate between letters and other patterns before they learn to read and write. Lavine (cited in Gibson 1970) presented preschool children with a set of drawings, scribbles, and written words. She found that by the time her subjects were four years old, they were able to distinguish among the three categories of stimuli and correctly identify them. Preschool children are able to correctly discriminate letters from nonletters.

How does the ability to discriminate letters develop? From the discussion of pattern perception, we might suspect that distinctive features of a letter are involved. Gibson has done much to investigate this hypothesis, and her work demonstrates that both children and adults distinguish among letters on the basis of sets of features that form unique clusters for each letter of a set. Children and adults were asked to make same–different judgments of pairs of capital letters. A pair of letters was projected on a screen, and the subject was asked to indicate whether the two letters were identical or different. The amount of time taken to make this decision for each pair was measured (Gibson, Shapiro, and Yonas, cited in Gibson 1970).

These judgments of similarity and difference yielded a pattern of responses that could be used to determine the "confusability" of certain letter pairs. According to feature testing theory, the more similar two letters are, the longer a subject should take to discriminate between them. Conversely, if two patterns are very dissimilar, they should be discriminated quickly. Response latencies were subjected to a statistical analysis, which revealed the features underlying the subjects' discrimination ability. Figures 8–4a and 8–4b show the organization of features for both adults and seven-year-olds.

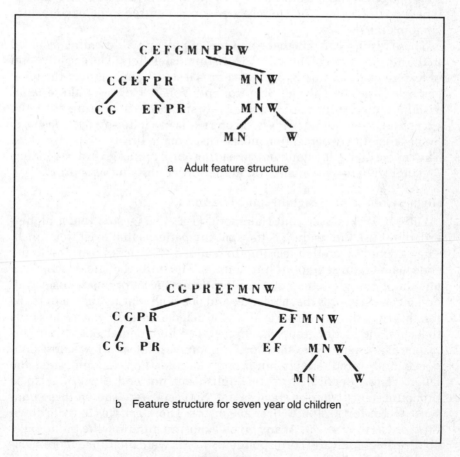

a   Adult feature structure

b   Feature structure for seven year old children

Figure 8–4

Feature hierarchies used by adults and by seven-year-olds in a letter discrimination task. (After Gibson, 1970.)

In the adult data, it appears that the tests that distinguished among the letters in the set involved differentiating diagonal letters, then curved versus straight letters, then angular letters with loops from angular letters without loops. The feature structure of letter discrimination was quite similar for the seven-year-olds, however several differences were apparent. With children of this age, straight versus curved was the first feature distinction made. At the second level, curved letters were split into round and looped, and straight letters separated on the basis of right angle versus diagonal.

Although only a small set of nine Roman capitals was used in this experiment, the results show clearly that letters are distinguished on the basis of specific sets of distinctive features. Furthermore, there seems to be a change over age in the order in which feature tests are made. Gibson et al. suggest that children do a sequential processing of features, whereas adults may come to rely more on structured, organized feature combinations.

These results indicate that some sort of perceptual learning occurred in the development of the ability to distinguish letters. The organization of feature tests, and perhaps the features tested, changed over the wide age span used by Gibson, Shapiro, and Yonas. However, these latter discrimination abilities play a relatively small role in reading. With the exception of beginning readers, no one reads in a letter-by-letter fashion. Some other unit of perception must be used in reading by skilled readers. The course of the development of reading ability must go from a reliance on single letters to a reliance on higher-order units in perception.

Higher-Order Units—Bigrams and Trigrams

Gibson, Pick, Osser, and Hammond (1962) suggested that a higher-order unit used in reading is the spelling patterns that exist in English. They hypothesized that learning to read may consist of learning to decode visual representations into sounds. The units that are decoded are not simply single letters of a written language but consist instead of organized structures that are larger and of a higher order than letters. To test this hypothesis, Gibson et al. constructed a series of nonsense words that contained letter groups having either a high degree of spelling correspondence (and were therefore pronounceable) or a low correspondence (and were therefore not pronounceable). For example, since the letters *gl* can begin a word in English but not end a word, *glasp* is pronounceable, whereas *spagl* is not. Subjects were shown these nonsense words for 50, 100, 150, or 250 msecs. Their task was to write down the word as they saw it. At any given exposure duration, the pronounceable (orthographically correspondent) words were identified more accurately than were the unpronounceable ones.

Why might such results be obtained? Assume for the moment that bigrams that followed English spelling patterns come to function as units in word perception. In a word that is unpronounceable, each letter must be functioning as a unit. Consequently, in a six-letter word, six individual units must be processed for the entire word to be perceived. In words in which bigrams (letter pairs) can function as the unit of word perception, fewer units (fewer bigrams) must be processed. Since fewer perceptual units are involved in pronounceable words, more of the word can be correctly identified during a brief exposure.

Gibson, Osser, and Pick (1963) extended this experiment to investigate the use of spelling to sound correspondence with first- and third-grade children. Three-letter words (put), pronounceable trigrams (tup), and unpronounceable trigrams (ptu) were presented for 40 msecs. Accuracy levels of third-grade children were consistently higher than those of first-graders. Of more interest, however, is the fact that words were correctly read more often than pronounceable trigrams, which in turn were read more correctly than unpronounceable trigrams. These results suggest that the use of spelling patterns as higher-order units in word perception occurs even in elementary school children. Processing units are organized on the basis of spelling correspondence.

Gibson et al. found also that with larger words of four and five letters, first-graders were unable to use orthographic structure in word perception. With words of this length, pronounceability did not affect the accuracy of perception. This result could occur because first-graders had not yet learned English spelling patterns.

Rosinski and Wheeler (1972) tested this hypothesis. Correspondent and noncorrespondent words were paired and printed on a card. First-, third-, and fifth-grade children were asked simply to indicate which of the two "was more like a word?" Using this procedure, no effect of word length was found. First-graders performed virtually at chance, indicating that words could not be discriminated on the basis of English spelling patterns. For third- and fifth-graders, such ability was present since their performance was significantly above chance.

It seems clear from these studies that children come to extract the orthographic structure of English in the course of learning how to read. When this ability develops cannot be answered conclusively at this time, but there is some indication of the developmental course that extraction of spelling patterns takes. The study by Rosinski and Wheeler tested children in the beginning of the school year and found that first-graders were unable to use orthographic structure in word discrimination. Some of the children were retested a year later (at the beginning of second grade) and were still found to be unable to use spelling patterns to discriminate words. In an extension of this study, Golinkoff (1974) used a similar task with second-graders at the end of their school term and found that these children were able to discriminate between words that did or did not follow English spelling patterns. Although the results of these studies must be regarded as tentative, the implication is that the use of spelling pattern clusters becomes an effective means of discriminating pseudowords at some time during the second grade.

If spelling patterns function as units in the perception of words, it is worth considering how perceptual processes might operate on these units. The first possibility involves the way words are segmented and taken into the perceptual system. When a word is seen, it may be broken up into spelling pattern units. Such segmentation would break a word into the largest possible units that the child could use. The segmentation of spelling pattern units must involve the position of the pattern in a word. Since a bigram that appears at the beginning of a word could function as a unit (for example, gl), but would not at the end of a word, segmentation must depend on location.

Once such segmentation has occurred, the unit may be analyzed by means of some feature testing scheme. For example, a skilled reader may have a feature hierarchy that can be applied to the cluster gl when it occurs at the beginning of a word. Then the entire spelling pattern, rather than just the individual letters, is differentiated by the feature tests. This would suggest that the feature test hierarchy would also be influenced by the position of the bigram in a word, since the occurrence of a spelling pattern is a function of its position. That is, there should be feature tests for certain bigrams that are specific to certain locations in a word.

In the original work by Gibson, Pick, Osser, and Hammond (1962), the authors suggested the possibility that spelling patterns come to function as units in perception because of their correspondence with sounds. It has been argued, however, that the ability to detect the correspondence between spelling and sound patterns is not a necessary aspect of this process. The perceptual advantage of letter combinations that follow English spelling patterns may result from visual familiarity rather than acoustic correspondences. Aderman and Smith (1971) point out, for example, that the pronunciation of a word must follow its perception, so that letter combinations must be learned before the correspondence with sound is noticed. Since the sound pattern follows the perception of a word, it could not affect initial perception.

To determine whether the extraction of spelling patterns requires experience with spelling-to-sound correspondences, let us look at the reading ability of the deaf. Gibson, Shurcliff, and Yonas (1970) investigated the ability of both deaf and hearing adult subjects to identify pseudowords. Pronounceable and unpronounceable pseudowords were tachistoscopically presented to these subjects for 100 msecs. The deaf subjects made more errors than did the hearing subjects, but in both groups, more of the pronounceable words than the unpronounceable ones were identified. The deaf subjects tested were congenitally deaf and had maximal hearing losses. Because of this severe hearing impairment, it is doubtful that the subjects had ever heard a spoken word. Therefore, they could not have experienced correspondences between the spelling patterns and their sounds. Yet, the results indicate that even deaf subjects use spelling patterns as perceptual units. Clearly, the correspondence between spelling and sound is not a necessary condition for the establishment of higher-order units in reading, since deaf subjects have also formed units based on spelling patterns.

Although spelling-to-sound correspondence is not a requirement for learning spelling patterns in reading, it is possible that children initially learn these patterns on the basis of sound correspondence. Continued experience with pronouncing words while looking at them, or hearing the teacher pronounce a word while the child looks at it, may emphasize the relationship between spelling and sound and draw the child's attention to this relationship.

Higher-Order Units—Words

The existence of bigram spelling patterns is not an adequate explanation of a skilled reader's perceptual abilities. Reading does not consist simply of stringing together spelling patterns into words and phrases. Segmentation and analysis must proceed on the basis of larger units than letter pairs. A clear demonstration of this fact has been provided by Hochberg, Levin, and Frail (cited in Hochberg 1970). Two kinds of texts were constructed. In a normal version, spaces were left between words. In a filled version, spaces were filled with a symbol consisting of an "x" superimposed on a "c" (**x**). One group of first- and second-graders and a second group of fifth- and sixth-graders were asked to read the passages, and their reading speeds were recorded. Hochberg et al. hypothesized that beginning readers, since they are reading on the basis of individual letters or bigrams, should be relatively unaffected by filled-in spaces between words. Older children, however, using words or phrases as units in reading, should read slower when spaces are filled. The results supported these predictions. Poorer readers showed little drop in reading speed as a result of the filled-in spaces. Better readers were slowed considerably in their reading.

Youxcanxgainxanxintuitivexappreciationxofxthisxresultxbyxcomparingxthextimexitxtakesxtoxreadxthisxsentencexwithxthextimex takenxwithxothers.

This example demonstrates one way a skilled reader segregates a passage of prose into units. The spaces between words can be picked up and used to determine the next word to be read. The fact that fifth-grade children were slowed in their reading indicates that they use blank space in this way. Our next question is how the words are processed in perception once they are isolated. Two alternatives can easily be ruled out. First, a reader could not identify each of the letters in the word and then string them together to form a word. A skilled reader reads much too fast for such a process to occur. If a word must be decomposed into individual letters, the letters subjected to a complete series of feature tests, and then recombined, reading would take much longer than it does. In addition, it has long been known that people do not perceive every letter in a word when reading. If the word *dangxr* is shown very briefly to a subject, he will report the word *danger*. The misspelling is not noticed (Pillsbury 1897).

A second, more common, example of this phenomenon is "proofreader's error." When you read through a paper for incorrect spellings, it is easy to miss these inaccuracies. As you read the words in the text, individual letters are not perceived, and spelling errors can go unnoticed. To proofread accurately, an unusual perceptual attitude has to be adopted. You must force yourself to pay attention to the letter sequences and to ignore the words and content. In fact, individuals who must pay close attention to spelling (for example, professional proofreaders and typists) often report that they "read" a long passage without knowing anything about the content. They read letters rather than words and meanings.

An alternative to letter-by-letter analysis of words is the analysis of the entire word as a unit. Just as an individual letter is perceived by the analysis of its features, one might suggest that feature networks develop for whole words. A set of feature tests might be set up, and each word would be identifiable on the basis of these tests. A five-letter word would be analyzed as if it were a single pattern. There are a number of objections that can be raised to such a scheme. To begin with, the total number of tests necessary to discretely classify every word in our sight vocabulary would have to be incredibly large. Even if each test eliminated half of the possible words, fifteen or sixteen individual tests would still be necessary to classify each word that was known, and each word would have a pattern of test results different from all other words.

In addition, if each word were treated as a separate pattern, the network of feature tests would have to be revised each time a new word was learned. That is, a set of feature tests would have to be constructed to differentiate that new word from all others in the vocabulary. Similarly, the perception of whole words as patterns would eliminate the advantages of an alphabetic writing system. If each word needed its own set of feature tests, unfamiliar words could not be read. Yet we are able to perceive unfamiliar ideographs and decipher their meanings from the context of the passage.

The actual way that a word is perceived in reading, then, must involve some compromise between these two extremes. Every letter cannot be analyzed separately, yet neither can every word be analyzed as a whole pattern. For the perceptual system to capitalize on alphabetic writing but not make all feature tests necessary for letter identification, word perception could rely on the redundancies of written language. A written word provides more information than is needed for its identification. For example, consider a word that begins with the letter *t*. A feature analysis may be done to determine the identity of that letter. A complete analysis of the second letter is unnecessary. In English, the letters *h, r, a, e, i, o,* and *u* are most likely to follow *t*. A small set of tests could then be done to determine which of these letters was present. Since the order of letters in a word is not random but follows certain rules, the number of feature tests necessary to identify a word is reduced.

Another way of stating this point is to say that the perceptual system generates a set of hypotheses in reading and analyzes the letters only enough to test these hypotheses. The generation of these hypotheses need not proceed from left to right in a word. Because the presence of certain letter combinations eliminates the possibility of other letters, some letter positions need not be checked at all. For example, if one saw the word thr__gh, the missing letters in the center need not be analyzed to read the word as *through*. Similarly if *thr* were seen, a number of hypotheses could be generated about the word, and analyzing the last letters could indicate which was correct. In this way, the number of analyses that need be performed to identify a word is greatly reduced, and many letters need not be feature tested at all.

A further kind of redundancy that reduces the perceptual processing necessary to identify a word comes from the context in which a word is found. If you are reading a passage about bank loans for houses, a word that begins with an *m* and has two *g*'s near the end is very likely to be *mortgage*. The context helps define a set of hypotheses that are appropriate, and little perceptual analysis is needed to confirm a hypothesis. Similarly, if in this passage on loans, we were to read that it is advisable to consult the vice-president of your local _____, then we would need only a small number of feature tests to verify that the last word is *bank*. A quick check that the first letter was *b* would be all that was necessary. The other letters in the word need not be read.

A perceptual system that read by using the redundancies of spelling and context to generate hypotheses would allow a substantial reduction in the number of analyses necessary in word identification. Furthermore, when feature tests or whole letters are omitted in reading, proofreader's errors are to be expected. In the last example, verifying the hypothesis that the last word in the sentence was *bank* might involve only a test for a closed loop at the bottom of the first letter; the other letters would not be tested. If the word were then misspelled as *benk*, the error would most likely go unnoticed.

The hypothesis testing notion of reading suggests that some part of a word is sampled, and then hypotheses are constructed and verified. What portions of the word might be analyzed first? The effect illustrated earlier of filling in the blank spaces between words in a text suggests that the area around these spaces may be important in guiding reading. Since the blank space between words clearly marks the beginning and end of a word, the first and last letters may be the first sampled. This appears to be the case with beginning readers. When children were asked to pick one nonsense word that most closely resembled a previously presented nonsense word, first-grade children relied most on the first and last letters of the word (Marchbanks and Levin 1965; Williams, Blumberg, and Williams 1970). Kindergarteners, however, showed no reliance on a particular position (Williams et al. 1970). It appears that even at the earliest stages of reading, systematic strategies emerge in discrimination.

SUMMARY

The perception of patterns that have representational or symbolic content is an important aspect of perceptual development. Pictorial patterns may be perceived because they give information of the same kind as that available from real objects and scenes. Two complementary viewpoints about pictorial perception can be applied to explaining development. First, since pictures project monocular information to the eye, this information can form the basis of perceptual ability. Second, since some representations are based on arbitrary conventions, these conventions must be learned for an individual to perceive what is depicted in the representation.

The evidence available indicates that much of the development of pictorial perception is based on the development of the ability to use monocular information in perception. By the time a child is four or five months old, he is able to recognize a picture of a face mask even though he has never seen that picture before, since his ability to perceive a three-dimensional model of a face transfers to a picture recognition task. We know from one case study of an infant that the ability to recognize and identify pictured objects does not depend on previous learning with pictures. A child who has never been exposed to pictures (or to very few) has been shown to be able to identify common objects in photographs and line drawings.

From the knowledge that infants respond little to pictured layouts that are specified totally by monocular information, we can conclude that the perception of pictured space must develop later than the perception of pictured objects. The ability to use such information improves over the preschool and school years. The ability to perceive certain events and actions specified by moving pictures is present in infants, so developmental differences in perceptual ability must be related to the ability to use static, monocular information. When events are specified by static arbitrary symbols, young children lack the ability to interpret these symbols.

One of the most complex forms of symbolic learning is learning how to read. Part of this complexity stems from the fact that reading involves not only the development of perceptual ability but also the development of cognitive, linguistic, motoric, and organizational abilities. Even from a purely perceptual standpoint, however, we can see a number of developmental changes in the ways that children treat letters and words. On the level of single letters, the nature and order of the feature tests employed by a child differ from those used by an adult. Further perceptual changes that occur involve the segmentation of symbols into larger and larger units. Perhaps because of the regularities that govern English spelling patterns, certain letter combinations clump together and are treated perceptually as single units.

Another form of segmentation involves the use of whole words as processing units. Early in the course of learning to read, children learn to extract word units by using the spaces that define them. In addition to this simple method for perceptually segmenting word units, a child must also develop strategies that allow him to read without perceiving every symbol set. By using the redundancies of spelling, grammar, and context, he can generate hypotheses about the nature of the text and verify these.

Chapter 9

GENERAL PRINCIPLES OF PERCEPTUAL DEVELOPMENT

Many changes in perceptual abilities occur over the course of development. In each of the areas of perception we examined in the preceding chapters, new skills emerge and existing ones are refined. Such changes are apparent even on a gross level of analysis. In the context of spatial layout perception, for example, monocular, static information is used little in infancy but comes to play a large role in perception in later years. Visual-motor coordination becomes increasingly accurate during the early years of life. In pattern perception, discrimination and recognition ability both become more efficient.

Our understanding of why these changes occur and why perceptual abilities become more accurate and efficient with increasing age and experience is very limited. Given the present state of developmental psychology and our knowledge about perception, speculations about the actual reason a sequence of changes occurs have little meaning and are often untestable. For example, the underlying causes of perceptual development might be sought in evolution and biology. We might hypothesize that humans have evolved by developing perceptual abilities when they are most needed. Since the protected human infant has little need for complex perceptual abilities, infants do not develop these abilities until later in life. Such an answer, however, tells us little. It says merely that development occurs because people have evolved to develop. Unless there is some way to determine the perceptual abilities that a child "needs" at a particular age and to determine the relationship between this "need" and the course of development, this hypothesis is empty of meaning.

A similar criticism can be made of attempts to explain developmental changes on the basis of perceptual motivation. We could hypothesize, for example, that development proceeds the way it does because it is controlled by an internal motive to gain as much knowledge as is necessary to perform a task. The task demands placed on the perceptual system change as the child matures. When a child learns to walk and run, accurate spatial vision is crucial; when he begins to read, efficient discrimination and identification are important. Simply describing these changes, however, does not demonstrate that there is a motivating force at their base. An independent definition and measurement of this motive must be available before such explanations are theoretically meaningful.

A third possible explanation of perceptual change might be found in the developing physiology of the child's brain. Perceptual change may be allied with specific neural changes. Pattern integration may develop as a result of changes in the connections between neural analyzers. On some level, this hypothesis must be true. Visual physiology is the foundation of visual perception. However, we know little about the relationship between physiology and vision, and we know almost nothing about the relationship between physiological change and perceptual change. Without such knowledge, even a physiological hypothesis has little theoretical meaning.

Any or all of these explanations of perceptual development may prove to be true. All of them are certainly useful. They serve to direct and define an approach to the question of why perceptual change occurs. Each suggests a set of variables—ecological, motivational, task, and physiological—that should be examined. However, these theoretical views cannot be evaluated at present. Not enough is known about the suggested causes of change to determine their effects on perception. The statement, for example, that neurophysiological changes underlie perceptual development must be true, but what does it tell us of the specific neurophysiological changes that accompany developmental changes?

Although we cannot describe the causes of perceptual development, we can describe the changes in perceptual processes that underlie development. Although we cannot determine as yet *why* certain changes happen, it is possible to describe *how* they happen. Since information pickup and utilization are two important aspects of perception, these processes would be expected to play a large role in perceptual development.

CHANGES IN INFORMATION PICKUP

A change in the ability to select information from available stimulation—that is, to direct attention to certain aspects of the world— is one way that perception could change in development.

Eye Movements

Since vision is a directional sense modality, a restriction on information pickup involves simply the ability to look in the right place. A preliminary way that attention can be directed and information selected is through the direction of eye movements. In children, the development of attention is evident in the development of their eye movements. With increasing age, there is a parallel increasing ability to direct the eyes and systematically sample portions of the visual world. Newborns possess what might be called an innate attentive ability. Even the youngest infant is able to direct his eyes in certain ways. This primitive attentional ability forms the basis for all of the preference experiments discussed in earlier chapters, however, it is refined with age.

Although young infants are able to control eye movements, these movements seem to be very restricted. Salapatek and Kessen (1966) presented newborn infants with a large, black triangle and recorded the children's eye movements as they looked at the display. The eye movement records of the children in this situation revealed two things. First, the eye movements often appeared to drift or dart around randomly with no apparent relationship to the figure or its contours. When directed eye movements to the figure were observed, they resulted in fixation of a particular stimulus feature, in this case, one of the angles of the figure. There was a substantial orientation to the vertices of the triangle and virtually no orientation to the contours. The infants seemed captivated by angles, and little sampling of the rest of the figure occurred.

In a further study, Kessen, Salapatek, and Haith (1972) evaluated infants' ability to scan contours. A single black-white edge was shown to newborn children, while eye movement records were taken. The presentation of a vertical contour had a pronounced effect on the infants' scanning behavior; their eyes moved to the contour and scanned it. When the same contour was presented in a horizontal orientation, no effect on the infants' behavior was observed; neither orienting to the contour nor scanning it occurred.

Although both of these studies show that infants have some ability to direct eye movements, little fine control seems to exist. The eyes appear to wander about until they are captured by a specific characteristic of the figure being scanned. The gross features of an angle or a vertical line are scanned, but other parts of the displays are not.

There have been few attempts to plot out the developmental course of eye movement control. The results obtained with infants, however, stand in sharp contrast to the eye movement patterns found with older children. The studies of Zaporozhets (1965) and Vurpillot (1968), discussed in Chapter Seven, are relevant here. In older children, the use of eye movement and scanning in exploring a pattern changes dramatically. As Zaporozhets has shown, the scanning patterns of the eyes become more closely related to the contours of the object seen, and exploration becomes more directed and systematic.

The nature of eye movement control in infants demonstrates a primitive restriction on the ability to pick up information. Obviously, information cannot be used in perception if it is not sampled. Developmental changes in eye movement patterns are directly related to changes in information sampling. However, increasing control of eye movements is not the only basis for attention. Even language makes the distinction between "looking at" something and "paying attention" to it. In addition to eye control, another process is involved in attention.

Selective Attention

Changes in information pickup occur independently of eye movements. If an experimenter is assured that a subject is looking at a particular portion of an array (by asking the subject to describe or to name it), differences in attention are still observed. Beyond the selective aspect of eye regard, some other internal process must operate to select certain aspects of stimulation. Furthermore, we know that children are capable of such selection, and that the ability to attend improves with age.

The basic paradigm for assessing attention is a simple one. If two stimuli are presented to a subject and he can report or respond to only one of them, selective attention is inferred. Using this simple paradigm, several experiments have found that the ability to select one aspect of stimulation relative to another improves with age. Gibson and Shepela (reported in Gibson 1969) found an age-related change in selective attention. They presented colored capital letters to five-year-olds and colored artificial letters to nine-year-olds. After several practice trials in which the subjects were trained to label the stimuli, the subjects were tested on their ability to label the stimuli when the color was removed and to report what color each form had been. Gibson and Shepela found that although both age groups were able to label the forms, younger children recalled many more of the colors than did the older children. Performance of the nine-year-olds was at chance, and some subjects could not even recall which colors had been used. Younger children noticed and remembered the nondistinctive characteristic of the letters (their colors), whereas older children were able to restrict their attention to the form and ignore the color.

Other studies have also found developmental increases in children's ability to focus attention. Maccoby and Hagan (1965) presented first-, third-, fifth-, and seventh-grade children with an array of picture cards, each with a distinctively colored background. Each picture was shown to the child and turned over serially. The subjects were instructed to remember the positions of the cards. In a central attention task, they were shown a colored chip and asked to point to the turned over card whose background color matched the chip. After a series of trials, the children were asked which picture appeared on each background color (an incidental, nonattended task). Maccoby and Hagan found that recall on the central task increased with age. Recall of the incidental material did not increase from grades one to five and decreased between grades five and seven. The ability to focus on the central task and ignore irrelevant material improved with age.

In a further study, Hagan (1967) used a similar procedure. A series of cards, each containing a line drawing of an animal and a household object, was presented to first-, third-, fifth-, and seventh-grade children. Each card was shown to a subject and laid down in a row. The children's central (attended) task was to remember the spatial position of the cards. As the incidental task, the children were asked to show the way the drawings were first paired. Hagan found performance on the central task increased over grade level, but found no difference in incidental task performance over grade. When the task required attention to certain aspects of the stimulus display, performance on that task improved with age. Older children were better able to select that portion of stimulation for later recall.

From the studies reviewed above, it is clear that there are developmental changes in children's abilities to select information. In each of the experiments, the differences between children's performances on an attended, central task and on an incidental task increased with age.

What changes in the child's capacity to attend result in such performance differences? For several years, psychologists have been attempting to determine the nature of attention and what processes are involved when a person attends to something. Similar questions are important in developmental psychology. We must determine the processes involved in attention to determine the nature of the developmental changes that occur. Two alternative theories of attention have been advanced. The three previous experiments all relied on some measure of memory to determine whether the subject had attended to the stimulus. Consequently, the developmental changes observed could be simply the result of increasing memory ability over age. What might be occurring in these experiments is that all aspects of the stimuli are perceived, but only some are remembered. Since memory changes do occur in development, the age-related changes found may reflect changes in memory. In this view, attentional selection occurs in what is remembered, not in what is perceived.

The second view of attention relates to perceptual change. Attention may involve perceptual selection rather than memorial selection. Attention limits what can be seen, not what can be remembered.

The distinction between these two views can be related to the perceptual process involved in pattern perception. According to the notion that attention involves a selection of what to remember, all features of patterns in an array would be analyzed. Consequently, all patterns would be perceived, but only selected ones would be remembered. If attention involves selective perception, however, a different description is required. When a group of patterns is presented, not all are feature analyzed and perceived. Analysis occurs for only those patterns that the subject attends to. Selective attention consists of the selection of a set of analyzers for perception. Closer investigation of the course of attentional development in children will provide the answer to this theoretical question in addition to providing a description of the changes that occur in development.

Does the development of attention in children signify a change in perceptual selectivity or a change in memorial selectivity? Pick, Christy, and Frankel (1972) conducted an experiment in which second- and sixth-grade children were shown pairs of colored wooden animal shapes and were then asked to indicate whether a particular aspect was identical in the two stimuli. In one condition, subjects were told which aspect (color or shape) they were to judge, and the stimuli were then exposed for one second. In a second condition, the stimuli were exposed for one second, and the subjects were told which aspect to judge after the display could no longer be seen.

These two instructional conditions place different demands on the subject. When the subject is preinformed about the relevant dimension, he should be able to select that dimension for comparison and ignore the other dimension. When the subject is informed of the relevant comparison after stimulus presentation, both dimensions must be perceived and remembered until the instruction is given. The comparison that most interested Pick et al. involved the differences between conditions as a function of age. Preinforming the subjects of the relevant dimension allowed them to make quicker judgments of similarity than did informing them after stimulus presentation. This effect, however, was greater for the older than for the younger subjects. These results imply that the developmental improvement in attention is the result of an increased ability to select one part of the stimulus and reject another. The results of Pick et al. suggest that the selective aspect of attention operates early in the perceptual process itself, and not in a memorial process such as the organization of already perceived material.

Further evidence supports the notion that the age-related improvements in performance on attended tasks are not the result of the development of memory strategies in older children. Drucker and Hagan (1969) found that performance on a task that required recall of attended material improved with age. They also observed an increase with age in the children's tendency to label and rehearse the material. They suggested that the improvement in performance found with older children is the result of increased use of labeling and rehearsal strategies; that is, attentional improvements are the result of better memory.

To test this hypothesis, Rosinski (1970) assessed attentional changes in a recognition task that was constructed to rule out the effects of labeling and rehearsal on attention. First-, third-, and fifth-grade children were presented with cards that had animals and common objects drawn on them. The subjects were merely told to look at the animals (or to look at the objects). They were not told to remember them and were not informed that a test would be given later. After presentation of the drawings, a recognition test was administered. In this test, the child was shown a pair of drawings and asked to pick out the drawing that had been shown before. In this test phase, the drawings differed in posture and orientation, but both had the same name—for example, both were camels.

If increased attention in older children is due to increased labeling and rehearsal of the label, poor performance should be obtained with this test. For example, suppose that a child saw a camel in the presentation phase of the experiment, labeled it "camel," and rehearsed that label a few times. If he relied on verbal memory in the test situation, he would not be able to distinguish between the two test alternatives. Therefore, if increased attention is the result of increased labeling and rehearsal, older children would do very poorly in this task. No such result was found. In spite of the fact that the labels could not serve to distinguish between test alternatives, older children performed significantly better than did younger children. Developmental increases in attention cannot simply be the result of increased use of rehearsal and verbal memory.

The changes that occur in attention should not be interpreted to indicate that young children are unable to attend to a display or that they suffer from some deficit of attention. Attention in perception involves the selective analysis of some aspect of stimulation. As pointed out in Chapters Six and Seven, these analytic mechanisms are present in elementary school children. The differences in attentional performance that have been observed between younger and older children do not result from the lack of a processing ability. Rather, younger children possess these abilities but do not use them spontaneously. When children are given a task that forces perceptual analysis to occur, age differences in attention are reduced or eliminated.

In another experiment, Rosinski (1970) presented first-, third-, and fifth-grade school children with animal and object drawings. Each stimulus card consisted of a common animal and a common object. For each subject, one of these classes was chosen, and the child was told to circle the part of the drawing that he would touch if it were real. To perform this task, the child had to determine what the drawing depicted and which portion of it could be touched. In other words, the task forced the child to attend to what was depicted.

In recognition testing, no age differences were found. Subjects at all grade levels were able to recognize most of the attended (circled) stimuli. Recognition of the unattended stimuli was uniformly poor across all grade levels. Similar effects have been found with other techniques for directing children's attention. When children were forced to label a drawing, recognition performance was high across all age groups, even though the label did not distinguish between the test alternatives. However, when children were told merely to look at the drawings, developmental differences were found; older children recognized more of the drawings than did younger children. These results demonstrate that the changes in attention that occur in development do not involve drastic changes in perceptual mechanisms. First-grade children have the same ability to perceive, attend to, and recognize visual patterns as do fifth-graders. They simply do not use this ability spontaneously; its use must be directed. Older children do not possess an ability lacked by first-graders; they are able to use an existing ability to advantage.

Differentiation

The ability to control scanning eye movements and to attend to relevant aspects of stimulation underlies one aspect of perceptual development. A second aspect of development involves learning what to attend to—that is, differentiating the parameters of stimulation that are informative. A restriction on the ability to differentiate stimulus information exists in early infancy. The ability of the eye to focus an array on the retina is very limited in newborns (White 1971). Prior to one month of age, the infant's eye does not adjust to differences in object distances. The eye seems to be locked at one focal length of approximately 19 cm. If objects are closer or farther than this focal length, they are increasingly blurred on the retina. By the age of four months, accommodation changes allow children to maintain a sharp focus on objects.

The exact relationship between this limitation on eye focusing and perceptual ability in infancy is not known. It is interesting, however, that one of the infant's earliest occurring perceptual abilities does not require precise focusing ability. Looming avoidance is present in neonates. The information that specifies looming (optical magnification) is only minimally affected by accommodation. Since it is the symmetry and rate of expansion of an object's contours that signals looming, even poor accommodative ability suffices. A blurry magnification is as informative for looming as a clearly focused one.

Even after clear vision develops and the accommodative system works normally, perceptual change is accompanied by the differentiation of stimulation. Children learn which aspects of a stimulus are important and must be attended to. An example of how such differentiation might work is provided by the perception of slant based on monocular information. On any slanted surface, there is a myriad of stimulus changes that could be present. Size, shape, brightness, and color of texture elements can all vary. The information for slant, however, is contained in the gradients of texture, the relative rates of change of angular size. To perceive slant on the basis of monocular gradients, a child must learn that information for slant is carried by the gradient and not by the other changes that occur over a slanted surface. The child must develop the ability to extract these gradients by comparing the angular sizes (or heights, widths, densities) of texture elements. To some extent, learning to use monocular texture gradients in perception involves learning to differentiate changes in texture parameters.

Other examples that show that perceptual development involves learning to differentiate aspects of stimulation can be drawn from experiments in pattern perception. An experiment by Yonas and Gibson (cited in Gibson 1969) clearly shows that subjects learn to differentiate specific aspects of stimulation for efficient task performance. Subjects were seated in front of a screen on which one of nine capital letters was projected. Certain of these letters were defined as a positive set, and the subject was required to press a lever in one direction whenever they were presented. If any other letter was presented, the subject responded by pushing the lever in the opposite direction. For one group, the positive set consisted only of the letter e; for a second group, aof made up the positive set; and for a third group, anv was positive.

In this task, the subject must make a set of feature comparisons to determine whether a letter that is presented belongs to the positive set. Since more comparisons have to be made with a three-letter set than with a one-letter set, we should expect that the time taken to respond would be longer for the larger sets. In fact, such a result was obtained. However, this was true only at the beginning of training. Subjects were repeatedly tested over thirty-five days. Response latencies decreased considerably over this time interval. The most striking finding of this experiment involved changes between groups. After the training period, subjects were able to respond to the three-letter set anv as rapidly as to the single letter set e. Subjects learned that this positive set was discriminable from the other letters on the basis of a single feature—diagonality. Over the course of training, they learned to base their recognition on that single feature and thus were able to respond quickly to any one of the three letters. The subjects had learned what specific information distinguished the letters and were able to use that information in their judgments.

Demonstration of a similar effect with children has been provided by Pick (1965). Using some of the patterns depicted in Figure 7–5 in Chapter Seven, Pick trained kindergarten children to discriminate between a set of standard patterns and three of their transformations. After this training was accomplished, three different kinds of transfer tests were administered. One group was given the same set of standards as in training, but with a new set of transformations. A second group was given a different set of standards, but the transformations were of the same kind used in training. A third group was given both new standards and new transformations. In testing, the second group made the fewest number of errors, the first group was next, and the third group made the greatest number of errors.

These results indicate that during the training period, subjects were learning the features on which differences could occur. For example, if a line-to-curve transform was used in both training and testing, subjects learned that this change in the pattern altered its identity with the standard. If a totally new transform was used in testing (such as a rotation), subjects made more errors since they could not tell whether this dimension of difference was permissible. Experience with relevant feature differences resulted in transfer of discrimination training.

CHANGES IN INFORMATIONAL SPECIFICITY

The underlying principles of perceptual development discussed in the previous sections are concerned primarily with the pickup of stimulus information. In the course of development, a child learns which variables of stimulation carry invariant information and learns also to attend to this information. Both of these principles are derived from the perceptual learning theory presented by E. J. Gibson (1969). Largely because of the work of Gibson, these two aspects of perceptual change are accepted as important by many developmental psychologists.

There is possibly yet another developmental change involved in perception. This process is one not previously discussed and about which little is known. Of course, the function of perception is that it provides an individual with knowledge of the physical world around him. For this function to occur, information must be picked up. In addition, however, this information must have meaning. For perception to have adaptive value, there must exist in the subject a correspondence between potential perceptual information and what it specifies. A child needs to be able to pick up information and to relate it to meaningful aspects of the world.

A distinction between stimulus information and stimulus meaning has not been drawn before in perceptual development. Some psychologists have argued that such a distinction is unnecessary. In J. J. Gibson's theory, for example, the notion of information pickup implies the pickup of meaning. When information is picked up, meaning is directly apprehended. Other psychologists (see Pick and Pick 1970) have also questioned whether the distinction between perceptual information and perceptual meaning need be drawn.

The crucial point here is whether it is necessary to suggest a third process to describe perceptual development. A general way to conceptualize perceptual development is to distinguish between potential and effective information, as we did in Chapter One. In the course of development, potential information becomes effective information. A source of information such as the gradients of texture may potentially specify distance. For the infant, this information is only potential information. In the course of development, texture gradients become a more effective determiner of perception. The important theoretical question is how this change from potential to effective information occurs. Are only changes in information pickup involved, or does the specificity of potential information change?

It is appropriate to distinguish between these two factors in development on both logical and empirical grounds. Logically, the ability to register a certain kind of stimulus information does not necessarily imply that the meaning is apprehended. It is possible that the stimulus variables can be registered but not specify anything about the world. One could, for example, conceive of an organism that can discriminate the changes in motion and size that specify looming but could not know that collision was imminent. In fact, such an animal exists. The Syrian golden hamster is able to perceive motion and is able to use motion parallax and motion perspective to locomote, find feed, and avoid cliffs. Yet this animal does not avoid a looming object (Rosinski and Keselica 1976). Since no other animal that lacks this ability has been found, three different measures were used to test the hamster.

In the first condition, looming was specified by the expansion of a shadow on a screen—only optical magnification was available. In the second condition, a textured square was dropped on an animal in a plexiglass-topped cage—both optical expansion and flow field information were available. In the third condition, an object was swung so that it would strike the animal on the head—all possible optical and nonoptical cues were present in this condition. In all conditions, with all animals tested, on all trials, not a single avoidance response was observed. Despite the fact that these animals can use motion parallax and motion perspective information, and despite the fact that they were oriented toward the object on each trial, no looming avoidance occurred. The stimulus information did not mean impending collision to these animals. There was no correlation between collision and information.

The logic of this example can be extended to human observers. An example of such an extension is the case of the perception of polarized light, described in Chapter One. Although polarization information exists, and although humans have a receptor system that can respond to this information, it is meaningless to us.

These two examples demonstrate that a distinction can be drawn between perceptual information and perceptual meaning on logical grounds. If such a distinction is appropriate for psychological as well as logical reasons, one aspect of perceptual development could involve the establishment of stimulus-specific correlations between information and meaning. There are indications that changes in information meaning are involved in development.

The visual cliff experiment of Campos, Langer, and Krowitz (1970) suggests that development may involve changes in stimulus meaning. When fifty-five-day-old infants were placed on the shallow or the deep side of the cliff, their heart rate responses indicated that they could discriminate between the two sides. Surprisingly, however, the children showed a substantial deceleration of heart rate when placed on the deep side. Being placed over the deep side elicited curiosity and orientation rather than fear. This response contrasts sharply with the results obtained with other animals. Gibson and Walk (1960) found that infant cats, goats, and monkeys showed pronounced fear when placed on the deep side of the cliff.

Why should such differences between the responses of human infants and those of other animals be found? One possibility involves the infants' ability to perceive the meaning of the different information available from the shallow and deep sides of the cliff. Head movement on the cliff would result in two different patterns of motion parallax. The array displacement of the shallow side would be greater than that of the deep side. Infants could discriminate between these two array displacements and thus show an ability to distinguish between the two sides of the cliff. The fact that no fear of the deep side was observed suggests that some aspects of depth were not perceived as such. These results may have been obtained because the children were able to register the stimulus information but did not know that the information specified a dangerous falling-off place.

A second experiment that suggests changes in the meaning of stimulus information is the kitten carousel experiment of Held and Hein (1963). The deprivation experiments discussed in Chapter Four show that kittens deprived of the opportunity for self-produced movement can discriminate array motions. As Held and Hein show, however, such kittens cannot use array motion (motion parallax) to discriminate depth of the cliff. This experiment suggests also that the specificity of information plays a role in perception. The passively reared kittens did not avoid the cliff although motion parallax was able to be registered, because this registered, potential information did not specify depth to the kitten.

Neither of these two experiments provides conclusive proof that stimulus-specific correlations between information and meaning are involved in development. Although both sets of results suggest the existence of such a factor, other interpretations are possible. One could argue that the infants tested by Campos et al. were simply not afraid of depth. According to this argument, human infants are able to perceive depth, but unlike other animals must learn to fear it. An alternative explanation for the Held and Hein results is that under normal rearing conditions, stimulation carries its own meaning, and no separate correlation between information and meaning is necessary. The unusual rearing conditions of the experiment may have resulted in a degeneration of the ability to use information, but under normal conditions no correlation with meaning is necessary.

In spite of these possible alternative explanations, the results of Campos et al. and of Held suggest that stimulus-specific correlations may play a role in development. In addition, however, there are experimental results dealing with spatial layout perception that point to the effect of stimulus-specific correlations between information and meaning. One of these experiments involves the perception of slant on the basis of monocular texture gradients. Slant is specified by four sources of potential information: the gradients of compression, linear perspective, size, and density.

Let us consider the processes that are necessary for the differentiation of these texture gradients. The perspective gradient involves the relative rate of change of the angular width of texture elements. To differentiate the perspective gradient, a subject must be able to measure the angular size of one dimension (width) of the texture elements and compare the widths of successive texture elements. The compression gradient is formally equivalent to the perspective gradient. The compression gradient involves the relative rate of change of the angular height of texture elements. To differentiate the compression gradient, a subject must be able to measure the angular size of one dimension (height) of the texture elements and compare the heights of successive texture elements.

As these parallel descriptions of the two gradients show, the same abilities are necessary for each. It should be expected, then, that once angular measurements of texture elements can be made and compared, both compression and perspective gradients would be differentiated. If slant perception depended only on the differentiation and pickup of information, both gradients should be equally effective in perception, and both should follow the same developmental course. But they do not. Although first-grade children are able to use perspective gradient information in slant perception, compression gradients are of little use. Although the information provided by the two gradients is equivalent, and both require the same abilities for differentiation, one gradient specifies slant, the other does not.

A similar conclusion can be drawn from considering the gradients of size and density. Both involve the same parameters of stimulation, and both provide the same potential information. The size gradient is the change in angular area of a number of elements; the density gradient is the number of elements over an angular area. If slant perception depended only on the pickup of information, these two gradients should be equally effective in perception. However, they are not. Even first-grade children can use size information for slant (Levine, Rosinski, and McDowell 1973), but density information cannot be used even by adults (Braunstein 1968). Again, the appropriate conclusion seems to be that a correspondence or specificity exists between size information and slant, but not between density information and slant.

SUMMARY

The developmental changes that occur in perceptual ability are the result of changes in the way stimulus information is picked up and used. A child must learn to differentiate information from available stimulation. He must learn which aspects of stimulation are invariant and potentially informative and which are not. In addition to discovering stimulus information, the child must also learn to pick up this information. The development of eye movement and scanning strategies influences the effectiveness of information for perception. Internal attentional strategies must also be developed to enable the child to select certain features of the array and to reject others.

In addition to these two major factors in development, there is an indication that changes in the specificity of registered information influence perceptual ability. A further aspect of development involves establishing appropriate correspondences between physical stimulation and perceptual specificity.

REFERENCES

Aderman, D., and Smith, E. E. 1971. Expectancy as a determinant of functional units in perceptual recognition. *Cognitive Psychology* 2: 117–29.

Appel, M. A. 1971. Binocular parallax in the eight-week-old infant. Doctoral dissertation, University of Denver, University Microfilms no. 72–16, 936.

Aslin, R. N. 1976. Development of binocular fixation and convergent eye movements in human infants. Paper read at the meeting of the Association for Research in Vision and Ophthalmology, April 1976, Sarasota, Florida.

Ball, W., and Tronick, E. 1971. Infant responses to impending collision: optical and real. *Science* 171: 818–20.

Benson, C., and Yonas, A. 1973. Development of sensitivity to static pictorial depth information. *Perception and Psychophysics* 13: 361–66.

Berlyne, D. E. 1958. The influence of albedo and complexity of stimuli on visual fixation in the human infant. *British Journal of Psychology* 49: 315–18.

Bower, T. G. R. 1964. Discrimination of depth in premotor infants. *Psychonomic Science* 1: 368.

———. 1965. Stimulus variables determining space perception in infants. *Science* 149: 88–89.

———. 1966. Heterogeneous summation in human infants. *Animal Behavior* 14: 395–98.

Bower, T. G. R.; Broughton, J. M.; and Moore, M. K. 1970. The coordination of visual and tactual input in infants. *Perception and Psychophysics* 8: 51–53.

———. 1971. Infant responses to approaching objects: an indicator of response to distal variables. *Perception and Psychophysics* 9: 193–96.

Brattgard, S. O. 1952. The importance of adequate stimulation for the chemical composition of retinal ganglion cells during the early post-natal period. *Acta Radiol* 96: 1–80.

Braunstein, M. L. 1968. Motion and texture as sources of slant information. *Journal of Experimental Psychology* 78: 247–53.

Brennan, W. M.; Ames, E. W.; and Moore, R. W. 1966. Age differences in infants' attention to patterns of different complexities. *Science* 151: 354–56.

Bronfenbrenner, U. 1968. Early deprivation in mammals: a cross-species analysis. In *Early experience and behavior,* eds. G. Newton and S. Levine. Springfield, Ill.: Charles C. Thomas.

Bruner, J. S. 1969. Eye, hand, and mind. In *Studies in cognitive development: essays in honor of Jean Piaget,* eds. D. Elkind and J. H. Flavell. New York: Oxford University Press.

Bruner, J. S., and Minturn, A. L. 1955. Perceptual identification and perceptual accuracy. *Journal of General Psychology* 53: 21–28.

Campos, J., and Langer, A. 1971. The visual cliff: discriminative cardiac orienting responses with retinal size held constant. *Psychophysiology* 8: 264–65.

Campos, J. J.; Langer, A.; and Krowitz, A. 1970. Cardiac responses on the visual cliff in prelocomotor human infants. *Science* 170: 196–97.

Casler, L. 1968. Perceptual deprivation in institutional settings. In *Early experience and behavior,* eds. G. Newton and S. Levine. Springfield, Ill.: Charles C. Thomas.

Chow, L. L.; Riesen, A. H.; and Newell, F. W. 1957. Degeneration of retinal ganglion cells in infant chimpanzees reared in darkness. *Journal of Comparative Neurology* 107: 27–42.

Dale, P. S. 1976. *Language development: structure and function.* New York: Holt, Rinehart and Winston.

Drucker, J. F., and Hagen, J. W. 1969. Developmental trends in the processing of task-relevant and task-irrelevant information. *Child Development* 40: 371–82.

Ebenholtz, S. M. 1966. Adaptation to a rotated visual field as a function of degree of optical tilt and exposure time. *Journal of Experimental Psychology* 72: 629–34.

Epstein, W. 1967. *Varieties of perceptual learning.* New York: McGraw-Hill.

Fagan, J. F. 1970. Memory in the infant. *Journal of Experimental Child Psychology* 9: 217–26.

———. 1971. Infants' recognition memory for a series of visual stimuli. *Journal of Experimental Child Psychology* 11: 244–50.

———. 1972. Infants' recognition memory for faces. *Journal of Experimental Child Psychology* 14: 453–76.

———. 1973. Infants' delayed recognition memory and forgetting. *Journal of Experimental Child Psychology* 16: 424–50.

———. 1974. Infant recognition memory: the effects of length of familiarization and type of discrimination task. *Child Development* 45: 351–56.

Fantz, R. L. 1958. Pattern vision in young infants. *Psychological Record* 8: 43–47.

———. 1961. The origin of form perception. *Scientific American* 204(5): 66–72.

———. 1964. Visual experience in infants: decreased attention to familiar patterns relative to novel ones. *Science* 146: 668–70.

———. 1965a. Ontogeny of perception. In *Behavior of nonhuman primates*, vol. 2, eds. A. M. Schrier, H. F. Harlow, and F. Stollnitz. New York: Academic Press.

———. 1965b. Visual perception from birth as shown by pattern selectivity. In New issues in infant development, ed. H. E. Whipple. *Annals of the New York Academy of Science* 118(21): 793–814.

———. 1967. Visual perception and experience in early infancy: a look at the hidden side of behavioral development. In *Early behavior: comparative and developmental approaches*, eds. H. W. Stevenson, E. H. Hess, and H. L. Rheingold. New York: Wiley.

———. 1972. Visual preferences as a function of age, gestation, and specified variations in form. Unpublished paper.

Fantz, R. L., and Fagan, J. F. 1975. Visual attention to size and number of pattern details by term and preterm infants during the first six months. *Child Development* 46: 3–18.

Fantz, R. L., and Miranda, S. B. 1975. Newborn infant attention to form of contour. *Child Development* 46: 224–28.

Fantz, R. L., and Nevis, S. 1967. Pattern preferences and perceptual-cognitive development in early infancy. *Merrill-Palmer Quarterly of Behavior and Development* 13: 77–108.

Farber, J. M. 1972. The effects of angular magnification on the perception of rigid motion. Doctoral dissertation, Cornell University. University Microfilms no. 73–7134.

Flock, H. R. 1964. A possible optical basis for monocular slant perception. *Psychological Review* 71: 380–91.

————. 1965. Optical texture and linear perspective as stimuli for slant perception. *Psychological Review* 72: 505–14.

Flock, H. R., and Moscatelli, A. 1964. Variables of surface texture and accuracy of space perceptions. *Perceptual and Motor Skills* 19: 327–34.

Flock, H. R.; Tenney, J. H.; and Graves, D. 1966. Depth information in single triangles and arrays of triangles. *Psychonomic Science* 6: 291–92.

Foley, J. E. 1974. Factors governing interocular transfer of prism adaptation. *Psychological Review* 81: 183–86.

Foley, J. E., and Miyanishi, K. 1969. Interocular effects in prism adaptation. *Science* 165: 311–12.

Friedman, S. L., and Stevenson, M. B. 1975. Developmental changes in the understanding of implied motion in two-dimensional pictures. *Child Development* 46: 773–78.

Gibson, E. J. 1963. Development of perception: discrimination of depth compared with discrimination of graphic symbols. In Basic cognitive processes in children, eds. J. C. Wright and J. Kagan. *The Society for Research in Child Development Monographs* 28, no. 2.

————. 1969. *Principles of perceptual learning and development.* New York: Appleton-Century-Crofts.

————. 1970. The ontogeny of reading. *American Psychologist* 25: 136–43.

Gibson, E. J.; Gibson, J. J.; Pick, A. D.; and Osser, H. 1962. A developmental study of the discrimination of letterlike forms. *Journal of Comparative and Physiological Psychology* 55: 897–906.

Gibson, E. J., and Levin, H. 1975. *The psychology of reading.* Cambridge, Mass.: MIT Press.

Gibson, E. J.; Osser, H.; and Pick, A. D. 1963. A study in the development of grapheme-phoneme correspondence. *Journal of Verbal Learning and Verbal Behavior* 2: 142–46.

Gibson, E. J.; Pick, A.; Osser, H.; and Hammond, M. 1962. The role of grapheme-phoneme correspondence in the perception of words. *American Journal of Psychology* 75: 554–70.

Gibson, E. J.; Shurcliff, A.; and Yonas, A. 1970. Utilization of spelling patterns by deaf and hearing subjects. In *Basic studies on reading,* eds. H. Levin and J. P. Williams. New York: Basic Books.

Gibson, E. J., and Walk, R. D. 1960. The "visual cliff." *Scientific American* 202(4): 64–71.

Gibson, J. J. 1950. *The perception of the visual world.* Boston: Houghton Mifflin.

————. 1966. *The senses considered as perceptual systems.* Boston: Houghton Mifflin.

————. 1968. What gives rise to the perception of motion? *Psychological Review* 75: 335–46.

Gibson, J. J., and Gibson, E. J. 1955. Perceptual learning: differentiation or enrichment? *Psychological Review* 62: 32–41.

Gibson, J. J.; Olum, P.; and Rosenblatt, F. 1955. Parallax and perspective during aircraft landings. *American Journal of Psychology* 68: 372–85.

Gogel, W. C., and Sturm, R. D. 1972. A comparison of accommodative and fusional convergence as cues to distance. *Perception and Psychophysics* 11: 166–68.

Golinkoff, R. M. 1974. Children's perception of English spelling patterns with redundant auditory information. Paper read at the meeting of the American Educational Research Association, 1974, Chicago.

————. 1975. Semantic development in infants: the concepts of agent and recipient. *Merrill-Palmer Quarterly of Behavior and Development* 21: 181–93.

Gordon, F. R., and Yonas, A. 1976. Sensitivity to binocular depth information in infants. *Journal of Experimental Child Psychology* 22: 413–22.

Gould, J. D. 1967. Pattern recognition and eye-movement parameters. *Perception and Psychophysics* 2: 399–407.

Graham, C. H. 1965. Visual space perception. In *Vision and visual perception*, eds. C. H. Graham, N. R. Bartlett, J. L. Brown, Y. Hsia, C. G. Mueller, and L. A. Riggs. New York: Wiley.

Grant, V. W. 1942. Accommodation and convergence in visual space perception. *Journal of Experimental Psychology* 31: 89–104.

Graybiel, A. M., and Held, R. 1970. Prismatic adaptation under scotopic and photopic conditions. *Journal of Experimental Psychology* 85: 16–22.

Guilford, J. P. 1954. *Psychometric methods.* New York: McGraw-Hill.

Haber, R. N. 1970. How we remember what we see. *Scientific American* 222(5): 104–12.

Hagen, J. W. 1967. The effect of distraction on selective attention. *Child Development* 38: 685–94.

Haith, M. M. 1966. The response of the human newborn to visual movement. *Journal of Experimental Child Psychology* 3: 235–43.

Hajos, A., and Ritter, M. 1965. Experiments to the problem of interocular transfer. *Acta Psychologica* 24: 81–90.

Hamilton, C. R. 1964. Intermanual transfer of adaptation to prisms. *American Journal of Psychology* 77: 457–62.

Harris, C. S. 1963. Adaptation to displaced vision: visual, motor, or proprioceptive change? *Science* 140: 812–13.

————. 1965. Perceptual adaptation to inverted, reversed, and displaced vision. *Psychological Review* 72: 419–44.

Hartline, H. K. 1938. The response of single optic nerve fibers of the vertebrate eye to illumination of the retina. *American Journal of Physiology* 121: 400–15.

Harway, N. I. 1963. Judgment of distance in children and adults. *Journal of Experimental Psychology* 65: 385–90.

Hay, J. C. 1966. Optical motions and space perception: an extension of Gibson's analysis. *Psychological Review* 73: 550–65.

Hay, J. C., and Pick, H. L., Jr. 1966. Gaze-contingent adaptation and prism orientation. *Journal of Experimental Psychology* 72: 640–48.

Hein, A., and Diamond, R. M. 1971a. Independence of the cat's scotopic and photopic systems in acquiring control of visually guided behavior. *Journal of Comparative and Physiological Psychology* 76: 31–38.

————. 1971b. Contrasting development of visually triggered and guided movements in kittens with respect to interocular and interlimb equivalence. *Journal of Comparative and Physiological Psychology* 76: 219–24.

Hein, A.; Gower, E. C.; and Diamond, R. M. 1970. Exposure requirements for developing the triggered component of the visual-placing response. *Journal of Comparative and Physiological Psychology* 73: 188–92.

Hein, A., and Held, R. 1967. Dissociation of the visual placing response into elicited and guided components. *Science* 158: 390–92.

Hein, A.; Held, R.; and Gower, E. C. 1970. Development and segmentation of visually controlled movement by selective exposure during rearing. *Journal of Comparative and Physiological Psychology* 73: 181–87.

Held, R. 1968. Dissociation of visual functions by deprivation and rearrangement. *Psychologische Forschung* 31: 338–48.

————. 1970. Effects of practice on visuomotor ability. In *Genetic and experiential factors in perception: research and commentary*, ed. R. A. McCleary. Glenview, Ill.: Scott, Foresman.

Held, R., and Bauer, J. A. 1967. Visually guided reaching in infant monkeys after restricted rearing. *Science* 155: 718–20.

Held, R., and Bossom, J. 1961. Neonatal deprivation and adult rearrangement: complementary techniques for analyzing plastic sensory-motor coordinations. *Journal of Comparative and Physiological Psychology* 54: 33–37.

Held, R., and Gottlieb, N. 1958. Technique for studying adaptation to disarranged hand-eye coordination. *Perceptual and Motor Skills* 8: 83–86.

Held, R., and Hein, A. 1963. Movement-produced stimulation in the development of visually guided behavior. *Journal of Comparative and Physiological Psychology* 56: 872–76.

Helmholtz, H. v. 1910. *Handbook of physiological optics,* vol. 3, ed. J. P. C. Southall. New York: Dover, 1962.

Hershenson, M. 1964. Visual discrimination in the human newborn. *Journal of Comparative and Physiological Psychology* 58: 270–76.

————. 1967. Development of the perception of form. *Psychological Bulletin* 67: 326–36.

Hershenson, M.; Munsinger, H.; and Kessen, W. 1965. Preference for shapes of intermediate variability in the newborn human. *Science* 147: 630–31.

Hochberg, J. 1962. The psychophysics of pictorial perception. *Audio-Visual Communications Review* 10: 22–54.

————. 1970. Components of literacy: speculations and exploratory research. In *Basic studies on reading,* eds. H. Levin and J. P. Williams. New York: Basic Books.

————. 1971. Perception II: space and movement. In *Woodworth and Schlosberg's experimental psychology,* eds. J. W. Kling and L. A. Riggs. New York: Holt, Rinehart and Winston.

Hochberg, J., and Brooks, V. 1962. Pictorial recognition as an unlearned ability: a study of one child's performance. *American Journal of Psychology* 75: 624–28.

House, B. J. 1964. Oddity performance in retardates, I: size discrimination functions from oddity and verbal methods. *Child Development* 35: 645–51.

Howard, I. P.; Craske, B.; and Templeton, W. B. 1965. Visuo-motor adaptation to discordant ex-afferent stimulation. *Journal of Experimental Psychology* 70: 189–91.

Howard, I. P., and Templeton, W. B. 1966. *Human spatial orientation.* New York: Wiley.

Hubel, D. H., and Wiesel, T. N. 1965. Receptive fields and functional architecture in two nonstriate visual areas (18 and 19) of the cat. *Journal of Neurophysiology* 28: 229–89.

Johansson, G. 1973. Monocular movement parallax and near-space perception. *Perception* 2: 135–46.

Johnson, B., and Beck, L. F. 1941. The development of space perception, I: stereoscopic vision in preschool children. *Journal of Genetic Psychology* 58: 247–54.

Julesz, B. 1971. *Foundations of cyclopean perception.* Chicago: University of Chicago Press.

Kabrisky, M.; Tallman, O.; Day, C. M.; and Radoy, C. M. 1970. A theory of pattern perception based on human physiology. In *Contemporary problems in perception*, eds. A. T. Welford and E. H. Houssiadas. London: Francis and Taylor.

Kagan, J. 1970. The determinants of attention in the infant. *American Scientist* 58: 298–305.

———. 1972. Do infants think? *Scientific American* 226(3): 74–82.

Kagan, J.; Henker, B. A.; Hen-Tov, A.; Levine, J.; and Lewis, M. 1966. Infants' differential reactions to familiar and distorted faces. *Child Development* 37: 519–32.

Karmel, B. Z. 1969. The effects of age, complexity, and amount of contour on pattern preferences in human infants. *Journal of Experimental Child Psychology* 7: 339–54.

Kepes, G. 1945. *The language of vision*. Chicago: Theobald.

Kerpelman, L. C., and Pollack, R. H. 1964. Developmental changes in the location of form discrimination cues. *Perceptual and Motor Skills* 19: 375–82.

Keselica, J. J., and Rosinski, R. R. Spatial perception in colliculectomized and normal golden hamsters (*Mesocricetus auratus*). *Physiological Psychology* (in press).

Kessen, W.; Salapatek, P.; and Haith, M. 1972. The visual response of the human newborn to linear contour. *Journal of Experimental Child Psychology* 13: 9–20.

Koffka, K. 1935. *Principles of Gestalt psychology*. New York: Harcourt, Brace and World.

Kohler, I. 1964. The formation and transformation of the perceptual world. *Psychological Issues* 3(4): monograph 12.

Kolers, P. A., and Perkins, D. N. 1969. Orientation of letters and their speed of recognition. *Perception and Psychophysics* 5: 275–80.

Kuffler, S. W. 1953. Discharge patterns and functional organization of mammalian retina. *Journal of Neurophysiology* 16: 37–68.

Kurtz, K. H., and Hovland, C. I. 1953. The effect of verbalization during observation of stimulus objects upon accuracy of recognition and recall. *Journal of Experimental Psychology* 45: 157–64.

Lacey, J. I.; Kagan, J.; Lacey, B. C.; and Moss, H. A. 1963. The visceral level: situational determinant and behavioral correlates of autonomic response patterns. In *Expression of the emotions in man*, ed. P. H. Knapp. New York: International Universities Press.

Levine, N. P. 1972. A developmental study of the detection of rotational invariances. Master's thesis, University of Pittsburgh.

Levine, N. P., and Rosinski, R. R. 1976. Distance perception under binocular and monocular viewing conditions. *Perception and Psychophysics* 19: 460–65.

Levine, N. P.; Rosinski, R. R.; and McDowell, E. 1973. Texture gradients in children's perception of surface slant. Paper read at the meeting of the Eastern Psychological Association, May 1973, Washington, D.C.

London, I. 1960. A Russian report on the postoperative newly seeing. *American Journal of Psychology* 73: 478–82.

Luneberg, R. K. 1947. *Mathematical analysis of binocular vision.* Princeton, N.J.: Princeton University Press.

Maccoby, E. E., and Hagen, J. W. 1965. Effects of distraction upon central versus incidental recall: developmental trends. *Journal of Experimental Child Psychology* 2: 280–89.

McGurk, H. 1970. The role of object orientation in infant perception. *Journal of Experimental Child Psychology* 9: 363–73.

Marchbanks, G., and Levin, H. 1965. Cues by which children recognize words. *Journal of Educational Psychology* 56: 57–61.

Meyers, B. 1964. Discrimination of visual movement in perceptually deprived cats. *Journal of Comparative and Physiological Psychology* 57: 152–53.

Miranda, S. B., and Fantz, R. L. 1971. Distribution of visual attention by newborn infants among patterns varying in size and number of details. *Proceedings of the 79th Annual Convention of the American Psychological Association* 6: 181–82.

Mittelstaedt, H. 1962. Control systems of orientation in insects. *Annual Review of Entomology* 7: 177–98.

———. 1964. Basic control patterns of orientational homeostasis. *Symposia of the Society for Experimental Biology* 18: 365–85.

Munsinger, H., and Weir, M. W. 1967. Infants' and young children's preference for complexity. *Journal of Experimental Child Psychology* 5: 69–73.

Neisser, U. 1967. *Cognitive psychology.* New York: Appleton-Century-Crofts.

O'Connor, N. 1968. Children in restricted environments. In *Early experience and behavior,* eds. G. Newton and S. Levine. Springfield, Ill.: Charles C. Thomas.

Ogle, K. N. 1950. *Researches in binocular vision.* Philadelphia: W. B. Saunders.

Ogle, K. N., and Reiher, L. 1962. Stereoscopic depth perception from after-images. *Vision Research* 2: 439–47.

Peiper, A. 1963. *Cerebral function in infancy and childhood.* New York: Consultants' Bureau.

Perlmutter, M., and Myers, N. A. 1974. Recognition memory development in two- to four-year-olds. *Developmental Psychology* 10: 447–50.

Piaget, J. 1946. *Les notions de mouvement et de vitesse chez l'enfant.* Paris: Presses Universitaire.

———. 1952. *The origins of intelligence in children.* New York: International Universities Press.

———. 1969. *The mechanisms of perception.* New York: Basic Books.

Piaget, J.; Feller, Y.; and McNear, E. 1958. Essais sur la perception des vitesses chez l'enfant et chez l'adulte. *Archives de Psychologie* 36: 253–327.

Pick, A. D. 1965. Improvement of visual and tactile form discrimination. *Journal of Experimental Psychology* 69: 331–39.

Pick, A. D.; Christy, M.D.; and Frankel, G. W. 1972. A developmental study of visual selective attention. *Journal of Experimental Child Psychology* 14: 165–75.

Pick, H. L., and Hay, J. C. 1965. A passive test of the Held reafference hypothesis. *Perceptual and Motor Skills* 20: 1070–72.

Pick, H. L.; Hay, J. C.; and Willoughby, R. H. 1966. Interocular transfer of adaptation to prismatic distortion. *Perceptual and Motor Skills* 23: 131–35.

Pick, H. L., Jr., and Pick, A. D. 1970. Sensory and perceptual development. In *Carmichael's manual of child psychology*, vol. 1, ed. P. H. Mussen. New York: Wiley.

Pillsbury, W. B. 1897. A study in apperception. *American Journal of Psychology* 8: 315–93.

Powers, W. T. 1973. *Behavior: the control of perception.* Chicago: Aldine.

Purdy, W. C. 1960. The hypothesis of psychophysical correspondence in space perception. *General Electric Technical Information Series no.* R60ELC56.

Richards, W., and Miller, J. F. 1969. Convergence as a cue to depth. *Perception and Psychophysics* 5: 317–20.

Riesen, A. H. 1947. The development of visual perception in man and chimpanzee. *Science* 106: 107–8.

———. 1966. Sensory deprivation. In *Progress in physiological psychology*, eds. E. Stellar and J. M. Sprague. New York: Academic Press.

Riesen, A. H., and Aarons, L. M. 1959. Visual movement and intensity discrimination in cats after early deprivation of pattern vision. *Journal of Comparative and Physiological Psychology* 52: 142–49.

Riesen, A. H.; Kurke, M. I.; and Mellinger, J. C. 1953. Interocular transfer of habits learned monocularly in visually naive and visually experienced cats. *Journal of Comparative and Physiological Psychology* 46: 166–72.

Riesen, A. H., and Mellinger, J. C. 1956. Interocular transfer of habits in cats after alternating monocular visual experience. *Journal of Comparative and Physiological Psychology* 49: 516–20.

Rock, I. 1966. *The nature of perceptual adaptation.* New York: Basic Books.

Rosenblum, L., and Cross, H. 1963. Performance of neonatal monkeys in the visual cliff situation. *American Journal of Psychology* 76: 318–20.

Rosinski, R. R. 1970. The development of attention and recognition. Doctoral dissertation, Cornell University. University Microfilms no. 71–7374.

Rosinski, R. R., and Keselica, J. J. 1976. Failure to avoid impending collision by the golden hamster *(Mesocricetus auratus). Bulletin of the Psychonomic Society* (in press).

Rosinski, R. R., and Levine, N. P. 1976. Texture gradient effectiveness in the perception of surface slant. *Journal of Experimental Child Psychology* 22: 261–71.

Rosinski, R. R., and Wheeler, K. E. 1972. Children's use of orthographic structure in word discrimination. *Psychonomic Science* 26: 97–98.

Saayman, G.; Ames, E. W.; and Moffett, A. 1964. Response to novelty as an indicator of visual discrimination in the human infant. *Journal of Experimental Child Psychology* 1: 189–98.

Salapatek, P., and Kessen, W. 1966. Visual scanning of triangles in the human newborn. *Journal of Experimental Child Psychology* 3: 155–67.

Schiff, W. 1965. Perception of impending collision: a study of visually directed avoidant behavior. *Psychological Monographs* 79(11), no. 604.

Schiff, W.; Caviness, J. A.; and Gibson, J. J. 1962. Persistent fear responses in rhesus monkeys to the optical stimulus of looming. *Science* 136: 982–83.

Schneider, G. E. 1967. Contrasting visuomotor functions in tectum and cortex in the golden hamster. *Psychologische Forschung* 31: 52–62.

———. 1969. Two visual systems. *Science* 163: 895–902.

Schwartz, A. N.; Campos, J. J.; and Baisel, E. J. 1973. The visual cliff: cardiac and behavioral responses on the deep and shallow sides at five and nine months of age. *Journal of Experimental Child Psychology* 15: 86–99.

Sedgwick, H. A. 1973. The visible horizon: a potential source of visual information for the perception of size and distance. Doctoral dissertation, Cornell University. University Microfilms no. 73–22, 530.

Selfridge, O. G. 1959. Pandemonium: a paradigm for learning. In *Mechanisation of thought processes,* symposium presented at the

National Physics Laboratory, November 1958. London: Her Majesty's Stationery Office, pp. 513–526.

Slater, A. M., and Findlay, J. M. 1975. Binocular fixation in the newborn baby. *Journal of Experimental Child Psychology* 20: 248–73.

Smith, O. W. 1958. Judgments of size and distance in photographs. *American Journal of Psychology* 71: 529–38.

Smith, O. W., and Smith, P. C. 1966. Developmental studies of spatial judgments by children and adults. *Perceptual and Motor Skills* 22: 3–73.

Smith, P. C., and Smith, O. W. 1961. Ball throwing responses to photographically portrayed targets. *Journal of Experimental Psychology* 62: 223–33.

Solomon, R. L., and Lessac, M. S. 1968. A control group design for experimental studies of developmental processes. *Psychological Bulletin* 70: 145–50.

Stenson, H. H. 1966. The physical factor structure of random forms and their judged complexity. *Perception and Psychophysics* 1: 303–10.

Tauber, E. S., and Koffler, S. 1966. Optomotor response in human infants to apparent motion: evidence of innateness. *Science* 152: 382–83.

Trevarthen, C. B. 1968. Two mechanisms of vision in primates. *Psychologische Forschung* 31: 299–337.

Vastola, E. F. 1968. Localization of visual function in the mammalian brain: a review. *Brain, Behavior and Evolution* 1: 420–71.

von Mickwitz, M. 1973. The effect of type and amount of familiarization training on pattern recognition. Doctoral dissertation, University of Pittsburgh.

Vurpillot, E. 1968. The development of scanning strategies and their relation to visual differentiation. *Journal of Experimental Child Psychology* 6: 632–50.

Walk, R. D. 1965. The study of visual depth and distance perception in animals. In *Advances in the study of behavior*, vol. 1, eds. D. Lehrman, R. Hinde, and E. Shaw. New York: Academic Press.

———. 1966. The development of depth perception in animals and human infants. *Monographs of the Society for Research in Child Development* 31(5), no. 107.

———. 1968. Monocular compared to binocular depth perception in human infants. *Science* 162: 473–75.

———. 1969. Two types of depth discrimination by the human infant. *Psychonomic Science* 14: 253–54.

Walk, R. D., and Dodge, S. H. 1962. Visual depth perception of a 10-month-old monocular human infant. *Science* 137: 529–30.

Walk, R. D., and Gibson, E. J. 1961. A comparative and analytical study of visual depth perception. *Psychological Monographs* 75(15), no. 519.

Wallach, H., and Kravitz, J. H. 1965a. The measurement of the constancy of visual direction and of its adaptation. *Psychonomic Science* 2: 217–18.

————. 1965b. Rapid adaptation in the constancy of visual direction with active and passive rotation. *Psychonomic Science* 3: 165–66.

Wallach, H.; Kravitz, J. H.; and Lindauer, J. 1963. A passive condition for rapid adaptation to displaced visual direction. *American Journal of Psychology* 76: 568–78.

Weiskrantz, L. 1958. Sensory deprivation and the cat's optic nervous system. *Nature* 181: 1047–50.

White, B. L. 1971. *Human infants: experience and psychological development.* Englewood Cliffs, N.J.: Prentice-Hall.

White, B. L.; Castle, P.; and Held, R. 1964. Observations on the development of visually-directed reaching. *Child Development* 35: 349–65.

White, B. L., and Held, R. 1966. Plasticity of sensorimotor development. In *The causes of behavior: readings in child development and educational psychology,* 2nd ed., eds. J. F. Rosenblith and W. Allinsmith. Boston: Allyn and Bacon.

Wickelgren, L. W. 1967. Convergence in the human newborn. *Journal of Experimental Child Psychology* 5: 74–85.

Wiesel, T. N., and Hubel, D. N. 1963. Effects of visual deprivation on morphology and physiology of cells in the cat's lateral geniculate. *Journal of Neurophysiology* 26: 978–93.

Wilcox, B. L., and Teghtsoonian, M. 1971. The control of relative size by pictorial depth cues in children and adults. *Journal of Experimental Child Psychology* 11: 413–29.

Williams, J. P.; Blumberg, E. L.; and Williams, D. V. 1970. Cues used in visual word recognition. *Journal of Educational Psychology* 61: 310–15.

Wohlwill, J. F. 1960. Developmental studies of perception. *Psychological Bulletin* 57: 249–88.

————. 1963a. Overconstancy in distance perception as a function of the texture of the stimulus field and other variables. *Perceptual and Motor Skills* 17: 831–46.

————. 1963b. The development of "overconstancy" in space perception. In *Advances in child development and behavior,* vol. 1, eds. L. P. Lipsitt and C. C. Spiker. New York: Academic Press.

————. 1965. Texture of the stimulus field and age as variables in the perception of relative distance in photographic slides. *Journal of Experimental Child Psychology* 2: 163–77.

Yonas, A. 1973. The development of spatial reference systems in the perception of shading information for depth. Paper read at the meeting of the Society for Research in Child Development, March 1973, Philadelphia.

Yonas, A., and Hagen, M. 1973. Effects of static and motion parallax depth information on perception of size in children and adults. *Journal of Experimental Child Psychology* 15: 254–65.

Zaporozhets, A. V. 1965. The development of perception in the preschool child. *Monographs of the Society for Research in Child Development* 30(2), no. 100.

Zeigler, H. P., and Leibowitz, H. W. 1957. Apparent visual size as a function of distance for children and adults. *American Journal of Psychology* 70: 106–9.

AUTHOR INDEX

Aarons, L. M., 80, 81, 82, 85, 119
Aderman, D., 186
Ames, E. W., 138, 141
Appel, M. A., 35
Aslin, R. N., 32

Baisel, E. J., 28
Ball, W., 43–44, 45
Bauer, J. A., 90, 95, 116, 119
Beck, L. F., 35
Benson, C., 177
Berlyne, D. E., 138
Blumberg, E. L., 189
Bossom, J., 112, 113, 119
Bower, T. G. R., 28–29, 35, 36, 37, 38, 44,
    45, 60, 62, 66, 149–150, 177
Brattgard, S. O., 80
Braunstein, M. L., 60, 61, 204
Brennan, W. M., 138
Bronfenbrenner, U., 93
Brooks, V., 175, 176, 179
Broughton, J. M., 35, 44, 45, 62
Bruner, J. S., 116, 119, 134

Campos, J. J., 27, 28, 202, 203
Casler, L., 93
Castle, P., 93
Caviness, J. A., 42
Chow, L. L., 79
Christy, M. D., 197
Conezio, J., 167
Craske, B., 114, 119
Cross, H., 28

Dale, P. S., 143
Day, C. M., 131
Diamond, R. M., 45, 87, 90, 92, 116, 117,
    119
Dodge, S. H., 36
Drucker, J. F., 197

Ebenholtz, S. M., 119
Epstein, W., 100

Fagan, J. F., 140, 142, 143, 152, 173–175,
    179
Fantz, R. L., 14, 15, 60, 77, 119, 124,
    134–135, 136, 137, 140, 141, 142,
    148, 151, 152, 153
Farber, J. M., 72, 73
Feller, Y., 69, 70
Findlay, J. M., 32
Flock, H. R., 59, 62
Foley, J. E., 118, 119
Frail, 187
Fraisse, P., 69
Frankel, G. W., 197
Friedman, S. L., 180

Gibson, E. J., 3, 25, 26, 27, 28, 37, 76, 78,
    84, 100, 154, 156, 157, 158, 159, 164,
    167, 182, 183, 184, 185, 186, 195,
    199–200, 201, 202
Gibson, J. J., 3, 6, 20, 21, 39, 40, 42, 59, 65,
    67, 68, 69, 156, 157, 158, 164, 167,
    171, 184, 201
Gogel, W. C., 31

Golinkoff, R. M., 179, 185
Gordon, F. R., 36
Gottlieb, N., 112, 113, 116, 119
Gould, J. D., 163
Gower, E. C., 45, 84, 87, 90, 92, 119
Graham, C. H., 31
Grant, V. W., 31
Graves, D., 62
Graybiel, A. M., 117, 119
Guilford, J. P., 10

Haber, R. N., 167
Hagen, J. W., 195, 196, 197
Hagen, M., 66
Haith, M. M., 69, 136, 194
Hajos, A., 118, 119
Hamilton, C. R., 119
Hammond, M., 184, 186
Harris, C. S., 108, 115, 116, 119
Hartline, H. K., 130
Harway, N. I., 51–52, 53
Hay, J. C., 72, 112, 118, 119
Hein, A., 45, 83, 84, 85, 86, 87, 88, 89, 90,
    92, 112, 116, 117, 119, 203
Held, R., 83, 84, 85, 86, 87, 88, 89, 90, 92,
    93, 95, 112, 113, 116, 117, 119, 123,
    124, 203
Helmholtz, H. v., 37
Henker, D. A., 149
Hen-Tov, A., 149
Hershenson, M., 31, 32, 138, 147–148
Hochberg, J., 34, 63, 171, 175, 176, 179,
    187
House, B. J., 13, 19
Hovland, C. I., 126
Howard, I. P., 89, 100, 114, 119
Hubel, D. H., 80, 131

Johansson, G., 111
Johnson, B., 35
Julesz, B., 35

Kabrisky, M., 131, 132
Kagan, J., 18, 149, 152–153
Karmel, B. Z., 139
Kepes, G., 170
Kerpelman, L. C., 159
Keselica, J. J., 123, 202
Kessen, W., 136, 138, 194
Koffka, K., 2, 3, 4, 5
Koffler, S., 69
Kohler, I., 115, 124
Kolers, P. A., 132
Kravitz, J. H., 111, 114, 115, 116, 119
Krowitz, A., 27, 202
Kuffler, S. W., 130
Kurke, M. I., 81, 119
Kurtz, K. H., 126

Lacey, B. C., 18
Lacey, J. I., 18

Lambercier, M., 67
Langer, A., 27, 28, 202
Lavine, L., 182
Leibowitz, H. W., 66–67
Lessac, M. S., 88, 89
Levin, H., 182, 187, 189
Levine, J., 149
Levine, N. P., 52, 60, 61, 62, 73, 177, 204
Lewis, M., 149
Lindauer, J., 114, 119
London, I., 82
Luneberg, R. K., 32

Maccoby, E. E., 195
McDowell, E., 204
McGurk, H., 16, 17, 19
McNear, E., 69, 70
Marchbanks, G., 189
Mellinger, J. C., 81, 119
Meyers, B., 82, 83, 85, 109
Miller, J. F., 31
Minturn, A. L., 134
Miranda, S. B., 137, 140
Mittelstaedt, H., 103, 104, 110, 113
Miyanishi, K., 118, 119
Moffett, A., 141
Moore, M. K., 35, 44, 45, 62
Moore, R. W., 138
Moscatelli, A., 62
Moss, H. A., 18
Munslnger, H., 138
Myers, N. A., 167

Neisser, U., 4, 132
Nevis, S., 15, 60, 137, 152, 153
Newell, F. W., 79

O'Connor, N., 93
Ogle, K. N., 31, 32
Olum, P., 39, 40
Osser, H., 156, 157, 158, 184, 185, 186

Peiper, A., 36
Perkins, D. N., 132
Perlmutter, M., 167
Piaget, J., 36, 69–70
Pick, A. D., 156, 157, 158, 184, 185, 186,
    197, 200, 201
Pick, H. L., 112, 118, 119, 201
Pillsbury, W. B., 188
Pokrovskii, 82
Pollack, R. H., 159
Powers, W. T., 101, 106
Purdy, W. C., 59, 62

Radoy, C. M., 131
Reiher, L., 31
Richards, W., 31
Riesen, A. H., 77, 79, 80, 81, 82, 83, 85,
    119
Ritter, M., 118, 119

Rock, I., 100
Rosenblatt, F., 39, 40
Rosenblum, L., 28
Rosinski, R. R., 52, 53, 60, 61, 62, 123,
    126, 167, 177, 185, 197, 198, 202, 204

Saayman, G., 141, 142
Salapatek, P., 136, 194
Schiff, W., 41, 42, 43
Schneider, G. E., 122–123
Schwartz, A. N., 28
Sedgwick, H. A., 65
Selfridge, O. G., 129
Shapiro, F., 183, 184
Shepela, S., 195
Shurcliff, A., 186
Slater, A. M., 32
Smith, E. E., 186
Smith, O. W., 37, 52, 65, 67, 177
Smith, P. C., 37, 52, 67, 177
Solomon, R. L., 88, 89
Standing, L., 167
Stenson, H. H., 139
Stevenson, M. B., 180
Sturm, R. D., 31

Tallman, O., 131
Tauber, E. S., 69
Teghtsoonian, M., 66
Templeton, W. B., 89, 100, 114, 119
Tenney, J. H., 62
Trevarthen, C. B., 123

Tronick, E., 43–44, 45
Twain, M., 76

Vastola, E. F., 123
Vautrey, P., 69
von Mickwitz, M., 154, 155
Vurpillot, E., 160, 161, 162, 194

Walk, R. D., 26–27, 28, 36, 37, 45, 78, 202
Wallach, H., 111, 114, 115, 116, 119
Weir, M. W., 138
Weiskrantz, L., 79–80
Wheeler, K. E., 185
White, B. L., 36, 44, 45, 93–97, 108, 116,
    119, 199
Wickelgren, L. W., 31, 32, 36
Wiesel, T. N., 80, 131
Wilcox, B. L., 66
Williams, D. V., 190
Williams, J. P., 189, 190
Willoughby, R. H., 118, 119
Wohlwill, J. F., 10–11, 12, 49–50, 51, 62,
    67, 177
Wundt, Wilhelm, 1

Yonas, A., 36, 44–45, 66, 173, 177, 183,
    184, 186, 199

Zaporozhets, A. V., 165, 166, 167, 194
Zeigler, H. P., 66–67

SUBJECT INDEX

Abstraction
  in concept formation, 143
  in discrimination, 159
  in recognition, 164, 167
Acoustic patterns, 181
Action perception, in pictures, 178–181
Acuity, visual, 22
Adaptation, 99–101, 102, 124
  control systems and, 107–109
  development compared to, 107–120
Ambient vision, 124
Angular size, 21–22, 47–49, 62–63
Anxiety, stranger, 144
Apparent motion, 68–69
Array motion, 85, 86, 109–112, 119
Art, communication through, 171
Attention
  eye movement and, 194–195
  selective, 195–199

Behavior, visually guided
  adaptation of, 124
  control of, 99–121
  development of, 75–98
Bigrams, 184–185, 187
Binocular disparity, 32–37, 62, 120
Binocular vision, 30–37, 46, 47
Bits, 6

Cataracts, 82
Categorization. See Identification
Classification. See Identification

Closed-loop systems. See Feedback
  systems
Cognitive demons, 129, 131
Collision avoidance, looming
  information and, 41–46, 75, 87
Communication, pictures as medium for,
  170–171
Comparison mechanism (comparator), in
  feedback systems, 103–104
Complexity, infant perception and,
  137–140
Compression gradient, 48, 61, 203, 204
Computers, similarities to human
  information processing, 6
Concepts, identification and, 126, 143
Conditioning, 76
Cone system, 92, 117
Contours
  children's perception of, 165
  infants' perception of, 136–137, 138,
    140, 194
Control systems, 101–120
  changes in, 115–120
Conventions, artistic, 171
Convergence, 30–32, 36
Converging operations, 19–20

Dark rearing. See Deprivation, visual
Density gradient, 48, 61, 203, 204
Deprivation, visual, 124
  effects on perceptual development,
    76–97 passim, 117–118

Depth perception, 25–56 passim, 60
   control systems and, 110
   kinetic, 70–74
   effects of light deprivation on, 77, 78,
      79, 85, 124
   physical growth and, 119–120
Development, language, 143
Development, perceptual, 2–5, 8, 9–19
   adaptation compared to, 107–120
   control systems in, 107–109
   effects of light deprivation on, 76–83
   principles of, 192–205
Differentiation, 199–200
Diffuse light experience, 80–81
Direction of motion, 69
Discrimination, 1, 12–13, 76, 81, 123,
      134–140, 146–153 passim, 154–163
   as type of pattern perception, 125, 126,
      127, 134–140, 146–153, 153–163
Dishabituation, 17–19
Disparity, binocular, 32–37, 62, 120
Display, 21
Distance
   motion perception and, 70, 86
   size perception and, 63, 64
Distance perception, 25–56, 57, 58, 62
   physical growth and, 120
Distortion, optical
   adaptation to, 99–101, 102
Disturbances, in feedback systems, 104,
      105, 106, 107

Efferent command, 110
Emotionality, sensory deprivation and,
      93
Event perception, in pictures, 178–181
Evolution, perceptual development and,
      192
Experience
   pattern perception and, 151–153,
      164–165
   pictorial perception and, 175
   role in development of visually guided
      behavior, 75–98 passim
   See also Learning; practice
Eye-limb coordination, 90–93, 116
   See also Hand-eye coordination
Eye movement, 193–195, 199
   discrimination and, 160, 163
   perception of form and, 147, 148
   recognition and, 165, 166

Familiarity, in infant pattern perception,
      141–142, 143, 151
Feedback loop, opening of, 104, 106
Feedback (closed-loop) systems, 103–120
   proprioceptive, 113–118
Focal vision, 124
Focus of expansion, 40–41
Focusing, 199

   of attention, 195
   lack of ability in infants, 44
Form, perception of, 147–151

Generalization, in language
   development, 143
Gradients. See Compression gradient;
   density gradient; perspective
   gradient; size gradient; texture
   gradient
Graphic design, communication through,
   171
   See also Pictorial perception
Growth, physical, perceptual
   development and, 119–120

Habituation, 16–19
   of response to looming, 43
Hand-eye coordination, 96
   feedback system and, 103–107, 108,
      109
   open-loop system and, 102–103
   See also Eye-limb coordination;
      Visual-motor coordination
Hand watching, 95, 96
Heart rate, as measure of discrimination
   capacity, 17–18, 27, 28, 202
Horizon, size perception and, 64–65

Identification
   in infants, 143–144
   as type of pattern perception, 126, 127,
      143–144
Identity, pattern, 159
Ideographic writing systems, 182
Information, 5–6
   pictorial perception and, 171–172
   potential and effective distinguished,
      4–5, 201
Information pickup, 8
   changes in, 193–200
Informational specificity, 132
   changes in, 201–204
Intelligence, sensory deprivation and, 93

Judgmental methods, 12–13

KDE (Kinetic Depth Effect), 70–72
Kinetic depth, perception of, 70–74
Kinetic Depth Effect (KDE), 70–72

Labeling, effects on attention, 197–198
Language, 170
Language development, identification
   and, 143
Learning
   discrimination, 12–13, 76
   looming information and, 42, 75
   in perceptual development, 80
   of spatial perception, 78

symbolic. *See* Reading
Letters, perception of, 182–184
Light deprivation, 76–97 *passim*,
   117–118
Linear perspective, 62
Localization ability, 123
  light deprivation and, 78
Locomotion, 124
  visual development and, 76, 78, 81, 82
Looming, 41–46, 69, 201–202
Looming avoidance ability, 42–46, 75,
   87, 90, 199, 202

Maturation, pattern perception and, 146,
   151–153, 154
Meaning, 201–203
  pictorial perception and, 170–171
Memory
  attention and, 196, 197, 198
  discrimination and, 125
  reading and, 181
  recognition and, 125–126, 140–142,
   151, 164, 167
Methods, 9–19
  converging operations, 19–20
  discrimination learning, 12–13
  dishabituation techniques, 17–19
  habituation techniques, 16–19
  in infant studies, 134
  judgmental methods, 10–12, 67–68
  preference methods, 13–16, 134–137
  in study of size-perception, 67–68
  in study of visually-guided-behavior,
   88–89
Minification, 111–112
Motion
  apparent, 68–69
  array, 85, 86, 109–112, 119
  direction of, 69
  pictorial representation of, 180
Motion parallax, 37–39, 46, 47, 59–60,
   62, 66, 81, 85–86, 110, 119, 120, 202,
   203
  minification and, 111
Motion perception, 68–70
Motion perspective, 39–46, 75, 81, 85, 86
Motivation, perceptual, 192–193
Motor coordination, effects of light
   deprivation on, 80–81, 88–97
Movement, self-produced, 82, 83–89,
   109–115, 119, 203

Number, infant perception and, 140, 152

Object perception, in pictures, 172–175,
   179
Object recognition. *See* Recognition
Open-loop systems, 102–103
Optic array, 20, 83, 85
  pictorial, 172

Optic tract, effects of light deprivation on,
   79
Optical distortion, adaptation to, 99–101,
   102
Orientation discrimination, in infants,
   17–18, 19
Overgeneralization, in language
   development, 143

Pandemonium model, 129
Parallax. *See* Motion parallax
Pattern discrimination, in infants, 14–16
Pattern perception, 122–145, 146–168,
   160–170
  differentiation and, 200
  in infants, 134–144, 146–153
  information for, 130–134
  models of, 127–130
  reading and, 181–190
  selective attention and, 196–197
  spatial perception contrasted with,
   122–125
  types of, 125–127
  See also Pictorial perception
Pattern vision, restriction of, 80–81
Perception
  action, 178–181
  defined, 2
  distance, 25–56, 57, 58, 62, 120
  event, 178–181
  form, 147–151
  kinetic depth, 70–74
  motion, 68–70
  object, 172–175, 179
  size, 62–68
  spatial and pattern, contrasted,
   122–125
  study of, 1–23
  veridical, 3
  See also Depth perception; Pattern
   perception; Pictorial perception
Perceptual development. *See*
   Development, perceptual
Perceptual motivation, 192–193
Perceptual redundancy, 46–47
Perceptual selection, attention and,
   196–197
Perspective
  linear, 62
  motion, 39–46, 75, 81, 85, 86
  transformation of, 72–73
Perspective gradient, 48, 61, 203–204
Phi phenomenon, 69
Photopic system, 92, 117
Physical growth, perceptual
   development and, 119–120
Physiology, perceptual development and,
   193
Pictorial perception, 170–181
  communications theory of, 170–171

Pictorial perception (*continued*)
    surrogate theory of, 171–172
Placing response, 45
Polarization, 5, 202
Practice, effects on children's
    recognition, 164
Preference methods, 13–16
Premature infants, pattern differentiation
    in, 151–152
Presentation, recognition and, 165
Prism adaptation experiments, 99–101,
    102, 112, 113, 114, 118, 119, 124
Pronounceability, 184–185, 186
Proofreader's errors, 188
Proprioreceptive feedback, 113–118

Reaching, visually directed, 95, 96
Reaction times, feedback systems and,
    104, 105–106, 107, 108–109
Reading, 181–190
Reafference, 110
Recognition
    limits of, 167
    as type of pattern perception, 125–126,
        127, 140–143, 144, 146, 151,
        163–167
Redundancy
    perceptual, 46–47
    in written language, 188–189
Rehearsal, effects on attention, 197–198
Response effector mechanism, 110
Response mechanism, in feedback
    systems, 104
Retina, effects of light deprivation on,
    79–80
Retinal size, 62–63, 66
Reversal, of feedback signal, 104, 105, 107
Rod system, 92, 117
Rorschach Psychodiagnostic Test, 1

Scanning, *See* Eye movement
Schemata underlying pattern
    recognition, 153
Scotopic system, 92, 117
Selective attention, 195–199
Self-produced movement, 82, 83–89,
    109–115, 119, 203
Semantic categories, 181
Semantics, 170
Sensory deprivation. *See* Deprivation,
    visual
Size
    angular, 21–22, 47–49, 62–63
    discrimination of, 13, 19, 66
    infant perception and, 140, 152
    perception of, 62–68
    retinal, 62–63, 66
    See also Looming
Size discrimination, in infants, 13, 19
Size-distance hypothesis, 63, 64

Size gradient, 22, 48, 61, 204
Slant, perception of, 3–4, 6, 57–62, 199,
    203, 204
Socialization, identification in infants
    and, 143–144
Sound, correspondence with spelling,
    186–187
    See also Pronounceability
Spatial layout, 24–74, 75–76, 175–178,
    179
    control systems and, 110, 119
Spatial perception, pattern perception
    contrasted with, 122–125
Specificity, informational, 132
    changes in, 201–204
Speed. *See* Velocity
Spelling patterns, 184–187
Station point. *See* Viewing point
Stereoscopic vision. *See* Binocular vision
Stranger anxiety, 144
Superior colliculus, 123
Surrogate theory of pictorial perception,
    171–172
Symbols, pictorial, 169–190 *passim*
Syntactic categories, 181
Syntax, 170, 181
System transfer function, 108
Systems, 102
    See also Control systems

Template matching models, 127–128
Texture
    perception of, 3–4
    size perception and, 63–64
Texture gradient, 46–54, 58–59, 60–62,
    120, 199, 201, 203–204
    minification and, 111
Transformation sequence, in kinetic
    depth perception, 70–74
Transformations, pattern perception and,
    156–157, 200
    See also Transformation sequence
Trigrams, 185

Velocity, perception of, 69–70
Veridical perception, 3
Viewing point (station point), 20–21,
    52–54, 55
    distance perception and, 52–54, 55
    size perception and, 64–65
Vision
    ambient mode, 124
    binocular, 30–37, 46, 47
    focal mode, 124
    pattern, 80–81
Visual acuity, 22
Visual angle, 21–22
Visual array. *See* Optic array
Visual cliff, 24–28, 36–37, 38, 76, 77, 78,
    83–84, 87, 123, 124, 202–203

Visual cortex, 123
Visual deprivation. *See* Deprivation,
    visual.
Visual-motor coordination
    control systems and, 107–120
    effects of light deprivation on, 80–81,
        88–97
    organization and reorganization of,
        109–115

Visual placing response, 45
Visually guided behavior
    adaptation of, 124
    control of, 99–121
    development of, 75–98

Words, 184–186, 187–190